Ten the Hard Way

An autobiographical memoir

by

Sanny L. Hermanson

Compiled, edited and published by

Ernest "Bud" Leonard Hermanson
Major, U.S. Army (Retired)

Author: Sanny L. Hermanson
Genre: autobiographical work

Published by
Ernest "Bud" Leonard Hermanson,
Major, U.S. Army (Retired)

For information, and copies in bulk, contact CreateSpace.com, a division of Amazon.com

First soft cover edition, August 2017

Manufactured in the United States of America

1 3 5 7 9 10 8 6 4 2

ISBN   978-0-9992316-0-9

Contents

Home   Page   1

Leaving Home   Page   37

Learning America   Page   47

Is This What You Had in Mind?   Page   51

The War Years   Page   139

The Post-War Years   Page   155

The Last Straw   Page   235

HISTORICAL FAMILY INFORMATION

The following information supplements information provided as content in the book **Ten the Hard Way** by Sanny L. Hermanson. Mrs. Hermanson provided the middle names of all her children in that book for her own purposes while it was being written. Since that protection is no longer required, the following identity information is provided to enhance your reading enjoyment and to clarify the content of the book by providing the full names of each individual involved.

Identified in Book as:	Person's Real Name and Information
Pat	**Adolph** Patrick Hermanson Husband to Sanny Lindberg Hermanson Father Born: Norrkoping, Sweden, April 16, 1891 Port of Entry: Montreal, Canada, Oct 10, 1910 Died: Duluth, MN, September 5, 1976 Married to Sanny L. Hermanson: Duluth, MN, March 24, 1917
Sanny	**Sanny** Lindberg (Hermanson) Wife to Adolph Patrick Hermanson Mother Born: Stockholm, Sweden, August 7, 1896 Port of Entry: New York, NY, Oct 3, 1913 Died: Sacramento, CA, September 2, 1994 Married to Adolph Patrick Hermanson: Duluth, MN, March 24, 1917

Identified in Book as:	Person's Real Name and Information
Linnea	**Alice** Gunborg Linnea Hermanson (White) Firstborn, married to George White, K.I.A., WW II, April 13, 1945 Born: Duluth, MN, December 22, 1917 Died: Sacramento, CA, February 10, 2003 Married to SGT George White, K.I.A., Madenburg, Germany Rcv'd the Silver Star for direct combat action against the enemy on April 13, 1945 at offensive on the Elbe River Professional: B.A. and Master's in law from the University of Chicago. Graduated Cum Laude. Phi Beta Kappa. Appointed Administrative Law Judge by Edmund Brown, Governor, State of California. Noted in Who's Who Dir
Violet	**Doris** Violet Gwendolyn Hermanson (Morgan) Born: Duluth, MN, July 10, 1919 Died: Sacramento, CA, February 22, 1989 Professional: Registered dental hygienist Career professional, County Clerk and State Offices
Raymond	**Gunnard** Raymond Hermanson Born: Duluth, MN, November 19, 1920 Died: Duluth, MN, September 9, 1963 Professional: Coast Guard, U.S. Naval Vessel during WW II Business owner, sheet metal and HVAC installations Studying medicine in college at the time of his death

Identified in Book as:	Person's Real Name and Information
Albert	**Ray** Albert Hermanson (1st born of twin brothers) Born: Duluth, MN, October 17, 1922 Died: Bloomington, MN, March 27, 2003 Professional: C.P.O., U.S. Navy, WW II, Pacific Theater Korea, Italy, Northern Africa Battleships and destroyers B.A. Mechanical Engineering, University of Minnesota Space program design, Minneapolis Honeywell Entire career was devoted to Minneapolis Honeywell
Harold	**Roy** Harold Hermanson (2nd born of twin brothers) Born: Duluth, MN, October 17, 1922 Died: Virginia, MN, November 5, 1993 Professional: U.S. Army/Air Corps, WW II, Italian, European Campaign Business owner, Texaco services United Steel Mining, Union Supervisor, Mining Operations
Walter	**Bernard** Walter Hermanson Born: Duluth, MN, December 24, 1923 Died: Chatsworth, CA, January 25, 2011 Professional: U.S. Army/Air Corps, WW II, European Campaign B-17 bomber crew, 25 missions over Germany Then sent to the Pacific Theater until the end of the war B.A., Hydraulic Engineering Career service appointment to Los Angeles Dept of Water

Identified in Book as:	Person's Real Name and Information

Mildred

Helen Mildred Dolores Hermanson (Kilby)
Born: Duluth, MN, June 12, 1926
Died: Sacramento, CA, May 24, 2013
Professional:
Executive Secretary, Technicolor, Inc.

Geraldine

Erna Mae Geraldine Hermanson
(Sr. M. Emily, O.S.B.)
Born: Duluth, MN, August 1, 1930
Died: Duluth, MN, January 11, 2015
Professional:
Registered Nurse
Registered Anesthetist
Registered Psychologist
B.A., Masters, Nursing, Medical, Psychology
Sister (Nun) M. Emily, Catholic Church, O.S.B.

Identified in Book as:	Person's Real Name and Information

Leonard

Ernest Leonard Bud Hermanson
Born: Duluth, MN, August 24, 1936
Professional:
Major, U.S. Army (Retired)
30 years service
Concert Master, 11th ABN DIV. post-war Europe
Field Engineer, Construction Management (Ret)
Pilot, multiple types of aircraft, 50 years experience
Concert clarinetist, multiple symphony orchestras

Jean

Gloria Jean Patricia Hermanson
(Dr. Gloria J. Heinemann, Ed.D)
Born: Duluth, MN, May 17, 1941
Professional: BA, Michigan State, MI
MA and Ed.D, University of the Pacific, CA
Career work: Director of Special Education
Dr. Heinemann is now retired and lives with
her daughter, an M.D. with a practice in Arizona

For

Sanny's children's children, who have heard variations of these stories all their lives, about the way their own parents struggled to grow up. So, here they are, the unvarnished truths, as recorded for each child by Sanny over a period of more than seventy years.

Ten the Hard Way

(An Autobiography)

By

Sanny L. Hermanson

Home

I was born on August 7, 1896 in Stockholm, Sweden into a farming and fishing family living in a rural setting. As the newest member of our family, it would take some time to learn that my character and upbringing would most certainly be influenced by my siblings; I just didn't know it yet. These siblings were brother Frank, the oldest at age nine, sister Fanny, age seven and brother Andrew, age four.

All of them had been born at home with a midwife in attendance but, as it happened, my mother was visiting some relatives in the "big city" (Stockholm) at the approach of my birth and, since she was suffering from chronic nephritis, the doctor insisted that she stay in the hospital until after my birth.

I'm told this was quite an event in itself, but I fail to recall the details of the situation as it was explained to me. Which begs the question, why even mention it?

Until reaching the age of ten, I was referred to at home as "ungen," which translated into English would be something like "brat," but the word itself didn't have any kind of malicious connotation. It was just a nickname, although I don't believe they would have been far wrong if they had meant it because, as a child, I was both mischievous and had a rather mean streak in me. Moreover, I was a good fighter and, for a girl, I was excellent and the boys in my village knew it.

Neither my mother nor my father had ever gone to school, but they could both read and write and could more than just hold their own in arithmetic calculations. They couldn't be cheated when computing our sales records.

My father wrote all contracts, wills and important papers and documents for the whole village, and he was a contractor who designed and erected buildings as well as a boat builder and cabinetmaker. I don't believe there was anything he couldn't do with his hands.

My mother could spin and weave our cloth and also sew for all of us, even the boys until they were about 15 years old. After that, the tailor made their suits, but my mother still made their shirts and everything else they wore. She also used to weave the rugs and we always had a new set of rugs for Christmas every year.

My first recollection of things going on around me was from the age of about three. We were living close to a river where we used to play on the shore, and logs made into floats came drifting by.

I also remember that, even at that early age, we were getting ready to move to another country, Finland, which was across the gulf. I recall we were visiting my father's sister and there were seven small children in the

2

neighborhood, some a little older than myself, some a little younger. I also remember that I was bored with the whole thing. I began to throw rocks at the others and every time someone got hit, they started to cry. That was great sport for me until someone went to tell my mother. That was the end of that and I was the only one crying for the next half-hour or so.

The most mental but totally visionary memory I had about our move to Finland was on the steamer going over. My brother, Andrew, told me they had rats on board ship. I guess he told me that so I wouldn't wander around, and it worked. I couldn't get the idea of the rats out of my head and I was so scared I wouldn't stir without holding onto someone's hand.

My mother's two sisters and my grandparents were already living in Finland so we stayed with my grandmother until our new house was ready, which actually took less than a month to complete.

Our house was right on the coast amidst beautiful surroundings but also included a great deal of brush. My mother got lost that first day we were there, just going to the spring for water. And it was fun standing by the shore and watching all the boats going by for six months out of the year. The other six months of the year, we had an unobstructed view of all the snow and ice we cared to look at.

My mother started to teach me to read when I was four, and by the time I was five I was already an excellent reader. I could read all the books my brother Andrew read in school, which was very aggravating to him because I memorized most of it and would be a line ahead of him most of the time.

The first sad memory I have of my youth is something that occurred shortly after we moved to Finland. My father lost some of the fingers on his right hand in an accident. He was in the city at the time and immediately went to the hospital. Unfortunately, neither the hospital nor the doctors had the necessary tools or training to handle his injury.

They bandaged his fingers and told him to come back in three days. He went to another city by boat in the meanwhile to see about a contract, but by the time the third day rolled around his fingers had all developed blood poisoning. He made the mistake of going back to the same hospital, where the same doctors compounded their lack of skill by removing all of his remaining fingers at the next joint.

He was a very strong man and they had to give him a great deal of chloroform just to keep him from lifting the doctor off the floor and over the operating table while the doctor was trying to give him chloroform over his nose, before they finally got him to succumb to the drug. Nevertheless, he kept going back to that same hospital for the next ten days.

Finally, a friend he knew in the city told him to, "Get out of that hospital and away from those doctors before you lose your whole hand!" He took his friend's advice and went to a private doctor in another town closer to home, but it was still too far to go home every day, since the doctor insisted that he come in to his office every day to see him and look at the wound. He ended up renting a room in town and he and the doctor began a five-month battle to undo the damage that had been done by the hospital doctors. In the end, the doctor saved his hand, but it was often touch and go, day by day to see how things were developing.

Only once during that entire period did my dad ask the doctor if he could go home, just for one day so he could see his family. The doctor gave him approval to stay home overnight but, he added, "If you see any sign of pus around the sore, get back here before 11:00 o'clock the following morning without fail."

4

Early the next morning, Mother lifted the bandage and the pus squirted out. Dad went to one of the farmers and asked if he could take him into town with the horse and sleigh (it was winter and no boats were running), and the farmer said, "of course. But let's have some breakfast first."

Dad was worried, of course, but didn't want to appear unreasonable so he sat down to breakfast with the farmer. He did mention that he had to be in town before 11:00 o'clock. The farmer asked his 17-year-old son to get the horse ready and, when that was done, he handed the boy the whip and said, "Now, son, don't spare the whip and don't spare the horse; get to the doctor's office before 11:00 o'clock."

They arrived just in time, but Dad said it was the fastest ride he had ever had, or would ever hope to have. The doctor took one look at the hand and said, "Thank God that you got here in time."

After everything was completely healed, the doctor told Dad how close he had come to losing his whole arm and, perhaps, his life as well.

Meanwhile, we had a struggle at home just to survive. We had some vegetables because we always kept a garden during the summer. Frank and Andrew were fishing through the ice to get a few fish. Fanny, my sister went to stay with my aunt because they had no children. It was supposed to be a temporary thing, but she ended up staying there until she was fully grown.

Dad was never the same after the accident. He wasn't able to work on buildings any more. His hand wasn't strong enough to do the work he used to do and he developed ulcers that he suffered with for many years. The worst part, by far, however, was that he took to drink as a part of his depression. He wasn't exactly an alcoholic, but he drank far too much. Worse yet, when he was drunk, he was miserable to work with and also just to live with. To his credit, however, he had one thing that favored him: he was never unjust. None of us children ever got a slap unless we deserved it. He also tried to provide for his family to the best of his ability. We had decent clothes and we had enough to eat.

Naturally, there were no luxuries. We never got anything for Christmas as the neighbor's children did, but we did have our Christmas tree and we got new skates and skis early in the fall when we needed them, because that would be our only means of transportation throughout the entire upcoming winter. Even so, we still managed to have our fun just like the rest of the neighborhood children.

We were forbidden to go down steep hills on skis because there were so many trees and it was dangerous; but, we did it anyhow on our way to school when we were sure that we were not being watched. I'm still wondering why we were not killed, because it did happen from time to time to someone we knew.

Ice was another hazard in the early fall when the first cold spell came, and again in the spring when it first began to thaw. All the children wanted to skate as soon as a thin coat of ice formed. With us, it wasn't too bad because we were not allowed on the ice until Dad said it was safe, and in that case we had better listen, or else!

One fall, just before Christmas, three boys from our school were drowned because they didn't listen to their elders. It was such a sad affair. It ruined our whole Christmas and that of everyone else for miles around.

In the spring, after the first thaw, a lot of adults were drowned because they drove across the ice with horses and the whole rig went through. There wasn't a chance of getting out alive. I saw a horse and two men go through once, and I'll never forget it. It often comes to mind today when I see that watery coating of ice all these decades after the incident happened.

After Dad's accident, it was rather hard to make ends meet. We owed some money on the small plot of ground we had, and the farmer who held the mortgage wasn't always the best or easiest to deal with. His heart may well have been the size of an ice wagon, but it was just as cold, probably colder.

He came to our house one day with a stub of carpenter's pencil and a shred of brown paper, wanting Dad to sign over our property to him. Dad told him, "First, I wouldn't write on a piece of paper like that, and second, your pencil looks like something someone discarded in the dump!"

What the farmer didn't know was that just an hour before, a friend of Dad's had loaned him the money to pay off what he owned on the loan. So Dad threw the money on the table and said, "There's your money. Now get out and don't let me see you around my property again!"

Naturally, they couldn't bother us for money again after that, but they always held bad feelings toward us from that day on. To us children, that just made life more interesting.

Dad still built boats and furniture during the winter months, but in the summer, Mother and Dad did small-scale commercial fishing. At the age of six, I was left alone all day while they were out on the bay. We had been taught from an early age not to play with fire in any way, and also to stay away from the docks when we were alone. The only other thing I dreaded was a thunderstorm. I was deathly afraid of thunder at the age of six.

Frank hired out as a deckhand on a steamer at the age of fourteen and Andrew was a cabin boy at the age of nine. Reasoning quietly with myself in a pensive moment many years later, I thought, "Quite a contrast to

America, where they still have babysitters at the age of twelve."

Something happened when I was seven that hastened me toward adulthood. We had a small fishing schooner at the time, which was run by an old skipper and a young fellow, about twenty-one, as a deckhand. One day, Mother and Dad had promised one of my aunt's help in planting potatoes. Early that morning, we received a message that the deckhand fell overboard and was drowned. There was no phone and someone had to get the message to my aunt so she would know why my parents couldn't come. Mother and Dad had to go with a few other neighbors to hunt for the body (which was never found). Apparently, the current carried him out to the gulf. Once that happens, nothing is ever found. But, on this particular day, I was the only one available to take the message to my aunt. I set out in a small boat to go three miles across the bay. It was windy, but I was going with the direction of the wind so it wasn't too bad.

In all the excitement, my parents forgot to tell me that I could stay across the bay until the wind died down. After I delivered my message, I set out for home. Although I knew how to handle the boat very well, remember that I was only seven and not too strong. I was fighting the boat, trying to keep it going in the right direction.

After a two-hour struggle, I finally beached the boat, but I was still two miles away from home. I fastened the boat to make sure it would stay on the beach and then walked home, worrying all the time about what Mother and Dad would say about not tying up at our dock.

I needn't have worried since they were surprised that I had returned at all that day; they had completely forgotten that they didn't tell me to stay on the other side of the bay until the wind settled. But I'll never forget those two hours coming back across the bay. I cried and I prayed, and I wondered every time a heavy gust of wind came up if I was ever going to make it to the other side.

A couple of months later, Andrew was home for a day. Mother and Dad had gone to the village. We took the sailboat out while a heavy wind came up and almost swamped us. The boat straightened out, but not until it was half full of water. I started to cry naturally, but Andrew said, "None of that, Brat. We have work to do, so get the bucket and start bailing." That snapped me out of it. I felt I was really needed and I was a sailor at last.

Sometimes I'm filled with wonder that I'm still alive. Once, I was standing on the deck at the stern of a pleasure yacht. The boom struck me in the back and I was thrown overboard. I could swim of course but, since it was fall, it was cold and I had on heavy boots and a sheepskin coat. The yacht was at anchor, but it turned from the wind and I was dragged underneath. Somehow, I managed to get out from underneath and when I popped up at the side, the skipper grabbed me by my sheepskin collar.

Another time, I tried to do what the longshoremen did while loading the boats. In those days, everything was done by hand. They loaded the boats by wheelbarrow. They had a plank about twelve inches wide crossing the distance from the boat to the dock, and which ran above open water. Well, for men who ran hundreds of wheelbarrows across this span every day, it wasn't a problem. But for an eleven-year-old who had never done it before, she found it a little more than difficult, even if it was only half-full.

I was only three feet away from the dock when I went off the side of the plank, preceded by the wheelbarrow and the sand! It was a miracle that I didn't impale myself on the logs beneath the dockside water. I may have been lucky there, but I took an all-day ribbing from the dock crews because I had to use the cabin boy's shirt and pants until my own dried out.

That set aside, I was still a first-rate tomboy. I could climb like a monkey and I was always up on the rope ladder or climbing the mast. I was also a big tease and had to make myself scarce when someone came looking for that "little troublemaker!" I remember a longshoreman I didn't particularly like who, in turn, didn't like high places. The only logical solution was to swipe his jacket and make him go after it. I tied it to the mast some 60 feet above the deck. Then I disappeared. Unfortunately, he went around me. He paid the cabin boy to climb the mast and retrieve it for him.

One day, in an excursionary mood, I drank three full glasses of wine. I felt like I was among the bravest soles ever to walk God's Green Earth. I used to be deathly afraid of horses but, on that day, I went into the village about three miles from home to collect our mail. I walked through the meadow right in-between the horses, telling them that they would only get one chance to get out of my way before I started kicking them where it would do the most good. But after I reached home, my legs turned to rubber (or something like it) and my stomach said,"I never knew you!" while practicing circus-style summersaults.

To this very day, I can't stand the sight or smell of wine, new or old, bottled, kegged or casked, but especially in glasses. No wine please!

After the age of seven, there wasn't much play; it was mostly work, except for Sundays. We never worked on Sunday. But Sunday forenoon, between eleven and twelve o'clock, I had to be in the house without fail. We lived twenty-eight miles from church, so nobody went to church, except once a year for communion. But Dad

10

read the sermon every Sunday and I had to sit still as a mouse, not even being allowed to wiggle in my seat. That was torture for someone as active as I was all other hours of the day; but after I reached the age of ten, I was the one chosen to read the sermon. I didn't mind our home services nearly as much after that because the time went so much faster. And, I could also pretend that I was the minister!

In the winter, we had school of course, but that didn't promise any respite from problems, either real or imagined. Right away, there was the distance to school, some seven miles from home. When there was snow, we could ski and that reduced the time to get there. But during those periods when it didn't snow, we had to walk, some mornings in temperatures as low as twenty-five and thirty degrees below zero. For a seven-year-old, that was cold, even bundled clear over the nose. Of course, we had felt shoes, sheepskin coats, woolen scarves, homemade mittens and stockings which all helped, but it was still cold.

On the cold mornings, we didn't play around much, but on nice days children were bound to create their own brand of mischief. Sometimes we got into a fight and usually that had to be settled before we got to school. And also quite naturally, such antics made us late for school on more than one occasion, which started another round of trouble, this one a little more serious. First, we caught holy heck from the teacher as soon as we got there, followed by a second round as soon as we got home. And there was no time expiration on such things. If the teacher didn't have time to report our misconduct on the day it happened, we could be sure of getting a double dose of "correction" on the following day for not reporting it ourselves.

And what a teacher! She was in her early thirties, but I have never seen anyone in America at that age with a face like hers; it looked like she was on her way to an accident. She was cross-eyed and I really believe her tears ran down her back should she ever cry; but I wouldn't have believed that either, because she could obviously see everything that went on behind her. She didn't miss a thing – ever.

She didn't like any of her pupils, except the boys fourteen and fifteen years old. But they, in turn, were not much interested in her; they had more important things on their minds, so there was always trouble of some kind at the ready.

When I was twelve years old, I went to school for two weeks. Then I felt that I was not learning anything new in school. All we had was catechism, Bible history, history of our country and plain arithmetic. Since I knew all that by heart, I quit school. A few days later, I went to get my books and we had a big row. The teacher was going to tell the minister, who had all the say about everything in those days.

But, getting back to my story about school, it was a comedy at times. In those days, there were many people working on the big estates for very small wages. Both the mother and father had to work and they usually had a lot of children to support with no one to look after them. It seemed to me like they were always in rags and often not very clean.

Unlike major cities, school for us was always held in some spare room on a big farm. And that venue was often changed from year to year. Once during the school term, there was a fire in the wing where we had our school, so they made room for us in the maid's room. We just had to crowd in together the best way we could.

A few of us were sitting with our backs to the maid's bed. I looked over at the girl next to me and I saw a big louse crawling up her braid. It reminded me of a sailor climbing a rope ladder. It was a big louse with the ace of spades on its back. I picked it from her braid and was examining it between my thumb and forefinger. I was thinking, "Now that I've got you, what am I supposed to do with you?" It was another of those life's lessons of not always wanting what you get! Then, of all things, I saw the teacher approaching to collect our slates. I got panicky because I knew that she would ask me what I had in my hand, so I quietly slipped the louse into the maid's bed. Problem solved, except the maid probably wouldn't think so.

The ministers came around once a year (to the various villages) to see how people were getting on with their reading and religious learning. They put ads in the papers and each district had a certain day when everyone in the district was expected to attend and, more or less, depose themselves. The church played a major role in people's lives in those days. If a person was not confirmed, usually by the age of fifteen, he or she became an outcast. They couldn't get married and they couldn't get the papers necessary to do any kind of travel outside of their immediate area. They were essentially treated as children, and some, in fact, reverted to that form of life style.

Shortly after I had quit school, the day arrived for the minister to come around. I didn't know whether the teachers had "squealed" on me or not, but I really didn't care. About ten of us were standing in a circle with the minister in the center. When it came to my turn, he asked how far I had read in the catechism and the Bible history. I answered, "The whole thing." He then asked if he could ask me anything in either book. I nodded my head. So he skipped from here to there throughout his books, in a rather vigorous fashion I thought and, by the end of the session, I hadn't missed any of the correct answers to his questions. Not one!

When it was all over, he turned to the rest of the people and called my name and made the remark, "She was excellent." I saw my teacher sitting in the front row. I turned to face her and had a big smirk on my face and walked out very proud. I felt something like "One-Way Corrigan" must have felt when he returned to the United States after his flight.

There were also political flare-ups during my childhood. The first one I remember was a general strike and what a strike that was! All the children liked it because, safety first, they closed all the schools. But not far behind the schools, they also closed everything else. No trains ran, no boats left the harbor, no mail service of any kind was available and finally, all of the stores closed. Nothing was allowed to move that had anything to do with wages, including factory workers and shop clerks.

The leaders of the strike didn't bother the working class, but the owners of the big estates were treated as a problem and had to find ways to protect themselves. They kidnapped one estate owner that our family knew very well. They put him in a manure wagon and took him to the dump and left him there. Once he was able to free himself, he had to walk back home during a big rainstorm, and the dump was several miles from his house.

A couple of years later, there was the revolution, which came as a shock to most of us. Usually during the summer they were target practicing with cannons all day long, but their daytime military activities had little to no affect on us.

But one morning at 3:00 a.m. we heard the cannons booming away. We lived 56 miles out from the capital but the cannons made quite a rumble. In those days, there were no radios, televisions, newspaper extra editions or anything else that might have informed us of our situation. The closest telephone was three miles away. We couldn't imagine what was happening. Then, finally, one of the schooners came by and we flagged them over to get the news. The wind wasn't very strong, so Dad and I managed to latch onto them with our boat. They told us about the mess they were having in the capital. Later in the afternoon, the powder house blew up and it broke several of our windows (you'll remember of course that our house was 56 miles away)!

There were some 500 people killed and many more injured during the revolution, but it lasted only about four days. Some of our friends were right in the middle of the mess and told us about it later.

There was one neighbor on his little fishing schooner that was right in the harbor of the capital. He had his eleven-year-old daughter with him. When they entered the harbor, they thought it was just the artillery's daily gunnery practice and, considering the normal setup for target practice, the target practice area was out of any cannon fire distance in which an artillery shell could actually reach them.

The bullets started missing them by inches and it became immediately apparent that some adjustment in their thinking would be required. As the girl became more and more hysterical, the father dropped anchor right where he was to see if he could or should do anything.

They couldn't stay in the cabin because of the vibration caused by the detonations of artillery fire, so they ended up sitting on the deck, side by side, for nearly 48 hours until the battle was over. They were nearly insane with fear when the shooting finally eased up a bit and they were able to get out of the harbor and, thankfully, also out of harm's way too.

There was a young boy, in his early twenties, who was a pilot guiding foreign ships in and out of the harbor.

He was picked up at 1:00 a.m. one morning and taken into custody with eleven others. They were all rushed out on the street in their nightclothes and taken across town, also being forced to run the entire distance. The guards had horsewhips and didn't hesitate to use them if the prisoners lagged behind.

This young boy was put in a dungeon that had only a trapdoor and no windows of any kind. He was left there for fourteen days, fed black sour bread and some sort of soup once a day. Every time the guard came by to feed him, he also told the youngster, "You'll be shot tomorrow."

He was released on the fourteenth day without ever having been questioned or charged with anything, nor did he ever learn what had happened to the other eleven prisoners. The only information he did learn, was that many people that had been picked up in the same manner as him were executed during the time that he was imprisoned.

There are many other memories that return from my childhood. When we were small children, Andrew and I used to go to Sunday school during the winter. There was an evangelist living on one of the islands across the bay from us. He held Sunday school on Sunday afternoons in the winter for all the children in the archipelago. We loved it because he always told us such beautiful religious stories.

They had three children of their own. Then one summer, their oldest daughter (14 years old) died from T.B. They didn't hold Sunday school after that. T.B. was running wild in those days, and whole families died within just a few years.

Our closest neighbor had a little girl, a beautiful child. She was the apple of my eye. She became ill when she was 2½ years old. The doctor said it was T.B. of the stomach. She lingered for a year but finally died.

16

After that, I lost all interest in small children until years later when I had some of my own.

Many other memories roll by me from time to time, like watching some kind of personal movie. My pet tomcat disappeared one spring. That was my first real "heartbreak." A few months later, a small stray dog came by and made himself at home. He took the place of my lost cat. But the dog had a habit of chasing sheep. A farmer got angry one day and shot him. That was my second grief.

From the time I was six years old, I had to work. During the winter, I had to make hoop nets for the perch, pike, eel, etc. During the summer, I had to help clean the herring and sardines. We didn't can them. We salted them in those days. I also had to knit my own stockings and mittens.

When I was eleven, I was considered a grown up. I had to work with the adults. That meant getting up at three o'clock in the morning and getting out on the gulf to fish. I didn't mind it in the summer, unless we got caught in a thunderstorm. If the lightning was heavy, I always had the feeling that I was caught in a sea of fire and there was no way to get out. In the fall, late October and early November, it was miserable. If there was a storm, we were drenched with water. Our clothes froze stiff and our hands felt as if they were frozen to the oars. No motors were in use at that time by the average fisherman and we had to depend entirely on our oars to move about.

In the fall, everybody did some butchering. That was one thing I didn't want to see. As I was supposed to be grown up, I was also supposed to help. Twice, I pretended to have a very bad toothache, but the third time, there was no one else to help and I knew there was no way out.

When Dad was out in the yard, I went into the cupboard and made use of his whiskey. I took three big gulps that almost choked me, but it gave results in a very short period of time. I began to feel like I was in a fog and I really didn't care what happened. Dad was half drunk himself, so he didn't know there was anything wrong with me.

I still felt sorry for the ram that they butchered that morning, although it had given me a very black eye and a headache just a couple of weeks before. We had been trying to get the sheep into the barn. We finally had them all in, but this fool ram wanted back out while I was standing in the doorway. It came streaking out of nowhere (seemingly) and tried to jump over my head but not quite making it. I got the full force of a hoof right on my forehead. When I went to school the next morning, I had to explain my black eye, several times it seems. It was the funniest thing to them, but it really wasn't very funny at all, at least to me.

Growing up where I did, I enjoyed generally good health as a child. I did have the measles and chickenpox though (combined), at the age of six. I was delirious for two days. And it did take a little time to get back to normal after that illness. But poor Andrew was a lot sicker than I was. He was lying there as if in a coma for eight days. In all that time, he ate just four boiled prunes. Nobody ever called a doctor for a "little thing" like the measles and the chickenpox. If a child died, it was considered just one of those tough breaks in life.

There was also an epidemic of scarlet fever going at the same time, but we escaped that. The next winter, there was diphtheria, but we didn't catch that either, so we were very fortunate at the time.

I ran into some other annoying things though. There was the time I got an infection in one of my eyes and almost went blind. That time, Dad took me to the doctor. I had never been to a doctor and I was scared to death as the saying goes. All I could think of was that the doctor was going to operate on my eye. I didn't dare cry because Dad didn't allow any soft stuff; he wanted us to be tough. And that I was, without a doubt. I could beat up any kid my own age, sometimes two at the same time.

But, getting back to the doctor, after looking through half a dozen contraptions, he gave us a jar of some sort of ointment to put in the eye. It burned worse than soap and every treatment was torture. They put that in my eye once a day for four weeks. I wore a patch over my eye all of that time and, for three months after that. I had to wear a visor to shade my eyes but, in the end, my eye finally got back to normal.

Then there was the time that we were sliding down a very steep hill that had a bump at the bottom. We had a big sleigh that the farmers used for the horses. Six of us got on this sleigh and I was the last one on the end, sitting on a crossbar. When we hit the bump, I flew up in the air and came down on the crossbar with a whack, which fractured my spine at the very end.

The other children took me home, but nobody mentioned that I was hurt. I just told Mother that I suddenly got a terrible stomachache, which I had, but my back hurt even worse. Mother put me to bed and kept putting hot kettle covers (wrapped in towels) on my stomach all night and all the next day. Nobody bothered to call a doctor. It was just one of those things. I was in bed just two weeks and couldn't walk very well for several weeks after that. The pain finally disappeared. Since I grew up, I have had x-rays and the doctors have told me that my spine is crooked at the base, but since it doesn't bother me, they're not going to do anything about it.

One fall, in late November, I got a very bad toothache. I was then about ten years old. My face was swollen and I couldn't eat anything. There was only one dentist we knew of and he was in town, about 28 miles away. Dad decided that the tooth should be pulled. So early one morning, Andrew and I started out for town on our skates. Andrew had breakfast, but since I couldn't eat, I had to go without.

We were about 15 miles up the river when my skate hit a rock, taking the edge off my skate blade. It was impossible for me to skate with the blade in that condition, but we were only about a mile away from a small village at that point.

I removed my skates and walked to shore. It was about 5:00 a.m. and almost everyone there was still asleep; however, there was a bakery where the lights were on inside and, fortunately for us, we knew those people. We rapped on the door and were immediately admitted to the house. Andrew explained the problem to the owner, who loaned him a file to fix the skate. They offered us some coffee and rolls. Andrew had some but, poor me, I still couldn't eat. My tooth still ached and all I wanted was to get that tooth out of my mouth. In a very short time, we were on our way again.

When we reached the dentist's office, we learned that he was out of town. There was nothing for us to do but go to the regular doctor. If the tooth hadn't ached so much, I would never have had nerve enough to sit down in the chair. But I just wanted to get it over with in a hurry.

The doctor took a pair of pliers about a foot long in his right hand and grabbed hold of my neck with his left hand and told me to open my mouth. At that time, they didn't use Novocain or gas. It was just, "Open your mouth" and that was the end of preparation. I tried my best, but my mouth was really sore and it took a little time. I guess the doctor was getting impatient with me since he seemed to be a little rougher than I thought was necessary. He jammed the pliers around the tooth and gave one good pull. It hurt like blazes but I didn't even yell. I disposed of that tooth so fast that the doctor didn't even see it. He kept holding onto my neck and shaking me, saying, "Spit it out, Spit it out." I said, "Let go of my neck. You already have the tooth in the bowl. What do you want?"

And so it was; it was so wonderful getting rid of the tooth, toothache and doctor all at the same time that we celebrated by going to a friend's house for some lunch. By that time, I was starving but, after lunch and an hour's rest, we started the 28-mile skate back home.

Another incident that will always linger in my memory happened early in the fall when I was twelve. The husband of my mother's late cousin had been spending the summer at my aunt's place. He was a retired army general in his early seventies. He had been retired for a number of years, but during that era, they wore the uniform for the rest of their lives.

This gentleman loved to fish. He had gone out alone in the boat early in the morning and anchored his boat a little way off the island. About 10 o'clock that morning, Dad and I noticed that the boat was empty, but we thought that perhaps someone had taken him to shore for some reason. When he didn't show up for lunch, my cousin rowed out to check. She found him floating a couple of yards from the boat. He had apparently suffered a fainting spell and fallen out of the boat, but he was wearing his long uniform overcoat which had formed a parachute or float of some sort, so he didn't sink. Unfortunately, he was lying face down, drowned of course.

Only my fourteen-year-old female cousin and aunt were at home when this happened, and neither of them was very strong. They came to our place for help so Dad and I went with them. When we finally got to the boat, we turned him face up. He looked very different from the way I had seen him just the day before; but remember, I was only twelve at the time. It was a great shock. Dad and I lifted him into the boat (he was a rather small person). We had him lying on the bottom of the boat, right behind my back, while we rowed to shore. Then Dad and I carried him up to the shed. Everything had a nightmarish quality to it, but my real troubles wouldn't start until later.

His family lived in the capital, many miles away. We had to notify them. The nearest telephone was three miles away. There was just a small path through the woods. It was rather dark all of the way there. Brat (meaning me) was always sent on those errands. At that moment, I would have given anything not to go, but when Dad said, "You do this or that," there was no backtalk, no excuses. We went, no matter what. It was of no use telling anyone I wasn't scared, because I was.

It took a long time to reach any of his family, because they were all at work and hard to locate. It was getting dark before I reached home, and all that time I could see that face before me. Sometimes I imagined that he was right behind me. It was a terrible day and I'll never forget it!

A few months later, two other sad things happened. But first, I'll have to go back a couple of years and relate another incident that almost proved fatal to Dad. He was sort of an acrobat and was always teasing us children, because we usually landed in a tangled heap on the floor when we tried some of his tricks.

This incident happened one evening during the winter. Dad put a small piece of paper on the floor on top of a saucer. He put both hands on his back, bent down without bending his knees and picked up the paper with his tongue. We all tried to repeat this performance but none of us could do it. He didn't act as if anything hurt him, but I'm sure that he must have felt something.

We all went to bed. About one o'clock during the night, Mother woke Frank and asked him to get on his skis, go to the village, call the doctor and ask what to do. Dad had a hemorrhage and was bleeding from the mouth very badly.

Frank went at once. He had to wake the people who had the only phone in the village. Then he got the doctor out of bed. Of course, no doctor would go 28 miles out in the country in the middle of the night. He didn't even have a horse! We knew that, so Frank just asked him what to do. The doctor said to give Dad a teaspoon of salt. Perhaps that would stop the bleeding for the time being, but to be sure to be in the doctor's office at eight o'clock in the morning to get some medicine.

So poor Frank had to come home first and tell Mother what to do, and then start out for town. Dad lost a great deal of blood, but it finally stopped. Frank returned with the medicine about noon the next day.

Dad was very weak for months after and things were really tough. As Dad wasn't able to do anything, we had to live on what little the boys brought in from cutting cordwood. I remember the people that had the telephone once brought us two dozen eggs and that made it seem like Christmas. For a while, it looked as if Dad wasn't going to make it, but he finally did, and he didn't even see the doctor personally.

Now, about the other sad things I mentioned. The first one concerned an excavation in progress where a new building was going up. In one corner, there was an open space about four feet wide and twenty-five feet deep. Young teenage boys in the area made it a sport to jump the open space. What they didn't notice or pay attention to were several steel rods installed in an upright position at the bottom of this opening. As one can imagine, it was bound to happen sooner or later, that one of these teenagers would miss the jump and fall down the opening. The boy who did impaled himself through his stomach. He died two hours later and was sorely missed because everyone in the neighborhood knew him and his family. Naturally, the accident could have been totally preventable with only a little thought to the situation.

Only a week or two later, another accident happened to another boy from the same village. He was sliding down one of the steep hills on his skis. Usually when skiing on such a hill, we discarded our ski poles, but he decided to hold on to his. He fell and the ski pole rammed into his side. He lingered for a couple of days, but he also died. I understand now why we were forbidden to slide on the steep hills but, at the time, it didn't sink in.

I was eleven the summer that my grandmother died. But that time my thirteen-year-old cousin, Lucy, had all the nightmares. But, in order to understand everything, I have to spend just a brief bit of time explaining the setup.

My grandparents lived with my aunt and her husband, and Lucy, an only child. Lucy's father was an engineer on a steamer, so he was never home during the summer. My grandfather was crippled with arthritis for most of the last 15 years of his life, but he spent his last seven years as an invalid in bed. My grandmother was 82 at the time of her death, but until a week before she died, she was very active. She could almost run like a young girl.

One Monday morning, she came down with something that, today, we as family medical neophytes, would diagnose as stomach flu and we were sure she would overcome it. Moreover, the doctor, as well as the drugstore, was 31 miles away from my aunt's house. And while everyone thought that Grandmother would get better because, after all, she was a very strong person, Grandmother didn't get better. By Saturday, she was quite bad. My aunt then decided to go into town, talk to the doctor and perhaps get some medicine. She was to stay overnight and return the next afternoon.

There was a large double bed in the room where my grandparents slept, but no one had a large number of rooms in their homes in those days. Everyone had to "double up," whether or not a person was sick. So Grandma was right there alongside of crippled Grandpa.

My aunt's house was the only house on the whole island. The nearest neighbor was on another island about two miles away. Another cousin was staying with Lucy at the time (Cousin Lena, fourteen years old and the youngest daughter of the gentleman we have already noted as having drowned while fishing in the fall). The two girls were taking care of the two sick grandparents as best they could, but they observed that Grandma had been breathing very heavily all that day. The girls decided to stay up for a while just in case either of them needed or wanted something.

About 11:30 p.m. that night, Lena jumped up from her chair and called out, "I can't hear Grandma breathing!" Both girls rushed to the bed. Lena was right. Grandma wasn't breathing. She was, in fact, dead. Grandpa didn't realize as quickly as the girls did what had happened, but he did when the girls came to the bed.

There were no morticians. Every family had to take care of their own dead. The girls were not strong enough to lift Grandma out of the bed and they asked Grandpa what to do. He said, "Leave her there until morning. Then you can try to get help." So Grandpa was lying there all night beside his dead wife. The poor girls put the Bible under Grandma's chin to keep her mouth closed, and they sat in their chairs for the rest of the night.

Grandpa died two years later, but his death was not unexpected. He was in a coma for several days before his death.

We were thankful that they both died during the summer. When those things happened in the fall or spring, it was hard to get the bodies to the cemetery. The ice was too heavy to saw through, and it was too thin to walk on. In that case, it sometimes took two or three weeks before burial.

One fall, that happened on one of the outer islands. The fellow died and they had to store him in the shed for over two weeks. The rats got at him and messed up his face.

Many sad things happened, or could happen, at any time of the year.

One summer, one of our neighbors, who also owned a fishing schooner, had gone to the capital with a load of live fish. He had a fourteen-year-old boy with him as a helper. They stopped at our house on their way home and had lunch with us. We walked down to the dock with them when they left for home.

A sudden storm came up most unexpectedly. We were walking home from our friend's departure from our dock, and we were almost to our porch when we heard a cry for help. Dad ran down to the boat and rowed out a way. He couldn't see the schooner anywhere, but he did see something bobbing on the waves. He hurried over to the object and found the fourteen-year-old helper floating on a hatch cover. After my Dad helped him into the boat, the boy told my father that the schooner tipped suddenly and took in a lot of water. And since it had a lot of ballast, it sank immediately. The skipper went down with the boat.

Dad took the boy to his home and then went to tell the sad news to the skipper's wife. Another fellow came by and Dad told him what had happened, so he walked along with Dad. When they got there, Dad was trying to break the news the easy way. He told her at first that the skipper had taken ill very suddenly and he was in bad shape. The other guy wasn't very smart and he had a big mouth as a bonus. He blurted out, "Oh, why don't you just tell her he drowned?" The lady fainted right off the bat. Dad got so angry with the man that he almost slugged him. If he had, there would have been two of them unconscious.

There was a lot of rough and hard work all through the winter, as well as in the summer. We were heating as well as cooking with wood. Dad and Frank cut down the dried trees. Andrew and I were the ones that had to pull them home on a large sled. Then the boys cut it up and I had to pile it. Dad used to do a lot of hunting in the winter. There were plenty of seal, otter and fox. Poison was against the law, but there was a fox that was just too smart to be shot. Frank put out smelt with a poison capsule inside. The fox took it and dropped dead just two feet away.

We had an old lady staying with us at the time and she was a big gossip. Frank came in and got the gun and went into the woods where he shot at a target. Then he took the fox home. The old lady was so proud of Frank "shooting" that fox that she told everybody in the neighborhood. Frank was her favorite. If there was any dispute, she took his part, even if he was in the wrong. Sometimes Andrew and I wanted to shoot the old lady.

To make a few cents in the winter, we had to work in the woods cutting cordwood for the farmers. The boys cut the trees down, sawed them into four-foot lengths and split them in half. The rest was up to me. I had to do the piling. I had to pile it in rows, six feet high, six feet long, I managed all but the top layer, which was a little too high for me. The boys helped me with that one.

To pile a row like that, I got fifteen cents. Only it wasn't worth fifteen cents in American money; it was worth only three cents. The average was three of those rows a day, and it was all birch which was very heavy. No wonder I always came out the winner in a fight with the neighborhood boys. Once, seven of them ganged up on me. I tore the seat out of the pants on one of them and the rest of them scattered. I know that poor fellow had a lot of explaining to do when he got home, because pants were not easy to come by. Everybody was poor.

When I think back on it now, I realize there was sometimes comedy involved in the things we got into. I remember when Frank was supposed to baby-sit with me and also milk the cow. We didn't have a cow very often, but that summer we did.

Dad was away building a house for someone. Andrew had gone to spend the weekend with my aunt where Fanny was staying. Mother was going into town to do some shopping. This crazy cow wouldn't let anyone milk her except Mother. Frank thought he could fool the cow. He put on Mother's dress and scarf. Everything went fine until I came by like a tumbleweed in a tornado. I scared the heck out of the cow. When I looked back, the cow had one foot in the milk pail and Frank was sitting on the ground.

I had no hesitation about my next step; I climbed a six-foot fence although I didn't feel too safe up there. I was sure Frank would come up there and belt me, but he didn't. But he wouldn't talk to me the rest of the evening. I was a great talker and that really hurt, to be ignored. Perhaps that's the reason I remember the incident so well.

Another time, we were rounding up the sheep to have them sheared. Besides ours, there were about seventy-five from one of the farms nearby. They were usually sheared together. Sometimes it took a bit of doing to get all those sheep into the pen.

Well, this was one of those days. Some of them took off for the woods. Andrew was home from his job on the boat that day, so he tried to help. He jumped the fence, but slipped somehow and struck his head on a sharp rock. It cut a hole in his scalp about three inches long. The home remedy we used most for that kind of injury was a form of liquid called balsam.

Dad took hold of the hair on Andrew's head and tried to pour some into the open cut. He lifted the whole scalp on one side of Andrew's head. He poured the stuff into the cut. Andrew said that he wanted to lie down, so it must have hurt him badly. It was still bleeding when one of the girls from the farm that was having its sheep sheared said, "I know how to stop it. Take the skin that is right inside of the shell of a raw egg and plaster it right over the cut. The bleeding will stop."

We didn't have a raw egg in the house, so I ran three miles to the nearest neighbor to get one. I was so worried about Andrew that I really made it in record time. The girl did just what she said and that stopped the bleeding. Nothing else was ever done about the wound. He had the scar as long as he lived, but it never bothered him. He was lucky he didn't have a fractured skull.

There were a lot of elk in the woods all around us. The bull elk began to be a nuisance and sometimes we were afraid to go through the woods. One could see them swimming across the bay every day. One day, the elk came swimming right by where a man was fishing.

He threw a rope over the elk's antlers and rode to shore, but he hadn't thought about what to do when he reached the shore. It went so fast that he couldn't release the rope. He jumped out of the boat, but the elk took off for the woods. The boat splintered like a matchbox. Nobody else ever tried that stunt again, at least that I know of.

There was no open season on elk, but the people got so disgusted that they began to shoot them anyway, on the sly of course. The game warden tried to look the other way because the meat didn't go to waste. It made wonderful roasts and steaks. We salted it and then smoked it. One elk and a family had meat for a whole year.

The summer that I was almost thirteen, I caught some kind of a virus. Only the doctors at that time didn't know a virus from a hole in the ground. I went to two different doctors, but neither one knew what ailed me. I was sick for three whole months, in bed most of that time. One of our neighbors gave me an adorable black cocker spaniel puppy as a companion. She was my whole life for the rest of my stay at home which was four years from that time.

I felt very sorry for Mother during my illness. I know it was very hard on her; she had a chronic kidney ailment which caused her back to ache constantly. Dad drank heavily and was very hard to get along with. Mother had to help with the fishing as well as taking care of the house. I wasn't any help at all during those three months. But finally, I snapped out of it and, in a very short time, I was back to normal.

From that time on, I became dissatisfied with life in Europe. Especially in the spring when I had to get used to sixteen-hour work days. There was fishing in the morning. In the afternoon, it was helping to load the freight boats and that wasn't child's play. When I was through with that, I had to take the place of a horse for three hours or more to pull the plow, so we could plant the vegetables. I disliked that most of all. It was very heavy work and I was already tired from twelve or thirteen hours of the work that went before that. I began to dream of America. Of course, I was still too young to go at that time, but it didn't stop me from dreaming.

When I was fourteen, Mother had a stroke. The fishing had been heavier than usual that day. We were a little late getting home. When we got there, Mother was lying on the floor with her face all crooked. She was conscious, but she couldn't talk. I didn't understand what ailed her, but Dad knew. We lifted her on the cot. He tried to do what he could for her and told me to get in touch with a fellow that had a motorboat, the only one within many miles. There was no telephone and he lived five miles from our place.

I ran all the way to his house. I happened to catch him at home, which was just plain luck. He came almost at once. They put a mattress in the bottom of the boat and wrapped Mother in blankets, then took her to the doctor in town. Mother had been in the middle of baking when she was stricken. I don't mean baking two or three loaves of bread at a time; it meant thirty or forty loaves because we supplied the bread to the ships that came into the harbor.

I rolled up my sleeves, so to say, and got on with the job at hand. I had never done it before, so I was a little apprehensive, but everything turned out all right. I was just taking the last loaves out of the oven when they brought Mother back. Today, they would have put her in the hospital, but not at that time. The doctor just gave her some medicine and that was it. The stroke must have been a mild one, though, because she was up and around within three weeks. She didn't become paralyzed and her speech returned to normal; also, her face straightened out.

Confirmation. Fifteen was the age by which most people were expected to be confirmed. After that, a person was considered to be a fully-gown adult, except for the right to vote which remained at 24 years of age.

We had to live in town during the confirmation period. That was a lot of fun. It took six weeks, from nine in the morning to three in the afternoon, Monday through Saturday. I always went home on Saturday afternoon and came back Sunday evening. The school was held from the beginning of March until the middle of April. During March, there was still a lot of snow, so I skied home on weekends. In April, there was a thaw and the river was all right for skating. The last time I went home before the final day was a week before confirmation.

We had the kind of skates that clamped onto the shoe. There was a rough spot in my shoe. It began to bother me when I was a few miles out of town. But I wanted to get home before dark because the ice was a bit rough so I just kept going. It was beginning to be a torture the last few miles.

When I finally reached home, I had an open sore on my leg over two inches long and a half-inch wide. I had worn black stockings, which stuck to the sore. It's a wonder I didn't get blood poisoning. All I used was some home remedy that was common to most households at that time. I don't even remember what it was. But it worked and the sore healed up fine.

I had a choice of a confirmation gift: Earrings for pierced ears or a watch. I chose the watch. I didn't want holes in my ears. The watch had a long chain that went around the neck. It was my pride and joy for years.

I began to look forward more and more to the day when I could leave Europe for good. I couldn't stand the European laws. It seemed that the women didn't have any rights at all. With my independent nature, I just couldn't swallow anything like that.

32

Of course there were things that I knew I was going to miss. First, there was Mother, who wasn't too well. Then there was my dog, which meant a great deal to me. There were the three months in the summer when it was daylight all through the night. And finally, all the ship traffic in and out of the harbor. But the urge to get away was stronger by the day.

Everything went smoothly enough until a couple of months before I was seventeen. One day I had worked twelve hours helping load one of the schooners with sand. I had been picking boulders out of the sand in the wheelbarrow while the men filled them up. My fingers had been hurt a couple of times with the boulders and I was tired in general. When I reached home that night, Dad was drunk. He called me a name. That was all that was needed for me to lose my temper. I had never talked back to him before but that night I did and I told him plenty. Then I washed up, changed clothes, packed my suitcase and left. I didn't even eat supper. My appetite was gone.

I walked ten miles to a girlfriend's house and stayed there overnight. The next morning, I took the passenger boat into the capital. There were plenty of places to get work in the capital, so I wasn't worried.

The next morning, when Dad realized what a mess he had gotten himself into, he was frantic. He wasn't even sure that I would be willing to talk to him. He wrote a letter of apology and asked one of our close neighbors to look me up. He had an idea of where I was staying, so our neighbor brought the letter asking me to go to a nearby restaurant where we could talk in private.

An old biddy, who was also the village gossip, was in town and she happened to come into the restaurant while we were there. She took one look and went out faster than I could say "Eisenhower." She went home to our village and told everybody, including the man's wife, that she saw us together in the restaurant, "and what did they think of that?" She tried to start a scandal, but of course it didn't work. We all had a good laugh over it later on.

Anyway, Dad wrote in the letter that, if I would come home and help him with the work for the summer, he would sign my papers and pay my fare to America in the fall. I had nothing to lose and everything to gain, so I returned home and did what he asked of me. He behaved wonderfully all summer long.

There was an old lady living a few miles from us. She had been a very good friend of Grandmother's. She was also very good to all of us while we were children. I thought it was only "fitting and proper" (to quote Lincoln) that I should call on her and say goodbye before I left for America.

I called on her one Sunday afternoon and planned to spend several hours with her. The poor soul had failing eyesight and she was getting somewhat senile. At that time, there was a popular pancake that was all the rage. It was baked in a large pan, was about an inch thick, and then cut into squares. She had baked one especially for me. She set the table and cut me a generous square. It looked delicious and I noticed some small dark objects in the pancake. I thought, "Oh, my; blueberries." But somehow they just didn't look right. I scrutinized the objects and I noticed that they had legs. You guessed it. They were flies. I thanked her very much and said I was very sorry, but I had an upset stomach (which was true at the moment) due to some green apples I had eaten the night before. But I would have a cup of coffee with her. I drank the coffee black with a lump of sugar. Even that wasn't too much of a success, but I managed to leave without "disgracing" myself. I took my leave earlier than I had anticipated but I don't believe she ever knew there was anything wrong.

When the day of my departure finally arrived, I knew Mother was a person who kept her emotions inside. By nature, she was an angel. She had the kind of patience that I've never seen in anyone else except my sister. If she cried, she did so in secret.

Dad was more openly upset and, as for me, I felt like a criminal. I knew they both needed me, but the urge to go was very strong. We had a small warehouse a short distance from the house. There was a linen closet in one corner. I went in there and cried for a long time. I wiped my last tears on Dad's underwear that were lying on a shelf. Then I went in the house with a smile on my face.

The passenger boat that was to take me to the capital had a stop ten miles away at one of the islands. Dad took me there, but Mother didn't want to go. I said goodbye to her at home. When we got to the island, Dad took my suitcase up on the dock; then he disappeared. He must have gone off to cry in private. He didn't return before the steamer left.

I never saw him again.

Leaving Home

I was to spend a day and a night in the capital. My brother Andrew was then quartermaster on a steamer. My brother-in-law was also a seaman, a sailor in the merchant marine, but it so happened that their shi`ps were both in the same town. A few of my friends were also there. They took me out and tried to show me a good time. We had dinner in the best hotel in town and went to the theater. I tried to be cheerful, but behind that smile something really hurt. I felt that I had let my parents down.

The steamer that took me to England left the next night. Frank was an engineer on a steamship that belonged to the same company as the ship I was on. His ship had developed trouble with its rudder. We ran across them somewhere on the way and we escorted them into the nearest dry dock. I knew he was on the ship, but I didn't get to see him of course. He didn't know until I wrote to him from New York that I was on the other ship.

We ran into a storm on the Baltic. I didn't get seasick of course, but when I opened the porthole for some air, I got a good shower.

We reached Hull, England two days later. It was about 10 o'clock in the evening and it was very foggy. We could barely see the dock and certainly nothing of the town.

I was to sail on the S.S. Adriatic. I heard them calling "The White Star Line" so I just followed the sound and got in the right line. They piled us into a coach on the train. One boy had an accordion. After the train got underway, he played and we danced all the way to Liverpool. It was a little crowded, but we had a lot of fun.

In Liverpool, they brought us to a hotel that had no ceiling. There were walls to separate our rooms, so we all had "private" rooms; but it was during October and a little chilly. One morning, I discovered we had snow flurries overnight; I shook them off the blanket, but I wondered what they did when it rained. We stayed there for three days.

The next step was boarding the S.S. Adriatic. She was anchored out in the harbor and they used a small passenger boat to ferry out the passengers. It was rather crowded and some lady put a little boy in my lap. I held him until we reached the ship. Then I handed him to the person next to me. I don't know if he belonged to her or not. But I wasn't going to get stuck with someone else's responsibility.

Once on board the Adriatic, people were assigned to their cabins. In my case, they somehow made a mistake. I had a third class passage, but they tried to put me in steerage.

Steerage was somewhere down in the bottom of the boat. When I came into the room, there were fourteen other people; two women and twelve children. Four of those were boys, the oldest being about nine. This "mistake," intentional or otherwise, had to be corrected, and quickly.

I put my suitcase down on the floor and sat on it. I made up my mind right then that they couldn't do that to me. The steward, or whoever he was, came in a couple of times, but he didn't say anything. The people in the room weren't any of my countrymen. I didn't mind that, but they all looked as though they needed a bath.

Soon, all the others were getting ready for bed, but I was still sitting on my suitcase. Much later, the steward came in again. He looked at me and said something that I didn't understand. I made a sweep with my hands towards all my roommates and shook my head. My brothers were both sailors and I had heard enough to know the difference between steerage and third class.

The steward went out again but returned in a few minutes with a man who spoke my language. He looked over my papers. Then he said, "You're right; you don't belong here, so come along with me." He took me to a different deck and put me in a cabin with three other girls. They didn't speak my language, but I understood enough of their language to get along. I also knew a few simple words.

We stopped outside of Ireland to take on passengers. I thought that this was the most beautiful country I had ever seen from a distance. It was such an odd shade of green. There were a lot of red houses trimmed in white. It was all very colorful, the whole combination.

The first and second days out on the ocean I was having a ball. Between watching the sharks swimming nearby and watching the passengers leaning over the side and "feeding the fish," I was fascinated.

But the third day, things changed; the waves were getting very high. I was watching the ship go up and down with the waves. Pretty soon, my stomach was following suit. I went to my cabin and stayed put for the next two days without eating anything. The third day I felt hungry, but every time I thought of food, I just wasn't hungry anymore.

One of my roommates had brought along some hardtack and pickled herring. She gave us each a portion. I have never enjoyed anything so much. For the rest of the trip, she was the Number One person in our cabin.

On the fifth day, there was a fire in the coal bin. The ship was standing for a long time, but they wouldn't tell us what it was all about until they had the fire under control. I'm sure it was better to do so. I'm also sure it would have caused somewhat of a panic if we had known, because there was a ship that burned at sea only the week before. The rest of the trip to New York went smoothly and uneventful.

This all happened in the year 1913, about a year-and-a-half after the Titanic disaster. So you'll understand why I gave a big sigh of relief when we reached the harbor in New York.

We were carted off to Ellis Island within hours of our arrival. At Ellis Island, they had some form of roll call. They called a name and when the person answered, he was put in a large cage to await the arrival of whoever was supposed to meet him. We all had to have the name and address of someone in the United States. We also had to have ten dollars in cash. If the former vaccination scar didn't show, one had to be vaccinated. In my case, there was no problem. Vaccination was compulsory in my country and they made sure it worked. They put six **cuts,** not scratches in the arm with a sharp knife and one of those was bound to show.

I also had the addresses of a couple of girls from my neighborhood. I knew them by looks, but not very well personally. They were a lot older than me and they had been away from the neighborhood for years. They just came back for a visit now and then, and for the last three years they had been in New York.

I waited a long time but wasn't called, so I sneaked into the cage when the officer wasn't looking. After what seemed like hours, he called my name, but by then I was afraid to answer because I had gone into the cage without being told to go there. He called several times – no answer. Finally, one of the girls who were to meet me spied me in the cage. She walked up to him and said, "Say, Uncle, I believe the girl is over there in the cage."

He came over and gave me a lecture about answering when my name was called. Then we got out of Ellis Island and went into New York City.

The girl took me to a boarding house run by an old lady who must have been in her seventies. She was very brusque but had a heart of gold. She catered to immigrant girls only. The sister to the girl who met me worked in a town on Long Island. We went there to visit her the first evening.

I had heard so many stories about people being sold, kidnapped or what have you, that I was just plain scared. It took us an hour on the streetcar and all that time I was just sitting there in a cold sweat because I didn't know what was going to happen next. We finally reached her sister's place. I recognized her and the place didn't look dangerous, so I felt more at ease.

That was also the first time I had ever seen tomatoes. The sister made lunch for us and she had some sliced tomatoes. They looked nice and colorful so I thought I'd try some, which I did, but with a terrific surprise: I thought they tasted awful! I would have liked to dispose of the matter pronto, but that wouldn't have been very nice, so I was sitting there chewing "with long teeth" and I finally managed to swallow the horrible stuff. I didn't try another tomato for at least a year.

Shortly after I arrived, I got work at a religious home or school, whatever it was. And since I didn't know the language, I never found out. To this day, I don't know if they were Catholics or Protestants. There were only girls there, and a few older women who ran the place. A man came there every evening to conduct a religious service. But I don't know if he was a priest or a minister. At that time, they all looked alike to me. They had fish on Friday, though, and that was what bothered me.

After making a living by fishing for a number of years, I wasn't even on speaking terms with a fish. When it came to Friday and I had all those big pans smelling of fish, and there were plenty of them as there were about sixty people in the place, it was more than I could stand. I was the kitchen maid and I had to wash all those things by hand.

The second Friday, I quit. I hated to leave for one reason though. The people had been very nice. The first day on the job, one of the ladies handed me a sheet and said, "Fold it," which I didn't understand. "Fold" in my language meant a large enclosure without a roof, which they used for cattle in the summer at milking time. I couldn't see what a sheet had to do with that, so I just stood there with a big grin on my face. Finally, she started to laugh too, and folded the sheet herself.

My second place was with a family on Long Island. They were people of my own nationality and spoke my language, so I didn't have any trouble in that respect, but the lady wasn't exactly my idol. One night when I was wiping dishes, I took the saucers two at a time. She came charging into the kitchen like Hurricane Hazel and told me that I wasn't doing it right. I said, "Good. Perhaps you had better get someone that knows how to do it right." This was on Thursday. I told her that I would stay until Saturday night, which I did.

At that time, there was no trouble getting a job, and no trouble to finding someone who was looking for a job.

My third employment in New York was also on Long Island. The work wasn't too hard, but there was nothing to eat. I was hungry most of the time. One day, I was eating an apple peeling and the lady "broke down" and gave me a whole apple for once. Every noon, it was either potato soup or celery soup and that was every day of the week. At supper, it was mostly cold cuts, and not very much of that. I never saw a roast or a chop during the whole time I was there.

I was going to night school then to learn English, and I began to understand most of it, at least about my work and such.

By that time, it was the middle of December and there was no heat in my room. I was rather fed up with New York.

My brother's best friend had come to the United States the year before. He lived in one of the Mid-Western states so I wrote to him and told him that I wasn't really in love with New York or with doing housework. He said for me to come to where he lived and that they had some factory work there. So I put that planning in my "hope for a better future's pocket," knowing that I still had to exist for some time yet in the present.

One day, I had been cleaning out the coal bin for my lady. I looked like someone who had just come from the darkest part of Africa. I asked her if I could use the bath tub (they had no shower). She said no; that I would have to take a sponge bath in a little dish that was about twelve inches across. I said, "Thanks a lot." Then I added in my broken English, "I'm leaving the day after tomorrow."

Three days later I was on a train bound for Minnesota. In Chicago, I had to wait three hours for the train. I also had to change depots. They left me in the charge of a Negro, an employee of the railroad. I was a little frightened since I had never talked to a Negro before and, in my entire life, I had only seen one once in Europe. He was very nice though. He showed me where to sit down and told me I could go to sleep if I wanted to and he would call me when it was time to go to the next depot. He did just that. At that time, they had horse-and-buggy transportation instead of a taxi. The man with the horse took me to the next depot and put me on the right train. The conductor was a little friendlier than I cared for, so every time I saw him coming I pulled out my ticket and handed it to him. Finally, he took the hint and didn't bother me any more.

I reached my destination, Duluth, Minnesota two days before Christmas. It was cold and snowing; the town looked miserable. I began to wonder what was in store for me next. Andrew's friend got me a place to stay. There were many of my own countrymen there and they lived in an old house that was very cold. We had to dress at night to go to bed, not undress as one usually does. We put on cap and mittens too. Some nights it was 40 below zero and everything was frozen. They tried to keep warm with an old coal heater, but it was warm just around and within three feet of the stove. Every other place was like a refrigerator.

I found work right after Christmas at a woolen mill. We worked from 6:00 a.m. to 6:00 p.m., with an hour off for lunch. The pay was five dollars a week.

I started work on a Saturday, so the next week I got paid for that one day: eighty-three cents. Wow! When I came to this city I had exactly eighty-six cents and one empty suitcase to my name. My room and board cost almost as much as I made. I had to work at the mill for six months before I was able to buy myself a cheap dress.

About two months after I started work, I suddenly became ill one morning. About 10 o'clock, I had to go home from work. It was only about nine blocks, but I was just as if in a fog. It took a whole hour to reach home. When I finally reached my room, I just kicked off my shoes and dropped on the bed, fully dressed. I lay there all day and nobody even looked in the room.

About eight o'clock in the evening, my brother's friend and four other people came and wanted me to go to a dance. By that time, I had such a high fever that I didn't even bother to look at them. Andrew's friend took one look at me and asked the lady of the house, "What's going on here? She's really sick. Why hasn't somebody seen to her or even helped her to undress?" The girls who came with him finally put me to bed "in style."

I lay there for three days without even moving from the bed. In that time, I had only two glasses of water. Nobody bothered to get a doctor. It was just "one of those things." One either lived or died. In about ten days, my skin started peeling and my hair started falling out. Then I knew it was scarlet fever. My throat was still sore, but aside from that, I felt pretty good. After sixteen days, I was back to work. I probably carried it to somebody else, but that many decades ago, people were not very germ-conscious. There was an epidemic going around at the same time (Spanish Flu around the time of World War I).

A boy working next to me had come down with the disease just a couple of days before me.

I liked the work at the mill. We had a wonderful boss. Then he got a better position in another state. We got a new boss who suffered from ulcers. He was a miserable cuss. My English wasn't too good and I believe he held that against me. But I was going to night school and learning fast. After a few months, I talked with a heavy accent of course, but I could make myself understood very well.

The boss began to change his attitude toward me as my English improved. He saw to it that I got a raise in pay and we became the best of friends. In fact, I might say I was his favorite worker. I would also add here that he was the only person that I've ever known with whom I've ever been able to completely overlook the differences that we had in the beginning, mostly with respect to working relationships. As to anyone else with whom I've had a serious disagreement, that feeling has always remained, even after everything else seemed to resolve to a non-issue.

After a few months, I moved to a different place, about twenty-five blocks from where I worked. Two other girls and I rented an apartment. I liked the place pretty well, the only drawback being the washroom which was down in the basement. We lived on the second floor and it was very dark down there, especially when we had to go there at night.

There was an incident that I'll never forget. The head dyer at the mill was a very robust fellow, weighing about 260 pounds. One day he came to work with a boil on his neck. Evidently he got some foreign matter in there, because he got an infection and had to go to the hospital. He was in the hospital for six weeks before he finally died. His weight had dropped to 86 pounds! I went to the funeral and they had an open casket, which they should not have done. The way he looked by that time, he was totally unrecognizable and his appearance alone was enough to scare anyone.

That night, after the funeral, I had an urgent call to go down to the washroom. The light went out while I was there and I just happened to remember what I had seen that afternoon. I almost dropped dead myself.

In order to get to work in the mornings, I used to cut across the railroad yard because it shortened my walk to work by six blocks. If the train was standing, I crawled under the cars. Naturally it was a very dangerous thing to do. One morning, I came across something that cured me of taking that shortcut. A man had been run over by the train. He probably had done what I use to do, that is, crawl under the cars. The mess was still there and so were the police. I turned around and went back the way I had come. I never crossed there again.

Learning America

I loved the work at the factory and I began to have a few outside interests. And, I was progressing famously in English!

Someone in the neighborhood where I lived when I first came to Duluth gave a New Year's party. That's where I first met Herman. We had a few dates, but we didn't go steady until the following spring. He was a very nice boy. He didn't smoke or drink and he was a steady worker. I liked him a lot, but I didn't love him. There was only one thing about him that bothered me. He spoke my language, and that was all he ever wanted to learn. He'd been in the United States for five years, but his English was atrocious. And his own language was what one would call Hill Billy if we heard it in our own country. If he had been interested in learning, it would have been fine. But he wasn't.

He always talked of marriage and I would tell him to wait ten years and then I would let him know. He didn't give up hope, though, until.... But wait. I'm getting ahead of my story and that wouldn't be a good thing.

In the summer of 1915, the factory closed for repairs. As it was to be closed for three months, I had to get another job for the summer. After all, I had to live, so I got work in a match factory. The job turned out to be a torture to me.

The sulfur smell made me sick. I had a splitting headache day after day. I stuck it out those three months, but I lost about ten pounds in weight.

In the fall, the mill opened again on a much larger scale than before. They put on a few extra employees and I became a spinner. They needed several in the spinning department. There was one fellow who was from my country. He had been in the United States about five years. He had been a spinner in Europe about

47

ten years before, but had forgotten some of the "tricks" of the trade. The boss put him on my machine to get the slant on it again. After a couple of weeks, we seemed to hit it off just fine. For the first (and only) time in my life, I was in love.

I told poor Herman then that I was in love with someone else. He took it very hard and talked about committing suicide as a solution.

Pat was the name of my love. He seemed to be so nice; too nice in fact as it eventually developed. What I didn't know then was that he was the world's smoothest talker and the most convincing liar in the United States, at least as I knew them. Moreover, he was a schizophrenic of a sort. He could be very nice while having a normal conversation, then fly off into a rage for no apparent reason. When he finished his tirade, he would be all sunshine and smiles again.

His mother had died when he was a little over eight years old. His father was, more or less, a brute according to what his older brother told me. I just took it for granted that he had had a hard life and everything would probably turn out to be okay. And I must add here that his brother was a wonderful person. They just didn't come any better as far as I was concerned.

A couple of things happened to me over the next six months that should be included here. First, I fractured an ankle by hitting an iron bar accidentally. The fracture was never set. For two weeks I couldn't step on it but, after that, I hobbled along until it got well. Then I got blood poisoning in my finger. Well, that time I went to the doctor and he did a little carving with an instrument that wasn't too sharp, but he finally managed to get the "stuff" out of there. And finally, a few weeks after that, I swallowed some Lysol instead of cough medicine. That time someone else sent for the doctor in a hurry. Well, I guess they just can't kill one from my part of the world. I also fell down a whole flight of stairs at the factory without breaking a bone.

One day, I tried to take a short cut home by walking across the ice. This was in the middle of winter and the harbor was usually covered with thick ice then. But I didn't realize that there was a current in the canal that played havoc with the ice. I kept walking until I suddenly looked ahead and then about five feet in front of me was open water. My guardian angel must have been right there with me, because thirty-one years later, my six-year-old daughter and a seven-year-old neighborhood boy walked out on the ice in the same way. The boy's foot went through. To this day, I still wonder how they managed to turn around and walk away without falling through. If they had drowned, no one would ever have known what had happened to them. With all the trouble I've had throughout my life, I've been very lucky, and I'm very thankful to God for that.

I knew Pat was jealous to a certain extent, but he didn't show it too much at the time, though, until he did! I used to bring my ice skates to work and some of us used to go out during the lunch hour and skate when the ice was smooth enough for skating.

I skated around for awhile with one of the boys. Pat was watching by the window. When I returned to work, he exploded at me, "Did you have to skate with Stan?" I felt that it was none of his business, as I wasn't married to the guy. I said, "No, I didn't have to, but I did, and he's a good skater." Pat didn't talk to me for over a week after that. It didn't bother me so very much, because I was going to business college (night school) studying bookkeeping and typing. I had no time to date anyway, except on weekends, and by the next weekend he seemed back to normal. He quit the factory shortly after that, drifting from one job to another. Sometimes he didn't work at all. His brother was usually stuck with

Pat's board bill as well as his own. They lived in the same boarding house.

I had always been more like a boy, tinkering with machinery in a small way. The boss noticed that, because I always fixed my own instead of calling him for minor troubles. Sometimes I also helped the other girls in the same manner.

The boss couldn't see eye-to-eye with the superintendent. He finally gave his notice and got another place about 600 miles away. Before he left, he had a heart-to-heart talk with me one day. He asked if I was going to marry Pat. I said that I believed so. Suddenly he said, "I wish you wouldn't. He's not dependable." Naturally, I couldn't see the things that were clear to him because I was in love. Someone once said that when people are in love, they have potato peelings over their eyes. When I think back now, I know I had two whole potatoes, one on each eye.

A few weeks after the boss left, he wrote to me and asked me to come to the new place and work for him. The work was about the same, but the wages were a little higher. I don't believe it was the work or the wages that bothered him although we had gotten along beautifully while we worked together. I believe his main objective was to get me away from Pat. I probably would have gone, but it was right in the middle of my school year. I loved school and I wanted to finish. I thanked him for the offer and told him the reason.

A few months later, my parents sent me a one-way ticket home. I already knew that I never again wanted to live in Europe and I didn't have enough money for a return to America. So I told them I wasn't feeling too well just then and that the doctor didn't want me to make the trip. I thanked them kindly and returned the ticket. Perhaps I was wrong, because I never got to see my parents again. One of life's harder decisions.

Is This What You Had in Mind?

The next winter, Pat began to hint about setting the wedding date. He had a habit of saying, "When we get married, we're going to do this or that." I was still in love, but I had my doubts if we would ever really get along. He was nice at times, but other times he was just plain awful. We had a lot of arguments. But then, true love never runs smoothly; it just runs, and that was exactly our case.

One Sunday, we were fooling around with the Ouija board, which was all the rage at that time. Pat said, "Let's find out the date of our wedding." So, laughingly, we proceeded. I don't know what was in back of all that, but the board spelled out a date: March 24th. I said, "So be it." I felt that I had been leading him on and it would be a dirty trick to say "No." The date was about six weeks away. So we started planning.

We had a big wedding with about 300 guests in all. As there was no one else to pay for anything, we had to save every cent that we made. Pat was back working at the factory again. Pat had a little money coming from his mother's estate in Europe that he had never collected so he sent for that. I borrowed some from my parents so we made it just fine in the short time that we had.

My new boss was a man in his late fifties. He took a fatherly interest in me from the very beginning. He noticed all the extra things I was doing. He showed me how to weigh the yarn and adjust the machine so the yarn would come out a perfect thickness as well as many other little things about the position I held. If he had to go out for an hour or two, he let me take over.

I always put in a few minutes every day of my own time to keep the machine clean and in good order. This pleased the boss very much. In fact, when I quit some months later, he called the girl over, the one that was to take my place, and said, "This is the cleanest machine in the whole place. Let's keep it that way."

Anyway, back to the wedding. We hired a large hall. After the ceremony, there was lunch for everybody and a dance that lasted until six o'clock the next morning.

Everything went fine until the reception, when the best man kissed the bride. I could see the dark cloud on Pat's face, but he couldn't very well explode in front of all those people. He didn't say a thing until we got in our room. The first thing he said was, "Didn't you have any better sense than to let Rudy kiss you?" I asked him if he wanted me to make a scene right in the reception line. Then he slapped me in the face and said, "You are my wife now and you will do just as I tell you." That was all I needed. I asked, "And who the hell do you think you are?"

He pulled a gun from somewhere. I still don't know where he had it, or where he got it. I had never seen it before and I never saw it after that. The look in his eyes was all I needed. I had to think fast. I pretended that the shock of the gun made me go insane for a moment. I tore off my rings and threw them at him and I kept on staring straight ahead, sort of wild-eyed, I guess. I kept repeating, "You are a murderer. Let me out of here." That scared him, but good. He threw the gun in the corner and came over and started to call my name, just as one would talk to a child. He kept on saying, "I didn't mean it. See, I threw it away. Don't leave. You know what an awful scandal this would make. What would the people say?"

I guess people always remember their wedding nights. Well, I'll never forget mine, but for a different reason.

Pat picked up the rings and put them on the dresser. But they didn't mean a thing to me after that. I still have them, but have never worn them. Still, there is something magic about them. I would feel bad if I lost them. It's something I just can't explain. I have never believed in divorce, so I stayed.

Some time after that, I finished my course in bookkeeping and typing. I could then have gone to work in the office at the factory as an assistant, but I would have had to take quite a reduction in pay as a beginner and as I didn't know just how long I was going to work, I decided not to make a change just then.

Pat wanted to try changing our luck in another venue, Pittsburgh, Pennsylvania, a city more than 800 miles away. He told me he had been there and liked it very much. Well, I discovered later that it was just some more of his in-bred fantasy, just as he had told me that he was twenty-one years old when I first met him, and he was really twenty-four. I still can't fathom the purpose of that kind of lie.

I discussed leaving and going to the other place with the boss. He didn't have too much confidence in Pat (nor did anyone else for that matter). He advised me to take a leave of absence for a couple of months, but Pat wouldn't hear of it. He said that we wouldn't be coming back.

So, we went. When we got there, I discovered that Pat didn't know a thing about Pittsburgh and, worse than that, there was a big steel strike going on. No one was working!

Nevertheless, we stayed there for a couple of weeks until we were almost broke. Pat wrote to his brother, trying to get a loan. One night, we were down to our last pennies. We bought a few biscuits and some pickled herring. We had that for supper and there was a small amount left over. During the night, I got hungry, so

I got up and finished the rest of it. In the morning, Pat got up before me. I guess he was hungry, too. He looked all around for the herring and the biscuits. I told him that I had finished them during the night. I expected a big explosion, but for once in his life, he didn't explode. Instead, he started to laugh, finding humor in the situation. I never could figure that one out.

That afternoon the answer came from his brother. He sent a few dollars but there was also a very stern letter. He told Pat that it was the last time he would help him and that it was about time Pat grew up and started to face his responsibilities. He put it like this: "I've paid your bills and looked after you ever since we came to the United States. I'm not a gold mine. Wake up." Pat's brother was like a brother to me from the time I first met him and I agreed with him wholeheartedly.

There was just enough money for one fare back to Duluth with a couple of dollars left over. We decided it would be better for me to go back first. I knew I could borrow money to send for Pat, but with the credit rating he had, nobody would have loaned him anything. So I took the train that night and left for Duluth. When I got there the next day, I called my former boss. He said that they needed a helper, but of course that was a very low-paying job. Still, I agreed to take the job for a couple of weeks until something better came open. Then I went to a friend of mine that afternoon, borrowed the money and sent the fare to Pat.

The next morning, I showed up at the factory. The boss met me with a big grin on his face. He said, "I have some good news for you. Fred got drunk last night (Fred was one of the spinners) and called in this morning to say that he was sick. I know he has a hangover and, since I've had trouble of that sort with him several times in the past, he's all through. You can take his machine and start where you left off two weeks ago."

Pat came back to town several days later, but he didn't get work right away. He did get some work on the docks a couple of weeks later, but that was only two and sometimes three days a week.

We rented a small apartment up on the hill. The rent was cheap, but there were steps to climb for more than a block, and I'm not exaggerating. I also had a two-edged sword to deal with; we were down to a ten-hour workday by then, but after working ten hours, walking home, picking up groceries on the way and then climbing all those steps, I was what one would term "all in." I was also a couple of months pregnant.

Pat would already be there on the days he didn't work, but he hadn't done anything to help me with the housework or anything else around the house. His first question was always the same: "What's for supper?"

Pat was getting more jealous by the day. One Sunday, we had been across town to visit some friends. I borrowed a couple of books and he was carrying them for me.

When we were getting off the streetcar, I stopped for a moment to talk to the conductor. I had known his whole family for several years. When we were clear of the street car, Pat threw my books on the street and slapped me in the face. He blurted out, "I've told you not to talk to those fellows, but you still do it." I don't even know to this day what he meant by "those fellows." I picked up my books and turned around to face him and said, "Don't **ever** do that again." And I meant it. He didn't for about a year. The next time he tried it, it didn't work out so well for him, but that's something I want to cover in greater detail later on.

In the fall, we moved into a different apartment. It was still a couple of blocks up a hill but we got away from those terrible steps. The apartment was nice, but it was an old house and awfully cold. We had been there only a week when the plumbing froze up. We thawed most of it out, but the bathtub fixtures were ruined. So we couldn't use the bathtub for the rest of the time we were there.

It was Friday evening before Christmas. Two girls from the factory and I had gone downtown to buy the boss a Christmas gift from the whole department. It was 25 degrees below zero. I got home about nine o'clock. Pat had one of his bad-natured days and locked me out. I rattled the door so everybody in the house could hear me. There was a widow living in the basement flat. She was Irish clear through and wasn't afraid of anybody. She came up to investigate. She had to go outside to come up to our flat and in all that cold it made her mad. I told her that he wouldn't open the door. She talked clear and loud; when she was through with her "speech," she said, "and if that door isn't open when I count to twenty, I'll go downstairs and call the police." He didn't want anything to do with the police. The door was open before she got to ten. He grumbled all night about it, but I just let him talk to himself.

The next day was Saturday. We had Saturday afternoons off during the winter months. I expected my baby in three weeks so I turned in my stop notice for work that day. The boss wanted me to work one more week because they had some extra orders to get out, but I told him that perhaps I had better not. I was very small and my pregnancy hardly showed unless someone knew about it and looked for it.

We lived about three miles from the center of town. I walked downtown and back in the afternoon. Then in the evening, I walked downtown again to take a steam bath, as we couldn't use our own bathtub. When I got out from the bath, I didn't feel very well. I took the streetcar home. I must have looked rather bad when I got on the street car, because a lady got up and gave me her seat. I was twenty-one and she was in her sixties. I was very grateful. I began to feel worse by the minute. I had to walk two long blocks up the hill after I got off. It must have taken me at least thirty minutes to walk those two blocks. My back felt as if it was broken.

Pat had gone with his brother to the next town. When I reached home, I was too sick to do anything. I just threw myself on the bed fully dressed. We had no phone. The lady downstairs had gone out of town for the holidays. The people upstairs didn't know anything about us; they had just moved in. Finally, I began to scream. The people upstairs thought that we had a fight and they didn't want to get involved. Even today, people have the same excuse. Pat came back about an hour later and, walking up the hill, he could hear me screaming a block off. I guess he understood that I was in trouble. He came running the rest of the way. But when he came in, he was so rattled that he just ran around in circles calling himself names. Sick as I was, I knew he wasn't going to be of any help. There were two couples, friends of ours, living a block down the hill. I told Pat to go down there. I said, "Tell them to call the doctor and ask one of the ladies to come to the house."

She was there inside of five minutes. The doctor came in a little less than an hour. He took one look at me and said, "I'll have to put her under and use the forceps." The pains never stopped and I could hardly breathe by that time. The doctor finally put me to sleep and what a blessing that was. By the time I woke up, I was torn both inside and out. That was the way birthing was handled at that point in time, but he was a wonderful doctor and deserved a lot of credit. The baby was a girl, a cute little thing. I don't believe she weighed much more than five pounds, but she seemed healthy enough. Pat appeared to be very happy at first since he had wanted a girl. I did, too, for that matter. But several days after the baby was born, he got into one of his spells again.

For three days in a row, he didn't as much as look into the bedroom to say hello. Well, I was young and we'd been married a little less than a year, but I didn't think it was right for him to ignore me completely after the experience I had just suffered through. I wasn't even back on me feet yet, but I was worried. The next day when he came home from work, the doctor was there and my temperature had risen to 106 degrees. I was conscious, but everything was in a fog. I really didn't care about anything. The doctor didn't say anything, but the nurse had the feeling that I was on the way out.

After the doctor left, the nurse lit into Pat. She talked very quietly while saying a lot. She told Pat that it was just what he had been asking for. He was crying. His tears might have been real; they might have been crocodile tears. I don't know. He said he would do anything, anything, if I would only get well. The nurse kneeled down in the corner of my bedroom. She prayed aloud. I don't believe she knew that I was aware of what took place.

When I heard her praying for me, it gave me a shock. I was awake enough then to know that I was in bad shape. Then I began to pray myself. From then on, my recovery was progressing. It took almost three weeks before I was back on my feet. Well, Pat didn't behave very long after I was back to normal. When the baby was six weeks old, he gave her a slap because she cried.

I couldn't nurse the baby since my milk had dried up when I had such a high temperature. The doctor tried different formulas, but nothing really seemed to agree with her, so she cried most of the time. I had to try to keep her quiet because of Pat's violent temper. It was torture. I might also mention here that the baby's name was Linnea.

When Linnea[1] was three months old, a little girl about four came in to see the baby one day. She was coughing a great deal and I tried to get her out to leave as soon as possible, but I didn't want to be rude about it. The next day, a neighbor told me that the girl had the whooping cough. But, by then, it was already too late.

Ten days later, Linnea came down with the same thing and had pneumonia as a bonus. How she ever lived through it, I'll never know. God must have saved her for a purpose. The doctor ordered all the windows open. It was below zero weather and we were short of fuel. I had to keep on the alert at all times. If she got a coughing spell, I had to pick her up so she wouldn't choke. For two weeks, I never took my coat off and I never went to bed. I sat in an old easy chair and got a few minutes of rest between each coughing spell. Pat never relieved me once.

I had never had the whooping cough, so two weeks later I came down with it myself. And to make it more interesting, I was pregnant again. The illness brought on a miscarriage. It was just a few weeks but it still made me quite sick.

Pat had always been very conceited about his good looks. He had the mistaken idea that he was the best-looking man in town. He was handsome to a certain extent to be sure, but he was no Rudolph Valentino. Far from it. He was smart, though, and could learn anything he put his mind to, but he had no ambition to better himself. With all the time he had on his hands, he could have studied anything and learned it, but he didn't. He never worked nights so he could have gone to night

---

[1]For reasons of my own, I've used the middle names of everyone involved in this narration, but I've also decided to provide a full index of all names with the completed manuscript.

school. There were many free classes going on all over town. With the exception of two years out of forty-five during our marriage, he never worked for at least four months out of every winter. Worse yet, he spent that time doing nothing in particular while I worked to support him.

When Linnea was about five months old, they hired some new help at the factory. Among them was a sixteen-year-old girl. Her mother had just died and her father didn't provide much in the way of support. They were a large family and the poor kid needed a job.

Pat started hanging around the girl a lot more than necessary and she was sort of falling for his smooth talk. The other girls told her that he was married, but it didn't seem to help. The boss warned him, but Pat didn't pay any attention. One day they got into an argument about it and Pat was fired. I knew he was just going to lie around again for weeks without working, so I called the boss. He said that if I could get someone to care for the baby, I could go right to work where Pat left off. Two days later, I got a girl my own age to take care of Linnea, so I went back to work. Pat didn't like the idea, but he wanted to eat as well as I did and he wasn't working, so there was nothing he could do about it.

A few weeks later, he was up for the draft for World War I. Years before, he had left Europe because he didn't want to go into the army and he certainly wasn't going into the army here if he could help it, especially if he had to go to war. He lost no time in getting a job in the shipyard. They couldn't touch him there because the shipyards were essential to the war effort.

He had one bad habit which was a little hard to take. He chewed snuff. There was a gold watch he had wanted for a long time, but because he never worked for long, he could never afford to buy it. I told him that if he quit chewing snuff, I would buy it for him. I paid monthly installments and it took me months to pay for it, but I thought it was worth the struggle if he quit chewing. He chewed in secret until he got the watch and then he went back to openly chewing as if we had never had an agreement.

That in itself I could have taken along with all his other less-than-honest dealings with me, but this one made me see red: He showed the watch to someone that didn't know him very well and then he made up the fantastic story that he had been the foreman at a certain company and the employees liked him so well that they gave him the gold watch when he quit. He worked there all right, but he wasn't the foreman. And he didn't quit; he was fired. And the rest of the employees hated him. When the story came back to me about what he had said, I really blew my top. It was one of the very few times that I ever did.

Pat didn't get along very well with the baby sitter. He was always trying to run her business. She was wonderful with the baby, but after a few months, she couldn't stand him any longer so she quit. I got her a job where I worked and I got an older woman to take care of the baby. After three months, she couldn't stand Pat either, so she quit too.

I was pregnant again and I knew that I'd have to quit sooner or later anyway. I didn't bother to hire a new girl. I quit my job. There wasn't any money coming in as Pat had been laid off at the shipyard. The war was over and I really didn't care. If he couldn't get along with the baby sitters, I thought that he could at least go out and find work. But he was in a nasty humor.

We bought a second-hand sewing machine one day. There were a couple of scratches on it at the time. I noticed them but I didn't make an issue of them because the price was reasonable. I don't know if Pat noticed them or not.

About a week later, he accused me of making the scratches on the machine. I told him that they were there when we bought it. He gave me a black eye. I warned him about that a year before and I had had enough. I had him picked up the next day. When the police came, he said that he didn't hit me. I attacked him and he just put his hand out to protect himself and I ran into his fist. The police laughed and said, "You'll have to tell that one to the judge. I don't have anything to do with it."

There was the cutest article in the paper the next day, all about Pat "crying salted tears when faced by the frail wife." They set the bail at $150.00. Of course he didn't have it. He called every one of our friends but nobody would put up the bail. Finally, he called the landlord. The landlord said, "I won't put up your bail, but I'll talk to your wife. She might let you go if you'll promise to behave. There's no reason for a man to hit a woman at any time, and you'd better go to work if you get out. Your rent is due in two weeks. If you can't pay, what then?"

So the landlord talked it over with me and, in the end, I didn't press charges and Pat got out after spending a week in jail. He was very much subdued at first. He never hit me again; however, he did throw an alarm clock at me once. I was putting some wood in the stove at the time, so I had a piece of wood in my hand and it had a nail in it. I threw the piece of wood at him and it ripped a small hole on his neck. He never tried to throw anything at me again, but he surely took it out on the children. He always hit the first one that crossed his path, whether guilty or not, and I mean **_hit!_**. They would just fly across the floor. And that kept on until the boys began to defend themselves.

In the spring of that year, after he was in jail, we were buying a five-room house next door to where we lived. Pat was working then. We had to put $200.00

down on it before we could move in. A friend of ours said that we could stay with them for a couple of months to save the rent and we could put that on the down payment. We had just saved the $200.00 and were getting ready to move in. So what does Pat do? There was an old chassis of a car in the neighborhood. It really wasn't worth anything. Pat paid $50.00 for the old wreck. He was going to build a car out of it. I was just sick. My next baby was due within the month and I wanted to get into our home before that happened. We had to wait another three weeks before we had the full down payment.

We had just moved in a couple of days before it happened. I got sick early one morning but I thought it was a false alarm. I didn't wake Pat until it was time to go to work. He was eating breakfast when I realized that it was the real thing. I let him finish breakfast and then told him to call the doctor. He had to go about six blocks to get to a phone. He asked the two ladies next door to come in and stay with me. They came all right, but they took one look at me and saw that the baby was ready to come. One of them blurted out, "Oh, my gosh!" And they both took off running, as if the devil was after them.

Neither one of them ever came back but, the baby's head was already out and I had to finish the job myself before something else could happen. I wrapped the baby in a blanket that was lying within my reach. Pat came shortly after that, but he didn't know what to do, so we just had to wait for the doctor to arrive.

The doctor showed up about thirty minutes later but the baby had already been fully born by that time. The doctor cut the cord right away and told me the baby had gotten a little too much blood but, other than that, she was fine. I told the doctor about the two women next door and he was just furious. If they had come in just then, I believe he would have "laid them out."

Pat had shifted from one job to another all that year. He either got fired or quit himself because he got mad at someone. By November that fall, he had had thirteen jobs within nine months. The house was livable enough as it was, but Pat got the idea that he wanted to put a basement under it.

He got a contractor to raise the house and put it on cement blocks. When the fellow didn't get paid at that stage, he wouldn't go any farther. He left it as it was. Everything was wide open. Then we got a severe cold spell. Everything froze up. We had to carry water from our next-door neighbor's house for the next five months. That was really sweet with two little children to wash for.

Pat was out of work altogether at that time. We were very short of fuel when Christmas Eve came. We had two potatoes and half a loaf of bread; also, one can of milk for the baby. We had no regular milk, coffee, sugar or butter, and certainly no meat. We had our Christmas dinner of bread and potatoes. In the evening, a friend of ours came over after having guessed our circumstances. She brought us a few things in the line of groceries.

Our fuel situation was still very bad. A couple of days later, there was a raging blizzard. Our house was very cold. But we had a gas stove in the kitchen, which helped a little. Linnea got a bad case of tonsillitis that night. Her temperature was 105. We knew we couldn't get a doctor on a night like that. We had her lying on the kitchen table. Cold packs were on her head and her throat. Her feet were ice-cold up to her knees. We thought she was going to die on us. We heated hot water, put it in bottles and packed her legs in blankets after we had massaged her legs. It was a terrible night, but by morning her temperature began to drop and her feet got warm. The good Lord was watching over us.

Shortly after that, we got our second cold spell of the winter. I kept Violet (the baby) in bed with me so she would stay warm. We didn't have plastic pants in those days. One morning when I got up, I left her in bed. After breakfast when I came to pick her up, the seat of her diaper was frozen to the bed. She developed a slight touch of pneumonia, but we managed to get the doctor right away and she came out of it just fine. Nobody would believe this, although it's true. I froze my toes just walking around the kitchen doing my work.

Linnea had rickets. She dragged one leg and had a rough time walking at all. When she was ten months old, she had a very bad case of diarrhea. She was in the hospital for twelve days. The doctor put her on a buttermilk diet. She couldn't have anything else for several months. Later, when she could have other things, we just didn't have the things that she was supposed to have. It didn't take long before her joints were just big lumps. After she got the right treatment, she came out of it just fine. By the time she was three years old, she was back to normal.

By New Year's Day, we were out of fuel. We didn't have food. I got a job in a knitting factory where they also had some spinning. I was a part-time spinner and part-time elevator operator. I took the children to a day nursery. Pat had a few days' work now and then. The place where I worked was across town and the nursery was close by my work. I did that for two weeks but it was awfully hard, getting the children up at six o'clock in the morning and getting them ready, then taking them on the streetcar.

As I mentioned previously, Linnea had a hard time walking. After I got home in the evening, I had to do the washing and carry water from the house next door. No washing machines in those days. Everything was done by hand. I also had to carry in the coal and carry out the ashes. Pat was no good around the house. There were many things he could have done, but he absolutely refused. As much as I hated it, I had to put the children in a boarding home for a time.

The evening we took them there, a big blizzard came up. It wasn't so very bad when we left home, but after we rode across town on the streetcar and walked five blocks up the hill, the snow was about to our knees. The wind was terrible and we could hardly breathe. I carried Violet; Pat carried Linnea. Luckily, we had them wrapped in blankets and we covered their faces.

They were in the home for three weeks. Then one Sunday, when we went to visit, they were both sick. The Spanish flu was then raging everywhere. I suspected it was the flu. We took them home. I called the doctor as soon as we got home. He came and looked them over. He said, "It's either measles or the flu."

He came again early the next morning and by that time both the doctor and I well knew that it was the flu. I had it, too. That time, Pat had to do what absolutely had to be done, such as taking care of the fire and getting the water. There just wasn't any help to be had for us anywhere.

The girls got well a lot faster than I did. On the ninth day, I tried to get out of bed. Everything turned black and I almost fainted. If I hadn't grabbed the corner of the table, I would have gone down. I was sick for a long time and couldn't go back to work, and that put us right back where we were financially a couple of months before.

Heaping up the miseries, Pat wasn't working either, but I finally got a job at a rug factory, working nights, from eleven at night until five in the morning. As long as Pat wasn't working, I thought he could stay home with the children. They slept all through the night anyway. I always put them to bed before I went out and they never woke up until six in the morning, and by that time I was home. Pat had to be home by ten at night, though, which he didn't like. But I felt that if he wanted to eat, he could do that much.

I worked there for two months when Pat decided that he didn't want to be home by 10 o'clock anymore. I told him, "That's just fine with me, but then you go to work." I was pregnant again anyway. He couldn't support the two that he had, but he tried all the underhanded tricks that he could think of to get me pregnant. And as soon as I got pregnant, he refused to go any place with me. He wouldn't even go with me to visit our friends. I had to go alone with the children wherever I went. By that time, I had had it, so to speak, and I wanted out, but I was brought up to believe that marriage was for keeps. I have had ample reason to think differently since then.

Pat worked a few days here and there, not enough income to get proper food for the children, let alone pay anything on the house. Suddenly Linnea came down with a very bad case of diarrhea again. I took her to the doctor's office. He put his hand on her stomach and the finger marks stayed there. It was just like a piece of dough. The hospital was on the outskirts of town. The doctor said, "Get her to the hospital at once and don't wait for the streetcar; get a taxi." I was in a fog and I don't really remember what went on, but I believe the doctor gave me money for the taxi, because I'm sure I didn't have that much when I left home. She was very sick for two weeks, but with God's help, she pulled through.

We were behind several payments on the house. The fellow that we bought it from knew that we were never going to be able to catch up. He gave us until the end of October to move out. My next baby was due in November. Pat was getting in a worse humor by the day. He was griping about everything and everybody.

We rented a three-room apartment on the other side of town. There was no bathtub and we had to share the toilet with another family. But worst of all, it was overrun by roaches. They made me sick every time I saw one. Pat kept on selling one piece of furniture after another. I put up a fight about the icebox, though. I couldn't afford to buy ice, but that was the only place I could keep the food where the roaches didn't get it.

Pat's brother came to the house often. He loved the children and played with them as if he was one of them, and they just loved him.

One thing about Pat that aggravated me to no end was that he opened all my mail and went through my pockets and all of my drawers. If I wrote a letter to someone and sealed it before he had a chance to read it, he would tear open the envelope and read the letter. Once, I thought I would let him know that I didn't approve. I wrote on a sheet of paper: "Anyone who opens this letter except the one who it is addressed to is a mutton head." Then I put it in an envelope and addressed it to one of our friends. Naturally, he opened it. He had a very embarrassed look on his face. His only comment was, "It was a mutton head that wrote it, too." But it cured him of opening the outgoing letters. He still opened the ones addressed to me.

Raymond was born just three weeks after we moved into the apartment. He was a large baby and for the second time I was badly torn. I had the same doctor and the County gave us a nurse during the delivery. She also came for ten days, once a day. We were lucky enough to get a woman to stay for a week to look after the two girls.

The apartment was small, so we managed to keep fairly warm, except for the time when the fuel ran out before we could buy some more. Sometimes when

Pat's brother came, if he noticed that there was nothing in the icebox, he would hand me a couple of dollars.

Linnea had trouble with her tonsils. She had a sore throat all winter. Towards spring, the pus began to run out of her ears. The doctor said that her tonsils had to come out. So, finally, I brought her to the hospital one morning and left her there. I came back in the evening and picked her up. She got along just fine after that. I don't believe that she has ever been sick since then, except for the measles when she was about twelve years old, and an appendectomy when she was in her early twenties.

The street where we lived wasn't paved at the time, so there wasn't much traffic. But the street was two feet down from the sidewalk and there were a lot of rough and sharp stones in the gutter.

One day, the girls were playing on the sidewalk right outside of the house. They both had white dresses on. Suddenly they came in, both screaming and both covered with blood. With white dresses on, they were enough to scare anyone. I didn't know which one was hurt until I washed the blood off. Then I discovered that Violet had a large cut on her forehead, but it wasn't very deep. She had fallen on the rocks and got a cut. Linnea was trying help her up and she got just as much blood on her as the one that was hurt.

We lived in that place about a year and a half. Then I was pregnant again. Naturally, we moved into a basement flat of four rooms. It was below a grocery store and was overrun by rats. Sometimes the rats would run over the children in bed at night and they would wake up screaming. One day, I put my hand in the clothes bin and got my hand right on the back of a rat. I'm still wondering why it didn't bite me. Perhaps it didn't like "white meat." Anyway, it just scampered up the water pipe and disappeared. In the winter, the walls in the bathroom and pantry were covered with ice. I shouldn't call it a bathroom. There was no tub; it was a room with a toilet only.

My clothes were all worn out. I had one skirt that had a hole in the front. I had to wear an apron at all times. I had no shoes. I wore a pair of men's shoes around the house. One evening, the lady upstairs asked me to go to a show with her but I couldn't go because I had nothing to wear.

I was pregnant again and this time I was very large. I couldn't afford maternity clothes, so I wore an old middy. I guess I looked like something from outer space. The doctor suspected that I was going to have twins, but he didn't tell me. He said afterwards that he didn't want to worry me. As a result, when the twins were born, I had six diapers, two little skimpy blankets and two baby nightgowns. I had nothing to change them with, even the first time. They were born in the morning, one at five, the other one at five-thirty; both boys. Both weighed about six pounds. One was a blue-eyed blond; the other one had brown eyes, brown hair and a darker complexion. We had no fear of mixing them up. In fact, we called them Ole and Frenchie the first couple of years, although their names were Albert and Harold.

About nine o'clock that morning, after they were born, the nurse got in touch with the Masonic Clinic to get some baby clothes. The people from the clinic brought up two layettes.

When the babies were two days old, Pat decided to go hunting. The nurse came once a day in the morning, but the rest of the day I was left alone. I was in bed, naturally, and besides the babies, there were three others running around. The oldest was only four-and-a-half years old. To top everything, Pat had left the butcher knife on the kitchen table when he left hat morning. Raymond took the butcher knife and started chasing the two girls. The more they screamed, the faster he ran. I had to get out of bed pronto, although the doctor had told me to stay in bed.

It was the latter part of October and no fire in the heater. The floors were ice cold. I must have caught a cold somehow, because my stomach started to swell and I was running a temperature. I sent Linnea upstairs in the store to have someone call the doctor. When the doctor came, the first thing he said was, "You got out of bed, didn't you." The landlord was the one that ran the store. He came down to see what was going on. He hit the ceiling when he found out that Pat had left town to go hunting.

He didn't like Pat anyway. And that was just about the last straw. The landlord went upstairs and got some coal and some kindling and started a fire in the heater. He was such a wonderful person. He was Jewish and I've liked the Jewish people ever since, although I had nothing against them before this incident either.

Linnea was only four and a half, but she was already going to the kindergarten, so that left Violet to run all my errands at the time. She was only a little over three, but she was very capable. She also kept an eye on Raymond for me.

Albert began to lose weight. He couldn't keep any food down. All the neighborhood ladies began to tell me that he wasn't going to live. I was ready to slug the next one who opened her mouth. The doctor discovered that he had a small tumor and needed to be in the hospital for awhile. They didn't operate, but somehow, he began to keep food down and gain weight. He also had leakage of the heart and when I took him home, the doctor said to keep him separated from the others because he was very delicate. I kept him on the dining room table with chairs all around it so the others couldn't get to him.

71

Some months later, I put him on the bed one day and a cat jumped in through the open window. It scared him and he fainted, but he came out of that in a little while.

Then Harold began to be troubled with bronchitis. For a time, they alternated being in the hospital. I usually took one home and brought the other one to the hospital. The worst time for me was when I had them both at home and both sick at the same time. If they cried at night, Pat would go into a tantrum and I never knew what to expect next, so I had to walk all night with one on each arm. Just so the "Lord and Master" could sleep, even when he wasn't working. My back ached so I could have screamed.

We used wood for the cook stove, but Pat never split the wood. I had to do that, too. Once, a piece of wood flew up and broke my nose. Pat laughed and said I should have been more careful.

When the twins were five months old, Raymond had to have his tonsils out. The Masons had a surgery in an old building. They did minor surgery there. The day that was set for surgery, Pat just happened to get a couple of days work. I couldn't ask him to stay home because we needed the money to get something to eat. I tried to get someone in the neighborhood to baby-sit with the twins, but had no luck. One had a P.T.A. meeting, one had to wash, one had to go downtown, etc.

In desperation, I said a prayer, left the twins in bed and fixed the covers so they couldn't pull them over their faces. Then I took Violet and Raymond down to the clinic. Linnea was in school.

I told the nurse that I had left the babies alone. She said that I should stay during the surgery, but as soon as it was over, I could leave Violet in the lobby and I could go home. I could come back later and pick both of them up.

I did that, but I had to walk home. It was about eighteen blocks. I had no streetcar fare. When it was time to go back, Linnea was home from school so I left her to keep an eye on the twins. If something went wrong, I asked her to get the landlord. He was very good about providing a helping hand, if needed. But everything was all right. They were such good babies except when they were sick. I went back to pick up the children. Raymond was a little sick from the ether. I had to carry him, but the nurse gave me a token so I could take the streetcar home.

Pats disposition was getting worse. He began to beat the children. One night, Raymond walked in his sleep. Pat jumped up and paddled him without mercy. The poor little fellow never knew what it was all about. If I said anything, he beat them twice as hard.

One day, Violet poured a little cream on her dish of Jell-O. Pat beat her on the bottom with his big paws. She started bleeding from the bowels. It stopped after a while so I didn't call the doctor, but that little trick caused her to have three operations before she was twenty-eight years old.

One day, Raymond and the girls were playing on the davenport. Linnea accidentally kicked Raymond in the face. She only had a slipper on, so he wasn't really hurt. I had been practicing on the violin shortly before that, so I had set the violin and bow on the table. Pat grabbed the bow and whacked Linnea across the face. She put up her arm. She had a big red streak across her face and another one on her arm. The bow broke, of course. I had to wait several months before I could buy a new bow and then only a very cheap one.

Mother died shortly before the twins were born. That was a hard blow to me, but she suffered so much the last six months of her life that it was a blessing that she could go. She had nephritis and her body swelled to

73

double the normal size. The skin cracked and water ran out. She was in a sitting position the whole six weeks before her death.

Now, a year after that, I got the message that Frank had been murdered. Someone broke into his cabin on board ship at night while they were in the harbor in order to rob him.

Just at this time, Harold came down with bronchitis again. He had such a high fever that it brought on convulsions. That was a new experience for me. I had heard someone say that one should put the person in very warm water so that's what I did. He came out of it all right but, an hour later, he came down with another one. I called the doctor then and he ordered him to the hospital.

The next day, Albert had a high temperature. I didn't know the reason and, with his already weakened condition, I didn't want to take any chances. I took him to the doctor's office at once. The doctor prescribed some powders and told me to take him home and give him a cold sponge to get the temperature down as quickly as possible.

I had to go on the streetcar and then walk three blocks to get home. I was a block from the house when he went into convulsions. Luckily, I had left a full teakettle of water on the stove when I left the house. There was fire in the stove so the water was still hot. There were no hot water tanks at that time in the poorer sections of town.

Pat's brother had taken the three older children out in the country that day and Pat had gone with them. I had no one to send to the drugstore for the medicine. After Albert came out of the convulsion, I put him on the bed and ran to the drugstore. I ran all the way and was gone only about twenty minutes. When I reached home, he was in another convulsion.

I got him out of that one and gave him the powder. The temperature dropped and he never had convulsions again. Harold was in the hospital about two weeks. He didn't have any more convulsions either, after that. It was a terrible strain while it lasted.

It was time for me to be pregnant again, which I was, and the doctor that I had for my first five deliveries had gone to Europe and would be gone for a couple of years. This time I was going to have the county doctor. He was nice, but I missed my old doctor.

On Christmas Eve, I had been in pain all day, alone, taking care of the five other children; the twins couldn't walk yet. I was a wreck, physically, when evening came. Pat had been out all day.

Walter was born about six o'clock Christmas Eve night. Everything went fine after all. We had four rooms, including the kitchen, one living room combination and two very small bedrooms. The nurse stayed for a while and helped the other five children into bed. They all slept on the davenport, which opened up to make a full-sized bed. But just imagine: five of them in one bed. That sounds like something from another continent. The nurse put the baby in bed with me and Pat had the other bedroom next to mine.

Pat went to bed about nine o'clock. He never even looked in to see if I was all right. He just went to sleep. Period.

During the night, I heard one of those big rats walking towards my bed. I was really frightened because of the baby. Otherwise I'm not afraid of rats or mice. I started pounding on the side of the bed, which made a lot of noise. It must have scared the rat away because I heard it run the other way. I didn't dare to go to sleep though.

The baby didn't get anything but water for the first twenty-four hours. I kept his water bottle wrapped up with a hot water bottle and a towel to keep it warm.

I don't know if there's anything like a "simple" delivery, because they all have an affect on the body somewhere along the line. With Walter, I was flowing heavily that night and then the cold set in. Pat had carelessly let the fire go out in the heater. I tried to wake him up by rapping on the wall, but he slept too soundly for that. I didn't want to call him for fear of waking the children, so I just settled in for a long, shiver-filled night.

He got up about eight o'clock. He was cold by that time himself. He did come in then and ask if I was cold. I said, "Yes," but I didn't mention that I had tried half the night to wake him up. It wouldn't have helped matters any. So I kept quiet about it. He started a fire and tried to make some coffee for himself. The nurse came shortly after that to give the baby a bath and do what she could for me.

We had received a Christmas basket from some organization, so we had a bit of food on hand. The nurse helped the children with their breakfast, but I didn't feel so well. I couldn't eat just then. I got a little hungry later on in the afternoon, but Pat couldn't cook and wasn't very handy in the kitchen, so I just waited for something to turn up. A neighbor lady from across the street came in about six o'clock in the evening. She made some ham and eggs. I will always remember that meal.

When I first became pregnant with Walter, Pat made a remark that he had "good neighbors," meaning the baby wasn't his. He happened to say it at the wrong time.

I was clearing off the table and had just picked up a glass of jelly. I aimed it at his head, but he saw it coming and ducked. The glass hit the wall and shattered and the mess went all over Pat. He never made that remark again. But I made him feel very cheap about it later.

Walter looked more like Pat than any of the others, although they all looked more like him than they looked like me. When Walter was about a week old, the nurse remarked about the close likeness between the baby and Pat. She said that he was an exact miniature of Pat. I said, "That can't be possible; Pat said that it isn't his." The nurse gave him a very cold look indeed. That's the only time I ever saw Pat blush.

We still had no washing machine, so it was quite a struggle to wash for eight people with three in diapers. As we had no hot water, everything had to be heated on the stove. There was an awful lot of lifting, which was hard on my legs. When the baby was two weeks old, I got an inflammation of the blood vessels. That was the start. At this writing, that was forty-two years ago and I'll have trouble with my legs the rest of my life. When that first happened, I had to keep my feet in an elevated position for six weeks. The Welfare Department got a woman to come in for a few hours every day to do the heavy work.

Pat hadn't been working for several months. They had started to build a big hotel in town. Pat knew that if he had a dump truck he could get a few months work. He bought a five-ton dump truck on the installment plan. He got about eight month's of work at the hotel, which helped a lot, but with the big payments on the truck, there wasn't very much left over. Nevertheless, we managed.

Pat was about as mean-natured a person as I had ever known and the children were very much afraid of him. They tried to keep out of his way as much as they could.

One day, Raymond came in crying and sobbing, "Daddy is coming. Daddy is coming." I asked him, "What did you do?" He said, "Nothing. Nothing." He went into the bedroom and put his hands over his face, leaning over the bed just shaking and sobbing. It took me a long time to calm him down. He was just three-and-a-half. Imagine how hard it must have been for the poor little fellow to be that scared of his father. And he wasn't the only one. They all had the same fear.

When Walter was thirteen months old, he wanted to follow Linnea into the bathroom one day. When she shut the door, he started to cry rather loudly. Pat grabbed him and whaled the daylights out of him. When he noticed that Walter wasn't breathing he handed him to me. I said, "Well, you've finally done it; I think he's dead. But get the doctor anyway." I fully believed the baby was dead. I could see that it wasn't convulsions, but I tried the same method. Only the water was a lot hotter than I used for the others. I was scared to death.

I had some hot water on the stove but I knew that wasn't enough. I ran across the yard just a few steps, grabbed the neighbor's teakettle without saying a word, and ran home. Pat did the same thing with another neighbor. I don't know if he explained or not. He just brought the kettle in and put it in front of me. Then he ran out again.

I had the hot water in the washtub. I put the baby in there. The water was so hot that my arms turned the color of a boiled lobster. I was praying out loud and holding the baby in the tub when the fellow came in to see what happened to their teakettle He just stood there and watched me without saying a word. Walter was in the water for fully six minutes before he showed signs of life. That was the longest six minutes I have ever gone through.

Linnea was a very religious little girl. She was just six but she was going to Sunday school every Sunday. She was sitting on a little chair holding Albert when she heard me tell Pat that I thought Walter was dead. She yelled out, "Oh, my best child." She dropped Albert like a hot potato. She ran into the bedroom, kneeled down and started praying. She was still there praying when Walter finally came back to consciousness.

The doctor said the next day that it was tetanus. I didn't know what became of Pat after he left the house. I found out later that he had cut across three backyards and jumped a six-foot fence to get to a telephone. He must really have been frightened. Our regular children's doctor was out of town. Pat called another that we had used once in an emergency, but he hadn't been paid and refused to come. I can't fault him for that I guess, but it really didn't make any difference. If Walter had died, he would have been dead before the doctor got there anyway. It was just a miracle that he lived. I don't ever want to go through anything like that again. I had nightmares for three weeks after that.

Our regular doctor was in town the next day, so I took Walter to him. He said that Walter's tonsils were too big and that they were choking him. They had to come out. Walter had a tonsillectomy when he was only fourteen months old. Then his throat wouldn't heal. Six months later, we had to take him back to the hospital. The doctor painted his throat with something and kept him under observation for a whole week. He was all right after that.

A month later, the twins had their tonsils out, one week apart. It seemed that everyone in the family had trouble with their tonsils. Not long after that, it was Violet's turn. We lived only three blocks from the hospital. When the day came for her operation, I couldn't go, because I couldn't leave all the others by themselves. Pat happened to have work that day. So Violet walked down to the hospital all by herself. She wasn't quite six years old. When I got to the hospital several hours later, the tonsils were out and she was in bed. Not long after that, she got a kidney infection and had to stay in the hospital for seven weeks.

We were several months behind with the rent. The landlord gave us notice to move out. I didn't blame him, because he knew that he would never be able to collect the back rent. We couldn't rent a place with six children. Nobody wanted children, not even two, let alone six. So we had to buy an old place. The truck was not paid for in full; there was a $500.00 balance on it. But Pat put it up as security in some way, which he shouldn't have done. But more on that later.

We were getting ready to move into the house we had bought. The truck hadn't been used for some time so Pat was getting it ready for moving the next day. It was an old-style truck with a crank starter. Well, the truck kicked back and Pat got a broken arm for his effort. That's all he needed. He was miserable to get along with anyway and having a broken arm only served to make him impossible.

When they started carrying the furniture, he hadn't fastened the buffet drawers; they fell out and smashed all to pieces. And who got the blame. I did, naturally, although I wasn't within twenty feet of the thing. Then when we got into the new place, I had to go downtown to get the water and light meter straightened out. Pat was supposed to keep an eye on the children. When I returned home, at first I couldn't find Walter. He couldn't even walk, so I knew that he couldn't be very far away. I hunted a while and finally found him in a cupboard that was even with the floor. One of the other children must have shut the door on him. It wasn't airtight and he was fast asleep, so there was no harm done, although I had some anxious moments.

I checked the others and Albert was missing. I couldn't find him anywhere. So I went out and called the police and gave a neighbor's telephone number. We didn't have a phone. It seemed like hours later that the neighbor came and said that they had found him fifteen blocks away, sitting on somebody's porch, crying. He had started out for the old place. Instead of going up the hill at the next corner, he just kept on walking straight ahead. After all, he was only two-and-a-half years old.

One day, a friend of ours who worked for the City, came to the house and told Pat that they needed a man to run the street sweeping machine and the grader. Pat still had the cast on the lower part of his arm, but the fellow said to put his coat on and go down and apply for the job. The work wasn't very hard to handle and the man was sure Pat wouldn't have any trouble about the arm if they didn't see it. So Pat did just that and he got the job. It was easy and good pay.

Of course we were making monthly payments on the house and couldn't make payments on the truck. We were several payments behind and one fine day they gave Pat just twenty-four hours to pay up. That's when Pat was heading for trouble, because he had put up the truck as security when we bought the house. I felt sorry for him as usual, although I shouldn't have, because I never got any credit for my good deeds. I went to Andrew's good friend and told him the whole story. He paid the $500.00 to the company that owned the truck. Incidentally, Pat filed bankruptcy some time later, so that fellow never got his $500.00 back.

It was difficult to get any money from Pat for household use even when he was working. If I told him the coal was running out, he would say, "Go out and fight for it." Fine chance I had to fight for anything. We had six children between two and eight, and I was pregnant with the seventh.

The chimney hadn't been cleaned for years, and one morning we all woke up sick from coal gas. It's a miracle that we woke up at all. Another thirty minutes and none of us would have been here to tell about it. As soon as I realized there was something wrong, I got all doors and windows open and got everyone outside.

Pat began to slide behind with the payments on the house. A neighbor that we knew very well took it over so we could make the payments to him. He had a hard time on his own, as he had lost one arm in an accident several years before. The company had cheated him out of the insurance. He had a wife and five children to support. He was selling insurance for a living. Besides all his other bad luck, his twelve-year-old son was drowned one day. He was going down in health and spirit daily after that. He still stood by us, though.

Pat did crazy things that I was never able to understand. He was interested in music, just as I was. But when Linnea won a year's scholarship on the violin, he had one of his bad days. He picked up her violin and smashed it against the wall. Well, I wasn't going to let that scholarship go to waste. I went down to the music studio and told them the story. They let her use one of their violins and gave her a room to practice in. She went there every day after school for two years. Sometimes if Pat thought she should have been in the house sooner, he would scold her, but she never told him where she had been.

After those two years, she played rather well. So I thought I would try her at home again. She was then big enough to use the full-size violin that I had. So she played at home. Pat didn't bother her after that. In fact, he was trying to take all the credit for her doing so well. But when Violet got a scholarship on the piano, he locked the piano and kept the key. So she had to do the same thing; go to the studio and practice every day after school. They liked music, so I never had trouble getting them to practice.

One day, several neighbor boys from eleven to thirteen went into an unlocked warehouse in the next yard to ours. They took a couple of twenty-two caliber long guns and some tools. Being next door, Raymond tagged along with them. He was only five-and-a-half years old.

He didn't have any of the loot, but when Pat found out that he had been in the warehouse with the others, he grabbed Raymond and started to question him. The boy was scared stiff, as they say, and wasn't able to say anything. When he didn't answer, Pat gave him a hard slap in the face so he flew across the floor. He fell and his nose and mouth were bleeding. I guess Raymond was too scared to get up, so he just lay there. Pat went over and picked him up by the collar and put him on the chair. His only comment was, "I guess I hit him a little too hard." Then he walked out.

Raymond got an almost uncountable number of beatings all through the years while he was in grade school and I don't believe he ever forgot them. When he was nineteen, he happened to come into town one day. Pat had lost a finger the day before, and was in the hospital. I told Raymond about it and added, "Are you going to see him?" He looked at me and then he asked a question: "What do I want to see him for?" He didn't go to the hospital, and I understood perfectly.

We had a ten-room house and rented out the upstairs. There was a Jewish lady living in the upper rooms, but towards the spring, she was giving up housekeeping. It was hard to get help so she promised to stay during my confinement and take care of the other children. She was wonderful with the children, good-natured with others and I was very happy to have her.

The baby was two days overdue, the first time that ever happened to me. They were usually early. I had the same county doctor as I had when Walter was born. We couldn't get the nurse right away. It was one o'clock in the morning. The Jewish lady was going to give me the ether and she started to pour it on instead of dripping it and it was choking me. I had to take the anesthetic mask contraption off my nose and explain to her how to administer the anesthetic. The baby was very big and the doctor had to use forceps for the third time during my deliveries. I was badly torn by this one.

The baby weighed eleven pounds. The nurse got there before it was all over. We had four boys in a row, so it was a novelty to have a little girl again. We called her Mildred.

Pat was happy about the baby being a girl, so he called all our friends at three o'clock in the morning to tell them the news. The news could have waited, in my opinion, but that was his idea. Mildred, I guess, was always his favorite. He never slapped her and he never gave her a hard time like the others. When Walter woke up in the morning and heard the baby cry, he came walking up to my bed. He asked, "Is that your baby, Mother?" When I nodded my head, he asked, "Are you going to keep it?" I said, "Yes, you'll have to take good care of her." And he always did. If anyone picked on her at play or in school, he was always there to put up a fight. He never asked where any of his brothers were when he came in. If he didn't see her, it was always the same question: "Where is Sis?"

But, again, I'm slightly ahead of my story.

The day after Mildred was born Pat broke his arm again, fooling around with that old dump truck again. (No fool like an old fool?) Five of the youngsters came down with the measles. Linnea had gone to a health camp for the summer. She wasn't sick but she was terribly underweight.

It was the middle of June, but the weather was very cool. The poor Jewish lady was trying hard to keep the children in bed and keep them covered. The twins were not very sick but they had to stay in bed and away from the draft. Their bed was next to the window, so they got up and opened the window. She would look into the room and see the window open and the boys with their head out. She would rush over to the window and say, "Are you cr-r-razy?" and down went the window with a bang. Thirty minutes later, the performance would be repeated.

Not very long after that, Pat had a gall bladder operation. He was such a baby. I went to the hospital and sat with him the first day. He got along fine but he wanted everybody's sympathy. So he was telling anyone who would listen that it was an emergency operation caused by his lifting a piano by himself and thereby causing the gall bladder to burst, all of which was fantasy of course. Then again, later, he had a tonsillectomy, and again another fairy story. This time his tonsils "were so bad" that they had to pick them out in pieces. It would have been funny if it hadn't sounded so silly. I was embarrassed no end when he started telling those tales.

He missed about three months of work that year, but the City never deducted one cent from his wages. They were wonderful.

I had had several attacks of the gall bladder problem. The doctor said that surgery was the only solution. But where could I get someone to take care of the children while I was in the hospital? The Jewish lady had already gone.

One day I had a very serious attack that left me extremely weak for two weeks. That was the last attack I ever had. The doctor said that it could have been gallstones and that I may have passed them. In either event, illnesses have rarely been visited on me since then, with the exception of pneumonia, which I came down with the next winter after I caught a bad cold trying to clean out the coal shed preparing for a coal delivery. When I got through cleaning it out, I was already too sick to wash. I lay down on the bed fully dressed and just as filthy black as I was when I crawled out of the coal shed.

Pat called the doctor and the doctor said to take me to the hospital at once. The nurses were so busy trying to get my temperature down during the night that they hadn't really seen what I looked like. The next morning, when one of the nurses came to give me a bath, she made a noise like a deflating tire. In spite of still being very sick, I couldn't help laughing. I could only imagine what I looked like.

One very fine Sunday afternoon the following summer, Walter took Raymond's wagon for a ride down the hill. Nobody saw him leave. We started looking for him, but couldn't find him anywhere. Some neighborhood boy told Raymond that Walter had been killed and the wagon was smashed beyond repair. At the time, I believe that Raymond was more worried about his wagon than about his brother.

I couldn't leave the house because of Mildred and the twins. The girls were already out scouting for Walter. Pat was standing across the alleyway. I called to him to go and see what he could find out. He swore at me and made some remark about sending the kids out to look for him, so I didn't get any help from the boy's father either.

When we had collected everybody involved and the dust had settled, here's what actually happened: Walter rode five blocks down a dead-end avenue, gaining speed as he went until he crashed into some rocks and bushes at the end of the avenue, and right at the beginning the edge of a twenty-five foot drop to the street below. The bushes and rocks stopped the wagon but Walter continued over the edge and dropped to the sidewalk adjacent to the street below. It stunned him, of course, but a witness to the accident across the street saw him fall. He ran across the street and picked Walter up and naturally thought he had been killed. The witness then called the police, who actually got there in fairly short order and, while the police were questioning the witness, trying to discover who everyone was, Walter woke up. They asked him his name and Walter managed to at least give them his first name. I still don't know why they stayed on the street below asking questions instead of getting Walter to the hospital.

To discover something about the neighborhood he came from, they asked him the name of the store where he bought his candy! He gave the name of the drugstore a half a block from the house. The police brought him there. Linnea had just come into the store when the police came. They didn't even bother to bring the poor kid home. They left him with his sister. Walter was dizzy from the fall, so she half carried and half led him home.

I took him to the emergency room in the hospital a short distance away. Walter had a blue mark behind one ear, but the doctor couldn't find any fractures. He said to take him home and keep him in bed for twenty-four hours. If he started to vomit, I was to call the doctor at once. If he didn't, I was to bring him back for a check-up in forty-eight hours. He didn't vomit, although he said that he felt like it a couple of times. In fact, there were no further complaints from him. I was worried for several years afterwards though, for fear of something showing up later.

That was Walter's second close brush with death. The third time came years later when he was thirty-six years old. But more on that when I get to that point in the story.

After the Jewish lady moved out from the upstairs, there was an old German couple that moved in. They were the nicest people one could ever meet. The lady was not well. They had lost their only child, a daughter, through an operation two years before. The lady never got over the shock. But she loved our children. She was just like a grandmother to them. At Christmas time, the old German fellow played Santa Claus, and he was a natural if there ever was one. I enjoyed having them around. But it was too good to last. After Pat had worked for the City for a year-and-a-half, he got into an argument with the foreman one day. There was a fight and Pat got fired. I was surprised that he had kept the job that long, but it was still a blow when it fell.

Pat wasn't working, so naturally, he was minding everyone else's business. He got into an argument with the German fellow and they moved out. There was no money coming in, so I had to go to work. That wasn't easy with seven little ones. It was hard to get a dependable woman to stay with the children during the day, even if they didn't have to do any of the housework, which they didn't. Pat would always have something to say. I got one woman who was pretty good, but some days she would send her fifteen-year-old daughter instead. But some of the things the children noticed about Pat's behavior when the girl was there made me realize it wasn't safe for Pat or the girl. I didn't want a scandal of any kind, so I had to let the mother and the girl go.

I worked six miles from home. I got a ride to work in the morning with the boss, but I walked home every night, just to save a few cents. When it was Violet's birthday, I bought her a small doll buggy which she had wanted for a long time. I also bought an inexpensive wagon for Raymond because he hadn't gotten anything for his last birthday. I paid fifty cents a week, which was a little less than I saved walking home. Still Pat had a fit about it. He wasn't working and he wasn't looking after the children. Everything fell on me which was usual.

I never knew what to expect when I got home at night. One evening when I came home, Walter's eyes were swollen shut. Pat had hit him in the face. I took Walter to the hospital to have him checked and I told the intern what had happened. Both the intern and the nun said that Pat should be in jail. But in those days, there wasn't much done about it. Also, there was a lot of red tape to go through. Above all, I didn't ever want to put the children in an orphanage. I would rather go through any hardship. A couple of times, I called the police when Pat was breaking up things around the house while in one of his tantrums. But the police always seemed to have the same excuse. "We didn't see him do it." That was natural. He wasn't going to do it in front of the police. In fact, he disappeared every time he knew that I went out to call the police.

We were months behind with the payments on the house. I was praying that some way or somehow we would be able to pay up so we wouldn't lose the house. We were $450.00 in arrears. Help came from a very unexpected source. Truly, the Lord works in a mysterious way to perform His wonders.

The house was an old-fashioned one where the porch ran along two walls of the house. It really wasn't of any use to us – just a lot of work to keep it clean. The twins were in the kindergarten and it was fire prevention week. There were a lot of lectures in school about fires. Somehow, it didn't sink in to little ones thought processing, at least the way the teachers had intended.

Harold and a neighbor boy the same age decided to build a bonfire under the porch. Harold got some newspapers from the house and the other boy went to his home to get the matches.

Before anybody really knew what had happened, the whole porch was burning. Raymond just happened to come into the yard and saw the smoke. He ran to the corner where the alarm box was and turned in the alarm. He was only seven-and-a-half years old at the time.

There was an old lady babysitting at the time. She was a little lame and very stubborn. Mildred was in the house with the old lady. The children were yelling for her to come out and bring the baby, but she couldn't find her purse and she wouldn't come out without it. She was limping around looking for the purse; the fire wasn't important to her.

A boy of about thirteen, who lived a few houses away, came running into the yard. The girls yelled that the baby was in there. He kicked one of the windows out and brought Mildred out. The firemen came then and took the old lady out. She had not as yet found her purse.

The firemen put the fire out. No damaged was done to the house, except the broken windows. The porch was a total loss of course. I came home shortly after that, and saw that something had happened. My first concern was the children, but someone told me that they were all right. I gave a big sigh of thanks. Pat, of course, was a raving maniac. I told him to hush. "Nothing is hurt but the porch and that's covered by insurance, but don't tell that to the small ones, or they might take a notion to burn the whole place down." Of course I had a serious talk with Harold, telling him that he was not to start a fire any place at any time and how someone could have been very badly hurt.

The insurance company paid us $450.00 for the old porch, just what we owed at the time. Pat got some old lumber and put up a small porch and it didn't cost more than $25.00 for the whole thing.

Pat wanted to go into the dray business. He was hinting for a truck. I thought he might be able to do something if he had a small truck. I bought one on the installment plan. The boss backed me up; otherwise I might not have been able to get one. It took me a whole year to pay for it. My whole wage went for the truck and the baby sitter. The problem was to feed the family. It was a major operation to get money out of Pat, even when he had it. I didn't even get as much as a "thank you" for buying the truck. The only good part about it was that he couldn't sell the truck because it was in my name.

Pat's brother had been working in another state all summer. He came back in town two days before Raymond's birthday. Raymond had a small party just for his sisters and brothers. I had bought Raymond a second-hand saxophone, which I got very cheaply from a friend of ours. All of our children were musically inclined. They all managed to get scholarships to start them off.

Getting back to the birthday party, Pat's brother was there all day, playing with the children. They had so much fun and they'll never forget that day. When he left that afternoon, he said that he would come back the next evening.

So, the next evening, we were waiting for him to come. Instead, someone came to the front door and knocked. I remarked, "I wonder why he came to the front door," because that door was usually locked. Pat went to the door. When he came back to the kitchen, he got his jacket in a terrible hurry and called over his shoulder on his way out, "Ernie got killed," meaning his brother.

It felt like someone stabbing me with a knife. Linnea almost went into shock. She loved her uncle and they had been exchanging letters all summer. The police told the story on the way to the hospital.

Ernie had been crossing the street. There were no stop signs at that time. A taxi was coming down the hill, and another car was going up. The lights from the taxi blinded Uncle Ernie. He was hurrying to get away from the taxi and stepped in front of the other car. He was thrown against the curb and got a fractured skull, killing him instantly.

Then something very odd happened that I've never been able to explain, and I don't believe anyone else can either. As a child, Ernie's hair had been auburn, but as a grown man, his hair had changed to a medium brown. But when we saw him at the funeral, his hair was a bright auburn again.

He had always been just like my own brother. It took me five years to get over the shock. In all that time, I couldn't think of him without something hurting inside.

Harold got into trouble with his bronchitis again, so we took him to the county hospital, which was very poorly run at that time. All patients mixed together. There were some tuberculosis patients as well as others. They had, as the fellow down South told the health nurse, "One sanitary drinking cup, and they all done drink from it." Result: two months later, Harold had T.B. and had to go to a sanatorium; thank the good Lord that was run efficiently. He had to spend two-and-a-half years there. But he recovered fully, and has never again had any trouble with bronchitis or T.B.

One day, Raymond came home from school with a broken collar bone. He fell on the school ground and his shoulder hit a brick. I don't know why a brick was on the school playground to begin with, but there it was. The school nurse said that there were no broken bones. I could see the minute he came in the house that it was broken simply by the way he was holding his shoulder.

That was the first of many broken arms, collarbones and fractured necks. With a large family, that was to be expected.

Mildred had a tonsillectomy at the age of two-and-a-half years. Before that had healed, she got a bad case of stomatitis. The poor kid could neither eat nor talk, so it was back to the hospital. It took several weeks before she was back to normal.

There was a blind man, a friend of ours who was running a second-hand furniture store. He was very sharp; nobody could ever fool him on anything. Walter spent a lot of time in the store. The fellow was lonesome for company. He took a lot of interest in the boy. Pretty soon Walter spent most of his time at the blind fellow's house. During summer vacation, the fellow used to go out of town and he always took Walter with him. Walter called him his second Dad. He certainly got a lot more consideration there than he got from his real Dad.

He also got enough to eat and the blind man bought him clothes. After Walter got a little older, the fellow moved about sixteen blocks away. Walter liked his own school, so he walked the distance every morning and every night, just to be with the blind fellow because he thought he needed him.

Pat built a van body on the truck so he could do some long distance hauling. Sometimes when Pat was in his better moods, we did manage to have some fun. One Sunday, a friend of ours who was an artist, painted on both sides of the van in watercolor, "It's the gypsy in us." Then we took off for a picnic to a beautiful lake. We had seven children, a neighbor of ours had six, there were two older couples, so there were twenty-one of us. When we all got out of that van, some people really thought we were gypsies. Anyway, we had a lot of fun.

One week, I got a few days off from work and we took the children and went camping. We had a big tent. I got a terrible sunburn. I had to go back to work before it was healed. It was torture. And imagine working in a dusty place like a woolen mill. I'm surprised that I'm still alive.

I was pregnant again. Two weeks before the baby was expected, the doctor said it was going to be a breech baby. I didn't have much time to worry about that. Pat had had some dizzy spells. He also had a call for long distance hauling which was to a place 120 miles away. I was afraid to let him go alone. He couldn't afford to hire a man to go with him, so I took a chance on going myself.

On the way, the truck was empty as we were to bring the furniture back. Pat took a shortcut across some railroad tracks, which shook me up but good. I started getting pains but I didn't say anything. I just tried to live with it until we could get back home. The pains stopped after a couple of hours. Nothing more happened so I went back to the doctor the next day. The doctor said, "I don't know what happened, but the baby seems to be in the right position now." Well, I knew what had happened, but I wasn't going to tell him about that terrible ride across the railroad tracks.

Pat never used his head in an emergency. He always acted on impulse; sometimes it had damaging effects. As we had no hot water tank, we still had to heat all water on the cook stove, in which we used wood. It was a chore of several hours to get water for baths for so many.

One day, Linnea heated some water in the teakettle to wash out some small item. She brought the teakettle over to the sink and started to put the water into a small washbasin. Mildred came running, as small children will, and stuck her hand into the basin. She only touched it with her fingertips so she really didn't get burned, but she screamed, naturally, because it scared her.

Linnea was still holding the kettle when Pat jumped up like a hurricane at Linnea. The hot water went all over her leg. She carries the scar to this day.

It was time for my confinement. My regular doctor was back from Europe. I was happy about that because, in a way, I expected complications. I didn't have an easy time with any of them, but some were worse than others. The same county nurse was also there, so I felt more at ease with my two standbys.

The doctor came about three o'clock in the morning. Geraldine wasn't born until six, but he stayed right through the night. Everything went okay, but I was awfully weak for several days after. The doctor came twice a day for a whole week. By the way, the doctor died from cancer nine months later. I felt very, very bad about that.

When Geraldine was four months old, she had a very high temperature one morning when I picked her up to give her a morning bath. The day before, I noticed that she had cut her first tooth. Well, sometimes it happened that some of the other children had also run a temperature at the time they were cutting teeth, although the temperature hadn't been quite as high. There was a free clinic day once a week at the hospital. I decided to take her to the clinic.

When the doctor checked her, he tried to bend her head forward; it wouldn't bend. He looked at me in such a strange way. I blurted out the question: "Meningitis?" He nodded his head. They got a room ready for her and the Sister said, "If she hasn't been baptized, please get the minister to do it immediately." I called the minister at once and she was baptized within half an hour.

When I returned from the hospital, I saw

95

Raymond out in the yard. When I told him how sick Geraldine was, he started to cry. That was unusual, as he had been toughened with the frequent beatings from Pat. I hadn't seen him cry since he was about five years old.

I realized then that he was very much attached to his baby sister, although there were seven other children in the family. He had taken care of her for one whole Sunday afternoon when she was only six weeks old. We had gone to the sanatorium to see Harold and there just wasn't anyone else to leave her with that day. We hadn't seen Harold for three weeks and he was lonesome. Raymond did a good job, though, for a boy that was not quite ten. He always had a knack with children, even after he grew up.

Well, Geraldine recovered fully after a few weeks. She suffered with boils for about six months after she came home from the hospital. She could never lie on her back in all that time, as there was always a painful boil on her back. That finally passed, though. She was very active, but she didn't say a single word before she was two years old. I began to worry that she was going to be a mute. When she finally began to talk, we couldn't "turn her off." She knew all the answers.

The next spring, Mildred, then almost five, suddenly came down with pneumonia. She was then going to the kindergarten. There was a busy street to cross and no school police. I used to watch for her and she waited on the corner for me to pick her up. This particular day, they had let the kindergartners out a half-an-hour early. I was busy in the house and I had no idea that she was on the corner. There was a cold wind blowing and she was frozen clear through when I finally picked her up. The next morning she had pneumonia.

There was no such thing as penicillin at that time; they just waited for the crisis. One either lived or died.

On the night of the crisis, the nurse let me stay all night, although that was really against hospital rules. About five o'clock in the morning, she told me that I could go home. Mildred was over the worst.

Everything was going to pot, so to speak. The tires on the truck were all shot. Pat also had an old car in the same condition. Just to show how bad it was, I'll tell you about a couple of experiences we had.

A friend of ours who lived in another town was in the hospital in Duluth. He got out on a Saturday and he spent the weekend with us. Sunday afternoon, we were going to take him out for a drive. We got two miles out of town and got a flat tire. Pat fixed that and we started out again, only to have the same thing happen another mile or so down the road. That happened seven times in all before we were able to make it back home. I have an idea that our friend will always remember that ride, but certainly not with any fondness!

It was just as bad with the truck. We couldn't afford to buy spares and if we did, they were in bad shape too, so it was always patch, patch, patch.

One day, Pat was driving about thirty girls out to a camp. Linnea and Violet were in the group. Raymond went along for the ride. It was only about thirty miles. They barely got out of town when they had the first flat. That happened several times during the trip. The girls rather enjoyed it. Every time the truck stopped, they all piled out, got out their ukuleles, played songs and sang. They had just as much fun on that trip as they later had at camp.

One day we were moving some furniture to another state. It was about 300 miles away. I still went with Pat on those long trips. I realize now that we took an awful chance on that old truck, but it was a matter of "had to" because we had a family to feed.

We ran into a terrible rainstorm on the way. We couldn't stop because we were supposed to be there the next morning. The windshield wiper wouldn't work. I have had to pitch in for all kinds of emergencies since I was a child, so this time I just got up on the hood and was lying up there wiping the windshield while Pat was driving. I felt like a downed rat, but I stuck it out until the rain stopped. I still wonder what the people in other cars were thinking when they passed by us.

On the way home, something else happened. It was an old-fashioned truck and it had two shifting levers, although that arrangement could have been a home-made modification by a previous owner. I'll never know. Anyway, sometimes I'd have to take a turn at the wheel. I was driving and something suddenly fell across my legs. I looked down and one of the levers was lying on the floor of the cab and my legs were covered with grease clear up to my knees. It would have been funny if it hadn't been so frustrating. I just couldn't help it, though. I laughed out loud and long. I guess it bothered Pat a lot more than it bothered me because he got a severe headache. We had to stop for several hours until he felt better.

On Sunday, Pat drove a neighbor out to a farm; it was a little over 100 miles away. He used the old car. When they all piled in, there were ten people, nine besides Pat, six children and four adults. They left at 5:00 a.m. and Pat didn't return until 1:00 a.m. the next morning and he only stopped at the farm for dinner, which took about an hour. They had fifteen flats on the way to the farm. Cars like that wouldn't be allowed on the road today.

There was more trouble in store for us, as well as for Andrew's, (my brother's) good friend. Their youngest daughter was then eleven years old. Her name was

Margie. She had been very pale ever since she was six, at which time she had had scarlet fever.

They had never taken her to a specialist. They just didn't think there was anything wrong because she never complained. The old doctor they had said that she was all right. One day she got very sick and their own doctor was not available. I asked them to call the doctor that we had had for our children since Linnea was an infant, because he was a pediatrician. They did. This doctor told them that she had chronic nephritis and that she would not live more than a year at the very most.

In the meanwhile, some more trouble cropped up at home. We had a swing under the upstairs porch. If the children were swinging high, it would swing over the fence a few yards from the porch. One day Walter was on the swing and Mildred was walking the fence. Walter accidentally kicked her in the chest. She fell to the ground and it knocked the wind out of her. After she got her breath back, she just kept on playing. She didn't complain about anything.

The next morning, however, I noticed that she was very listless and she just wanted to lie down. I took her temperature and it was 105. I took her to the doctor at once. They took some x-rays. The doctor said that she had pneumonia, which was caused by the fall. It had torn the lining of her lungs. The doctor sent her right to the hospital.

She got along all right for the first few days, but it began to build pus in her lungs. The doctors tried to drain it. Then the inflammation flared up again. She was really in a bad way by then.

We were very much worried about the outcome. She was under oxygen for a whole week. We had private nurses all that time – three of them in eight-hour shifts. She finally snapped out of that, but she also had pleurisy and that hung on. She was in the hospital for six months.

Things were really tough. I was busy night and day. I went to the hospital twice a day to visit Mildred. Margie was in another hospital. I tried to manage to see her once a day. She was very much like one of my own.

I made clothes for the children out of old discarded clothes that people gave me. It wasn't quite as bad just then because I had finally managed to get a sewing machine. Before that, I sewed everything by hand. I sat up all night sometimes, trying to get something ready.

Once while I was still working out, I had worked all day Saturday, done my washing Saturday evening and sat up all night making dresses for Linnea and Violet. I finished at six o'clock Sunday morning. They were going to a children's party that afternoon and they didn't have anything that even resembled a party dress.

In the fall, I started night school four nights a week. I took a foreign language that I had always wanted to learn. I also wanted music. I wanted to continue on the violin, which I had started when Linnea was a baby. But they didn't teach the violin, so I settled for the mandolin.

Pat was getting more jealous by the day. He didn't want me to have any outside interests. He came into the language class several times and started to make a scene. It embarrassed me to no end, but I just let him rave on.

One night I said, "Well, come on in; there's always room for one more." The whole class burst out laughing. He didn't come after that, but he tagged me to the music class every time, and when I was going home he always popped up on the outside and started an argument. Once when we were going to play in a program, he hid my mandolin. I had to go to the library and borrow one. I wasn't used to the instrument and it was harder to play, but I got through the program all right.

I don't know where Pat got the crazy idea that I would be interested in another man. With the treatment I had received from him, I wouldn't have wanted one on a silver platter. I began to dislike all men and sometimes I was wishing that there was an open season on them, like they had on deer. So I could go out and shoot a couple.

A fellow living in the house next door was a good guitar player. In folk music, that is. He didn't play classical guitar, but his compliment of instrumental knowledge included the banjo and mandolin. Finally, he got Pat interested in the mandolin and banjo. Of course Pat couldn't read notes. He never cared to learn. But he learned to play by ear fairly well.

The first year they had a lot of arguments. The other fellow used to go out and play musical programs for local audiences, but he had another old fellow with him who played the violin. Pat wasn't ready to play for anything at that time. He was just learning. But every time they played out, Pat got mad and stayed mad for several weeks. Well, he finally got to the stage where he played with them for small gatherings.

All of our children played. They had a lot of calls, playing for lodges, churches and even on the radio, but of course there was no money in it. I even had to pay the streetcar fare for them. But the children enjoyed it and it kept them out of mischief.

About a year before, Walter had brought home a kitten that he had rescued from a dog while he was on the way home from his music lesson. He carried it about fifteen blocks. He also had his big guitar, so it was quite a load. But he was very proud of his good deed. The kitten looked like a big overgrown mouse. We called it Depression.

101

Now, a year later, it had an offspring, a beautiful back angora that was Mildred's pride and joy. We called him Tarzan.

Depression was exceptionally smart. She never called to be let in; instead, she stood on her hind legs and rattled the doorknob. She held the screen door open for Tarzan to get in and out when he was a small kitten. Later, there was a hole in the screen door that wasn't fixed right away. One day she caught a chipmunk and put it through the hole for Tarzan, who was inside.

Walter was very proud of Depression. That was his cat and nobody else's. One day he beat up a boy older than himself because the boy had put Depression in somebody's woodshed and shut the door.

Mildred was getting along very well at the hospital. One evening while I was visiting at the hospital, Violet came down to tell me that a street car had killed Tarzan.

Without thinking, she said it in front of Mildred. That was all it took to set Mildred off. The temperature went up that night and she was a very sick girl again for the next two weeks.

Violet had always said that she wanted to be a nurse until the incident with Tarzan. But when she saw the mangled remains of the cat, she changed her mind. She said, "If that makes me sick, what would happen when it comes to people?"

Shortly after that, she witnessed an accident where three young boys were killed in an automobile crash. It threw her into hysterics, and she has never forgotten the incident. She has never been able to drive a car in traffic because of it. Several years later, her daughter was describing a similar accident she had just seen. It brought back that accident which had happened thirty-some years before. She called me long-distance that same evening. She seemed very upset. She said, "I thought I had forgotten the incident, but I guess I never will. Whenever something like that happens, it always brings it back."

Margie died on Thanksgiving Day, about ten months after they first took her to the doctor. The first six months she was in and out of the hospital, but the last four she had been there steady. I spent an hour with her that afternoon. She died two hours later. Her parents really never got over the blow. Her father was never the same person after that.

It was hard enough as it was, and then to top it all, on the day of the funeral, a big blizzard came up. They couldn't take her to the cemetery. They had to take her back to the mortuary from the church. They had to wait three days before the roads were cleared. It was a strain on all of us.

Mildred had to spend Christmas in the hospital, but the doctor let her out on New Year's Eve. She had gone in on July 1st. We owed the hospital something over $800.00. I can't imagine what the bill would be today. Mildred had forgotten how to walk. It took her months to get back to normal.

The real depression was in full swing. Food was scarce. The "Relief" was giving out navy beans and salt pork once a month. There were days in a stretch when we had nothing else. The children would come home from school for lunch. It was always the same question: "What's for lunch?" And I would always reply, "Pork and beans." Then in chorus: "I'm not hungry." And off they would go, back to school. In the evening, they were usually hungry enough to eat pork and beans.

Pat, "The master of the house," would sometimes demand ham and eggs just to start trouble. Where would I get ham and eggs? I couldn't even get milk for the children. I used to dread breakfast-time because Pat was always there and was picking on the children enough to drive me crazy. Those poor kids. He had them all crying before they left for school. Raymond had gotten to the stage where he wouldn't have cried no matter what. But the looks he gave his father. I was worried that he would do something drastic someday. All the others were in the "Open Air Room" in the school because they were very much underweight. Raymond was always the sturdy one, large for his age.

Pat still had his flare-ups. One day when Albert was playing the violin, Pat gave him a cuff on the ear. I asked him what that was for. Pat said, "He played the wrong note." Pat didn't even know the piece and he couldn't read notes in the first place.

He discouraged them in every way he could. But I was right there behind them to build them up, because I knew they all had talent. Still, every time they played exceptionally well at a program or when they won a prize, Pat was right there trying to grab all the credit.

Linnea won a piano at the studio where she took her violin lessons, and Violet won an accordion at a contest that was put up by a club on Sundays, "just for the fun of it." Naturally, Pat felt that it was all on account of him. He was still talking about it 35 years later, if he could still find anyone willing to listen to such fantasies.

Once, Linnea, Violet and Raymond played in a park for a large festival. The Governor was there and made a speech. After the program, they all got a free dinner and they all sat at the Governor's table. Besides that, they each got $2.00. That was big money for children at that time. They were the happiest and proudest youngsters in town that day.

Sometimes there was comedy mixed with all seriousness. Once, Albert had a bad case of sinus trouble. He had been in the hospital to have his sinuses drained, and he hadn't as yet gone back to school.

The principal of the school liked him very much. One morning, the principal called and said that Albert's class was having a picnic out of town that afternoon and if Albert was able to go, he would be welcome. So Albert washed and dressed. He had a long-sleeved shirt on and he wanted me to roll up his sleeves. I folded the first sleeve a couple of times, when he suddenly said, "Don't roll them any higher; that's all the farther I washed."

When several of the children had "pink eye" and had to stay out of school, Harold wasn't one of the "lucky ones." He started rubbing his eyes in secret. His eyes were not only pink – they were bloodshot. The doctor couldn't really tell what was wrong but he asked me to keep him out of school, although he insisted that it wasn't "pink eye." Harold didn't tell me until several years later what he had done.

"Depression" had another set of kittens. We kept them upstairs. We were then using the whole house for ourselves. Geraldine brought all the kittens down one day and put them in the corner of the kitchen. I asked her why she had brought the kittens down. She said, "With all that smoke up there, I don't think it's good for them." I didn't know anything about smoke, so I went up to investigate. There was a big chimney fire going on and the upstairs was dense with smoke.

Another time, Linnea was scheduled to play in a recital one evening. She went to lie down on the bed in the afternoon, which was very unusual for her. After a while she said, "Will you get me some cupcakes at Dougherty's?" That particular store was a hardware store so it didn't sound right. I went in and looked at her and she seemed in a fog. I took her temperature; it was 104. She had come down with the measles. She escaped it when all the others had it because she was at camp. So now she had the measles all by herself.

The girls had long curls when they were small. They all looked very nice while they were in grade school, but Pat refused to let them have their hair cut as they grew older.

Linnea was fifteen. She played in the Senior Symphony Orchestra. With her long curls, she looked like a child. The business manager refused to put her name on the program because it was a **senior** orchestra.

Finally, the time came for the spring concert. The girls were going to wear formals. I bought an inexpensive formal and a girlfriend was going to put up Linnea's hair. But there was the problem of her shoes. Pat was "thumbs down" on dress shoes. All she had ever worn was sport shoes.

She bought a pair of heels. Pat was determined that she was never going to wear heels. I had this to say to Pat. "If she's going to wear sport shoes with a formal, you and I had better leave town because everybody will think that we're ready for the State Hospital."

Linnea wore dress shoes, but Pat didn't like it. He wouldn't talk to me for months after that. Of course, that was nothing unusual. He went as long as nine months in a stretch without saying anything except some nasty remark. Once when a neighbor man came in, the neighbor said something to me in the line of conversation. I answered. Pat turned around and said to the fellow. "Don't pay any attention to her. She is nothing but a goddamn whore." The man looked disgusted and walked out.

Linnea played in the orchestra in high school. She also played in a trio and in a quartet, playing solos for all the school programs. She was a senior and an honor student and graduated at sixteen. But she still had her long curls and looked like twelve. The other seniors were not very anxious to date her. She had a few dates, but nothing like I'm sure she would have had if she looked her age.

After graduation, she took a year of post-graduate work at the same high school. There were no scholarships at that time. The depression was still on. We had no money for college.

At the end of the post-graduate year, she got work at the City Hall through the welfare agency. She was very good in typing and shorthand. Pat wanted to know when her first payday was due. He was going to collect the check. I put him straight on that in a hurry. I told him that the only check he would collect would be anything he worked for and nobody else's.

When Linnea was eighteen and Violet was sixteen-and-a-half, they still had their long curls. The fellow next door to us, the one who was teaching Pat to play folk music, had a serious talk with Pat one day. He told him that Pat was ruining the girls' lives by forcing them to use fashions from many years back. He must really have made it sink in, because when Pat came home that time, he said that they could cut their hair.

One day when Raymond was about thirteen, Pat was mad at him for some reason I didn't even know about. He told Raymond that he was to stay in the yard all day. Well, Raymond wasn't about to be treated like a five-year-old. The minute Pat went out the gate on one side of the yard, Raymond jumped the fence on the other side and was gone. Pat bawled me out for letting him go. I told him that I had more important work to do than watch a thirteen-year-old, which was the truth.

Pat thought that Raymond had hitchhiked out to a farm about 30 miles away, where we had some friends. I knew better. Raymond wasn't going anyplace where he would get caught in a hurry. When Pat found out that he wasn't at the farm, I could see that he was worried. I never said a thing. I was a little uneasy because I didn't know where he was either. But I felt that was Pat's business and I wasn't mixing in. Pat didn't report him missing, but I could see that he was getting more worried by the day.

One day, three weeks later, Raymond walked in. I thought, "Oh,oh! Here comes the explosion." But I believe Pat was so relieved to see him that all he said was "Well, have you had enough traveling?" Raymond said, "For a while."

Mentally, the boy had gotten a lot older in those three weeks. Raymond told me about his trip later. He rode the rods under the freight trains to California some 2,000 miles away. He said that it was very cold and very tiresome. He said that he would never travel that way again. What little he had to eat, he got from some of the hobos that traveled the same way. They talked him into going back home. He hitchhiked on the return trip. Hitchhiking was very common at that time.

The following winter there were more broken bones. Violet got a broken arm skiing. Raymond got a broken collarbone on the skating rink, the same one that was broken before.

One Saturday afternoon, Harold went to the show with some other boys. In less than an hour he returned, white as a ghost. He went into the bedroom, flopped down on the bed and was moaning. I asked him what was wrong. He said that he had a terrible pain in his stomach.

I called the doctor and when he checked Harold, he said that the appendix was very bad and had to come out at once. The only place where we could go was the county hospital. Pat had filed for bankruptcy for the second time. He hadn't paid the hospital when Mildred was there and they wouldn't have any more to do with us.

At the county hospital, they tried to give Harold a spinal, but he kicked up such a fuss that they had to give him gas. He didn't wake up until five hours later. I stayed at the hospital all night. Harold got well quickly. Two weeks after surgery he was out fighting with his pals.

Only a month later, Albert came home from school one day in the early afternoon. He also complained of a stomach ache. I didn't think it was anything serious. I tried all the home remedies, all the things I know now that I shouldn't have tried, including a hot water bag. He was getting worse instead of better, so I finally called the doctor. It was the same verdict as Harold. The appendix had to come out.

Albert went to the hospital in the evening, but the surgery wasn't until the next morning. I don't believe that the doctors really knew how to give a spinal at that time. Albert had the same trouble as Harold. He said that he felt everything, which I believe he did, but he was such a good-natured fellow that he would rather suffer than make trouble. It took him much longer to recover. He never did get over the pain in his back – some thirty years later it still bothered him.

At home, it was an awful struggle to get something to eat. Even when Pat had money he didn't want to part with it. If he made a little extra, he would buy another old truck, until he had four of them. He didn't have enough work for one, let alone four. The only one that was any good was a little pickup truck, which we used instead of a car.

Pat used to hand out $5.00 once every three weeks for groceries. Even at that time $5.00 would not cover three weeks for ten people.

One Sunday, we hadn't had anything to eat for 24 hours. The only thing we had in the house was coffee, which hadn't as yet run out. Pat went to the store and bought himself six rolls. He sat down and ate three of them with a cup of coffee. The older children looked disgusted. The smaller ones looked longingly at the rolls He didn't give them any, though. He put the other three rolls in the icebox for later use. Nobody dared to touch them. So all the children and I took a walk over to the blind fellow's house. Walter was already there. We stayed the night. When we didn't come home Monday morning, Pat called the Humane Society. We came home just as the man got there. He wanted to know what the trouble was and I told him. He asked Pat if he had any money. Pat said, "A few dollars." The fellow said, "Well, give it to your wife." Pat gave me three dollars then, while the man was there. He had more, but that's all he would hand out. But I didn't argue.

Another time, Pat gave me four dollars instead of the usual five every third week. Harold happened to be right there at the time.

The next week, Pat tried to tell me that he had given me ten dollars. I asked Harold in front of Pat, "How much money did Dad give me the other day when you were here?" Harold said, "Four dollars." Pat struck him in the face and said, "How much?" Harold repeated, "Four dollars. You counted them out one by one." Pat hit him again. Then I yelled at him, "Now leave the boy alone, you know he's right." He had it in for Harold for a long time after that.

At that time, there was no strict law about getting a driver's license. Anyone who had 35 cents and looked somewhere near 15 years of age could get his license without any test whatsoever. All the boys in the family got their licenses when they were 12. Pat had never taught any of them to drive, but they learned from the other boys in the neighborhood. As soon as Pat knew that they could drive, he let them drive the trucks. He used to tell them to take the trucks to the gas station and fill them up.

One day he told Harold to "take the truck over there." But he didn't say where. So naturally Harold thought he meant the gas station. He drove the truck to the station and thought that his father would follow in the other truck, which he usually did. He waited a while, but when his father didn't show up, he drove the truck back home. Pat was there waiting for him with one of his brainstorms. He hauled Harold out of the truck and beat him up, saying, "Who told you to go to the gas station?" I don't think Harold thought so much about the beating in itself; he was used to that. But it embarrassed him because several of his pals were standing around. I know that he never forgot it, as he mentioned it several times after he grew up. There were other things, too, that he didn't forget.

The twins had trouble with their kidneys until they were about six years old. They wet the bed, so they usually got a beating before breakfast every morning. The more beatings Pat gave them, the worse the problems became. But nobody could tell Pat anything. He insisted that they were too lazy to get up.

Mildred had the same trouble, but Pat never noticed her trouble, because she was his favorite child. The only thing he ever said to her was when she was about 15. She had had a high school picture taken. One of Pat's cronies was scrutinizing the picture and remarked that she had used too much eyebrow makeup. Pat said to Mildred, "I see that you're beginning to use makeup." Mildred laughed right out loud and said, "Beginning to?" She had used makeup since she was 14. He never mentioned it again. Linnea and Violet wouldn't have dared to use makeup around the house. Pat would have "Mowed them down."

The winter before Linnea got the job in City Hall was a very tight one. We lived mostly on peanut butter and homemade bread. I usually bought a five-pound pail of peanut butter for a dollar and that would go about 10 days. I usually baked at night when everybody was in bed. About eleven o'clock, when I took the bread out of the oven, the children could smell the fresh bread and they would tiptoe downstairs very quietly to get a slice. They didn't dare to awaken Pat. He would have had another brainstorm.

I always had homemade bread until years later when Pat did something that he should never have done, at least to me anyway. He might have gotten away with it with someone else, but it was a "last straw" event with me. One day he was mad about something; I didn't even know what. He threw a loaf of homemade coffeecake on the floor and called me an S.O.B. I told him right then and there, "You'll never again eat any of the bread that I bake." And I stuck to that. I never baked again. There were only two of the children then left at home. They missed the homemade bread of course, but they were big enough to understand the situation.

Now, to get back to those giddy days of the depression....

There was an old black lady in our neighborhood, born into slavery and emancipated by President Lincoln with his famous proclamation during the Civil War. She was very odd in some ways, but she had a heart of gold. Sometimes when she got some stew meat or some other inexpensive cut at the butcher shop, she would bring half of it to me. She didn't have much herself, but she always divided what she had. She was also very good to the children and looked after them like a mother hen. Sometimes when she would take one of them for a walk, it happened that someone who didn't know her would remark, "Isn't that child awfully light for being colored?" And someone else would remark, "Oh, he'll get darker when he gets older."

We could have had a lot of fun raising the children if it hadn't been for Pat's nasty disposition. But he liked nothing better than to hurt the feelings of his own family. For example, when Violet was still in the lower grades, she put in a lot of extra time making a wastepaper basket as a Christmas gift for her father. We needed the basket and it was a beautiful thing. But on Christmas morning, Pat broke it up and put it in the stove. Naturally Violet went in her room and cried. I felt sorry for her.

There were three words that just weren't in Pat's vocabulary. They were "Please," "Excuse me," and "Thank you." And he would rather have died than say, "I'm sorry." If he wanted to get in some place where someone was standing in his way, he would never say, "Excuse me." It was always, "You there, get out of my way." or "You. Get out of there."

During the winter when there wasn't much to do, we used to get together with several other couples who also had children. We had a small gathering in someone's house. Everyone brought something, so there was lunch for everyone. This was always on a Sunday afternoon. Someone always played and sometimes the children put on a skit. Everybody had a good time, but every time it was at our place, Pat would either pick on one of our children or else he would pick a fight with me after the others went home. Someone's feelings were always hurt.

But outsiders didn't know that. They always got a kick out of those parties. There was always some funny little thing that happened to make people laugh.

When Mildred was eight and Geraldine four, it was their turn to perform one Sunday. Mildred was at the piano and Geraldine was going to sing. She got through her first song just fine, but when she started on the second one, she made a mistake. She stopped right in the middle of it, walked over to the piano, struck Mildred in the shoulder with her little fist and said for all to hear, "Start over again." That just about brought down the house.

Once, when our friends knew that we were very hard up, they had collected $12.00, which was supposed to be for groceries. I had gone out for a few minutes on an errand. Someone made the mistake of giving Pat the money while I was out. I never got any of it. He kept it all for himself. Many times I didn't have enough money to buy a stamp to mail a letter with. That was really living.

Father died about this time. The ulcers finally got the best of him. I had always hoped that I would be able to make a trip home even before Mother died. But at the rate the babies were coming, there wasn't a chance. Pat was the kind of fellow that would stay under the water the longest and drown rather than lose a bet.

Once, I had bought a few Christmas cards and I had them all written out and ready to mail when Pat had one of his famous brainstorms and tore up all the cards. Another time, he tore up my snapshot album and burned it. There went the only photos I had of Andrew and my Dad. It was getting a little harder each time to overlook those things.

The girls were babysitting a whole night for a quarter. The boys delivered groceries with a little wagon for ten cents a trip. Sometimes they had to walk over two miles for a dime. Albert wanted a pair of boots that cost three dollars. He used to come and hand me the dime after each trip until he had enough for a pair of boots.

Once, a lady came to the house and wanted Violet to clean an eight-room house for a quarter. That time I drew the line. I told her that we needed the money, but not that bad. If the woman had been sick, I would have let Violet do it for nothing, but she was just plain lazy. She didn't have a thing to do herself and she had a grown son and daughter.

114

When Raymond was 14 and in the ninth grade, he quit school and signed up for the C.C.C. camp. He passed for 19 and was driving a truck for a year-and-a-half before that. He didn't have to prove his age and he knew his work so there were no questions asked.

Violet had her first surgery. She also had a very bad case of sinus trouble. She had to drop out of school for a year, but she did go back the next year and finish.

Sometimes it was hard for the children to get their schoolwork done because of Pat. If they had to write about some article in the newspapers, he always made trouble. If any of them picked up the newspaper, he would come and snatch it out of their hands and say, "Study your lesson." Nobody could convince him that that was the lesson. Sometimes he would treat me the same way. If I took a few minutes' time to read the newspaper, he would throw something at the paper so it would fall to the floor. Sometimes it was an effort to control myself so as not to do something drastic.

Pat was not a drinking man. He couldn't stand the stuff. It made him very ill. It was a blessing that he couldn't drink because when he was drunk he was downright filthy. But sometimes he would go out and get plastered, just to make it miserable for me.

Once, just before Raymond joined the C.C.C., Pat was mad about something as usual. I never knew just what brought it on but it happened quite often.

This was on a Saturday night. He went out early in the evening. Two young boys that we knew – they lived about 30 miles away – came into town. One of them was dating Violet at the time.

I made coffee for them. We had coffee and rolls and were sitting there talking. The smaller children were in bed, but Linnea, Violet, Raymond and the two boys, as well as I were sitting by the table when Pat came in, drunk as all "get out." He started berating us for having a "wild party."

I knew that he was going to keep it up all night if I was there, so I just decided to get out. I asked Raymond to keep an eye on the younger ones until I came home in the morning. I knew that Pat wouldn't bother the small ones while they were in bed. He was just mad at the girls and me.

Violet went with the boys. I knew that she would be all right as I knew the parents of one boy and he also had three sisters who had been spending time at our house. The boys wanted Linnea and me to go with them also, but I wanted to get back home by the time the children got up in the morning. Linnea also had something to do on Sunday morning, so we decided to go to a hotel.

I only had three dollars, so we had to go to a very cheap one; but anyway, it was someplace to go. We got more than we asked for. The bedbugs kept us company all night. Linnea still had her long curls. She had just washed her hair. That was in the era before the hairdryer. The people used strips of cloth instead of curlers to put up their hair. She had nothing to put up her hair with and, if she didn't, she knew that she would look a mess in the morning. The night clerk at the hotel was an old fellow and he tried to be very helpful. He gave her a piece of cloth to rip and make strips out of. But it was such a small piece that it made the strips very narrow. She used them anyway. But in the morning when she took the strips out of her hair, she looked like the bride of Frankenstein. We just sat down and laughed.

When we returned home, Pat started right in on me again. He wouldn't let me fix the beds. When I finished one, he would rip the covers right off. When I put the roast in the oven, he took it out and threw it in the sink.

Finally, I called the police. The police came, but they had their usual excuse. "We didn't see him do it." But one of them did turn around to Pat and say very gruffly, "It seems to me that you would have enough to take care of around here without running around Saturday nights getting drunk." Well, that did the trick. Pat went to a corner and sat down. He was quiet for the rest of the day. In the evening, he drove out to the place where Violet was and brought her home.

It was a very frustrating time for the girls. Their friends didn't call on the phone unless it was something important, but if Pat happened to answer the phone, he would say, "Not home," even if they were standing right there. The girls didn't dare to say anything. If they did, he would have hit them.

The twins had always been so different in their likes and dislikes. Albert was the studious type. Harold liked to read, of course, but his whole life was tinkering with mechanical things. He could take anything apart and put it together again when he was only a small boy.

When he was about 12, one day Harold wanted to take the truck to the city dump, but Raymond didn't want him to. Raymond took the keys and came in the house to get himself a sandwich. He looked out the window and there was Harold on his way to the dump with the truck. He had crossed the wires somehow to run the truck without the key. Raymond's only comment was: "That kid is too smart for his own good."

The twins had been collecting aluminum scrap for several weeks. They had a nice little pile that they were going to sell. Suddenly, it disappeared. I asked Pat about it. No, he didn't know anything about it.

There was a big warehouse on the lot next to ours, where we kept the trucks. One day the boys were trying to straighten up the place because Pat always kept everything in such a mess. Lo and behold, there was the pile of aluminum, hidden in the corner under a lot of junk. Pat had taken it for his own selfish use. What could the boys say? They didn't dare to accuse their father, so naturally they had to let it go. Pat sold it and kept the money.

Pat kept those boys on the trucks moving furniture and had them lifting things that were much too heavy for them. But he was very tight with the money. One day, Albert wanted to go to a football game. It was only a quarter. He asked his father for the quarter and Pat started to give him a spiel about how broke he was. Albert said, "Never mind," and walked out. That day, I happened to have a quarter so I gave it to him. Most of the time, I didn't have so much as a penny. Pat even landed in jail once in a roundabout way because he never left any money, even for an emergency.

Pat had brought a load of furniture from another city. He ran into a big rainstorm. The top of the van was leaking and some of the linen that was packed in the corner of the van got spotted so he had to send it to the laundry. The people didn't pay the moving bill so Pat was holding the linen as security. The laundry delivered the goods to our house when they were ready but, as usual, I didn't have the money to pay for it.

Pat knew that they were supposed to deliver it that day, so there was no excuse for him not to be ready to accept delivery. The laundry man took the stuff back to the laundry. When Pat came home, I told him what had happened. He went to the laundry to pick up the linen, and in doing so, he committed a crime. If the laundry delivered it to our house, he was in the clear, but when he went to the laundry to pick it up, the owners of the linen swore out a warrant for larceny. Of course they had to let him go inside of 48 hours, but it was too late for our children because all the other children were reminding them that their father was in jail. Children can also be very cruel!

Harold got a job during vacation driving a small truck for an old fellow who was picking up scrap iron. The old man didn't know how to drive, but he was always on the truck. Harold was only about twelve-and-a-half at the time.

One day Albert and Harold had a boxing bout, without the gloves of course. Harold hit Albert in the head and his knuckles caved in. We were teasing Albert about his solid head. The doctor fixed up Harold's knuckles and he went back to his job.

It was an old-fashioned truck with the stick shift. When Harold tried to shift, his knuckles caved in again. The doctor tried a new method. He cut both ends out of a soup can and taped Harold's hand around the can. As both ends were open, all he had to do was to slip the can over the rod and shift away. It worked fine. He kept the can tied in the hand until his knuckles were healed.

Not very long after that, Albert got a small neck fracture diving in the pool at the "Y," and the same thing happened to Violet when she was riding in an old car that went over a bad bump in the street. Her head hit the roof. They were both walking around with very stiff necks for several weeks.

Mildred still had a little trouble walking after being in the hospital for six months. We had some friends who owned a large farm in another state about 700 miles away. They wanted us to send Walter and Mildred there for the summer. So one day I packed them up and sent them on the train.

They had to change trains in Chicago, about midway on the trip. But Walter was 11 and I knew that they would be all right. Our friends were supposed to pick them up at the depot in the closest town. The children got into that town about four o'clock in the morning. Our friends had gotten the schedule mixed up somehow and didn't come to get them until nine o'clock that morning.

In Duluth, where we lived, there was somewhere near a hundred-thousand people. But in this small town where they would spend the summer, there was only one main street that was more of a country road than a city street. The children had the most fun watching the cows walking all over town while they were waiting for the people to pick them up, so they really didn't mind the wait.

The next winter, Pat got on the W.P.A. with one of his trucks. To show what a coward he was at times, something turned up one day. He told me the night before that they were to haul dynamite the next day. The trip was about 30 miles. I really don't believe that there was any danger because it was just the sticks, not the caps. Anyway, Pat played sick the next morning and told me to keep Harold out of school that day and send him out with the truck. There was nothing I could do but go through with it. Anyway, nothing happened that day, but the foreman sent a very stiff note to Pat by Harold that evening and told him not to send the boy again. If he couldn't come himself, to let the truck stand. I was glad he did. Then Pat couldn't blame it on me.

I had a lot of trouble with ulcers on my legs. The sores broke open time and again and they were getting harder to heal all the time. I didn't have the money to have surgery done. The welfare wasn't too keen on paying for anything so I just suffered with it.

The next summer, it was time to have my ninth child.

Walter broke his arm roller-skating one evening. It was a very bad break. "When he came in with the arm twisted every which way, he wanted Harold to go with him to the hospital to have it set. Harold was not in a hurry. He was making himself a sandwich. Walter said, "Hurry up, hurry up. This thing really hurts." Harold kept on making the sandwich, mumbling, "Oh, wait a minute, can't you?" It didn't bother him as long as it was the other guy suffering, but he finally grabbed his sandwich and went along.

Raymond quit the C.C.C. camp and hitchhiked back to California for his second visit to the west coast. All he had was five dollars cash. He was only fifteen-and-a-half but he looked a lot older. He got along fine, though. He worked first for Western Union, and then he joined a carnival. He was somewhat of a clown, so he was just the right man for his job as a barker. They traveled all over the western states.

We had a severe hot spell in Minnesota that summer. With my bad legs and being in the last month of pregnancy, I really had a hard time. Walter, Mildred and Geraldine all went to the same farm again where Walter and Mildred spent the summer before.

Leonard was born a few days after they left. I had done a big weekly washing the day he was born. I had pains all day, but I had had them all week so I wasn't sure anything was going to happen.

I had just taken in the last of my wash when I realized that something **was** going to happen, and soon. Just then, two ladies came to see about some moving. They were chatterboxes of the worst kind. They didn't only talk about moving, they gave me their whole family history.

My immediate problem was how to get rid of them without offending them. I wanted to scream and still I had to stand there and try to pay attention. Finally, Pat came in. That was about the only time in many years that I was really glad to see him.

I didn't lose any time getting out of the room. I called the doctor. He came shortly after. The nurse didn't get there right away. Pat was never any good in any kind of emergency. But it was funny to say the least. Linnea was over 18 years old and Pat told her to go upstairs. She smiled politely and stayed on until the nurse came. Pat stayed away as far as possible until it was over.

Linnea was still working at the City Hall and Violet had a job for the summer out of town. But the nurse got me an older woman to come and stay a week until I got back on my feet.

Soon everyone came back home except Raymond, who was still on the west coast.

One evening, Geraldine was walking a high fence. She was a natural-born tomboy anyway. Usually she didn't have any mishaps, but this time she lost her balance and fell. She came in and went upstairs without saying a word. After a while, I heard her whimpers. I went up to investigate.

She just told me that she fell off the fence, but didn't tell me which fence. I took it for granted that it was the one in our backyard, which was only about three-and-a-half feet high. But it happened to be one six feet high a half a block away. I tried to keep her quiet so Pat wouldn't have another tantrum, but when she was still whimpering an hour later, I knew that something was wrong. Mildred walked down with Geraldine to the emergency room at the hospital and of course the arm was broken, so I just chalked up one more.

The next summer, Linnea was called to Washington, D.C. to work for the government. Raymond came back home to join the Navy, but he had to wait about three months as he was not yet 17. He was driving one of the trucks for his father. We also had another driver for one of the other trucks. This was a construction job and it was rather heavy work.

About this time, I developed an abscess on my breast and had to go to the hospital for surgery. I hated to leave Violet all alone with the whole mess. Pat was awfully mean to her. He was in seventh heaven when he could hurt her feelings in some way.

She was 18 years old and she was usually home by eleven every time that she had a date. One evening, it was eleven-fifteen when she came in. Pat had locked the door. I didn't know that. When she rapped, he went to the door. He grabbed her like a wild man. He tore the sleeve out of her coat and scratched her arm. Usually she didn't say anything. This time she did, though. She looked him straight in the face and said, "I hope that somebody poisons you someday." He was so surprised that he forgot to slug her. She walked right past him and went to her room.

It was very hard on Violet. She was all alone to do all the work, also to take care of Leonard. He was then only about eleven months old. I had always been with him and he just couldn't understand that I wasn't there. He would crawl to the bathroom door, sit down and cry, "Mommy, Mommy," all day long.

One day, Pat had extra help on the truck. We had some visitors from out of town, an old lady and her son. Violet had fourteen for dinner.

That night when she came to visit me and I could see that she was near tears. I asked her what was wrong and she told me how nerve-wracking everything had been all day. Mildred was at camp; otherwise she could have helped with the baby. I was supposed to stay in the hospital a couple more days, but I asked the doctor for permission to go home the next day.

Raymond joined the Navy as planned, that fall.

Geraldine had a tonsillectomy. She didn't have any trouble though. They had a special surgery in the clinic for minor operations. I took her there in the morning and picked her up in the afternoon. She was back in school a couple of days later.

Harold was then 15 and he took his turn at the C.C.C. camp. He stayed a year. Albert wanted to stay in school. He had a rough time getting along with Pat. Sometimes he had to stay out of school a half a day at a time to help on the truck, but he always made up his work. Albert was also a good carpenter, so he and four other boys built themselves a small cabin in the backyard of one of the other boys' houses. It was a neat little thing. They spent all their evenings in there. None of them were ever found on the street at night. They were all very good boys.

Linnea came home for Christmas for her first visit. Pat behaved fairly well for those few days, so we all enjoyed Christmas for a change.

The depression was still on, and food was not plentiful. During the winter, there was no work for the trucks. We had to live on what Harold made in the C.C.C. camp and a very small relief order.

Walter needed glasses but I couldn't afford to buy them. So he stayed out of school two weeks helping some fellow on a truck deliver potatoes. He got just enough to pay for the glasses. Then he went back to school. He had to work hard to catch up, but he could see better, so that helped.

Pat's musician friend had a son who had property by a lake about 100 miles southwest of Duluth. He lived there himself and had about 500 acres. It was a very good fishing lake. Pat and the old fellow decided to build a cabin so they would have someplace to live while they were fishing. They built the cabin out of old scrap lumber. They made a fairly nice cabin. The cabin had been there about two years before I was ever asked to go there. I finally went but I certainly didn't enjoy myself. It was no picnic for me. I had to carry the water for three blocks, get the wood for the cook stove, watch the children all day and have the meals ready when the two

"Kings" came in to eat. I went a couple of times, but finally washed my hands of the whole business.

Once when Pat was up there for a couple of days, he had Geraldine with him. The fellow that owned the property had a girl Geraldine's age. On the way home, they had an accident on the outskirts of Duluth. Pat called and said that they had an accident and that the police had taken Geraldine to the hospital and nothing more. He didn't even say where they were.

I called the police in our part of town but they had no record of anything. I was very much worried but couldn't do a thing. Finally, the hospital from the other part of town called and said that Geraldine had had emergency treatment and was ready to go home. Albert went to pick her up. She had been stunned for a few minutes and she had a big cut on her hand. The windshield broke and that's how she got the cut. She had a light dress on and that was covered with blood. I was glad that the hospital said that she was alright otherwise I might have passed out from fright. The truck never worked right after that.

Shortly after that, a young boy in his early twenties was driving it and it jackknifed on him. It was a dump truck. Pat owed the fellow two weeks' wages but he refused to pay him because of the accident, although it wasn't the boy's fault. I was very much disgusted with Pat because the boy was poor and needed the money. Pat never carried insurance on anything. He always took a very big chance.

The next summer, Walter stowed away on one of the freight boats on the Great Lakes. They ran into a big storm and he got deathly sick. He came out of hiding as soon as he was able to walk. They put him in the kitchen to peel potatoes. He could have stayed until the end of the trip, but he had had enough for the time being. He got off in the first town they came to and hitchhiked home. A year later, he worked as a deckhand for a while on a boat for the same company.

Albert was very much disgusted with Pat. As soon as school was out, he took off. He hitchhiked 700 miles to the farm where the other children had stayed two summers before. He worked there all summer until it was time for school again. Then he came back. He had his mind set on finishing high school. Although he almost quit once and took off a couple of times when Pat got to be too much for him, he stuck it out.

Raymond was on a battleship. One day we got a letter telling us he was a very sick boy. His appendix had ruptured and he had had emergency surgery. But there were no complications, so he got well very soon. Almost everyone in the family seemed to have a bad appendix and bad tonsils, with the exception of myself. I was always a healthy specimen, outside of varicose veins.

Pat used to have spells when he didn't talk to me for months, as I mentioned before. Well, this time we really hadn't had a conversation for about nine months. One day he decided to talk. He told me without any preliminaries that we were going to take a trip on the bus to the east coast. I was floored, so to speak, but I wasn't going to argue about it. If he had money for a trip to the east coast, it was perfectly all right with me. He never spent anything on me otherwise.

But, I'm a little ahead of my story again. The things I've just written about were in the period just before Harold joined the C.C.C. I'll go back to February, a few months before the trip east.

There weren't many calls for long distance moving in the winter, but once in a great while, it happened. This time there was a load going 150 miles. I went along to keep Pat company. He was much better natured out on the road than he was in the house. He never had a tantrum on the road. We were driving through the night. The temperature dropped to 25 degrees below zero and no heater in the truck. I have never been as cold as I was that night. Not even in Europe when we were fishing during the November snowstorms.

When we reached our destination the next morning, I discovered that I had come down with the German measles. There was an epidemic in Duluth. I wasn't sick except for a slight headache, but my face looked a mess. I had a rash all over. The way I froze that night, I fully expected to come down with pneumonia, but nothing happened.

It wasn't quite as cold driving back. When we reached home, there was another load going 150 miles in the other direction, so we were on the road for twelve hours more. Still, nothing happened. The germs just had to look out for themselves. But I kept away from other people. I didn't want to give it to anybody else.

One day Leonard almost suffocated. I left him sitting in the crib while I was doing the upstairs work. I heard him crying after I had been up there a few minutes, but I thought he cried because he didn't want to be left alone. But when the cry became a scream, I went down to investigate. He had pulled the crib blanket over his head. It had been hanging on the side of the crib. He was crying so hard when I got there that he was blue in the face and could hardly breathe. For a minute, I was just as frightened as he was. If I had waited a couple more minutes, he would have been gone.

In the late spring, we had another long distance haul. In the middle of the night we got a flat tire, five miles out from the nearest town. No spare. Pat walked into town, but everything was closed for the night. I was sitting alone in the cab of the truck for seven hours. No lock on the door of the cab. To say I was scared is putting it mildly. Those were some of the longest hours I have ever been through. There have been others, of course, but not as bad as that night. Pat finally got his tire and hitched a ride back to the truck.

There was also a little comedy that I remember from that spring. A friend of Harold and Walter had an old car. He was a couple of years older than the twins. He let the boys use the old jalopy for a few weeks.

The school was only a few blocks away – they could easily have walked. But they were big shots now. They had a car and they were going to use it. It takes gas to run a car. The only money they had was the nickel apiece that they had for their milk at noon. Naturally gas was a lot cheaper than it is now, but one still couldn't run a car on a nickel. But somehow, **they** did. In the morning, they ran into the gas station and nonchalantly said, "Put in five cents worth of gas." I don't believe they even said, "Please." The next morning, the same thing was repeated. The man used to say, "Oh, no," every time he saw them coming, but he never refused. Partly, I believe it was because Pat bought his gas at the same station.

Now, back to the story about our trip east.

We had set the date when we were supposed to leave. Two days before the time set, Mildred and Geraldine came down with the measles. Geraldine got pneumonia and had to go to the hospital. We had to postpone it for the time being.

The doctor didn't want Leonard to get the measles while we were gone, which naturally would have happened. So the doctor gave Leonard a shot of blood taken from my arm because I had had a good case of measles at the age of six.

To this day, several decades later, Leonard has never had the measles. Geraldine was out of danger and the doctor finally said that we could go. Violet was home. I also got the same old lady who was there when

Leonard was born to come and stay while we were gone. She didn't do much, but she wasn't working any place else, so I thought she might as well be there.

Pat didn't have very much money to leave for the family to get along on. But the boys were there and the trucks were there and I though they might get some small moving or delivery jobs to keep them going with food. It was risky because the boys were in their early teens and by law not old enough to drive a truck. Also, there was no insurance on the trucks. But that was a chance I had to take. If I had refused to go, Pat would have had seventeen kinds of fits. The boys did get a couple of long distance hauls which helped tremendously, but Violet was worried sick while they were out on the road. Their guardian angel must have been with them. They had no accidents.

We took the bus, first to New Jersey where I had some friends. They had been neighbors of mine in Europe. I had not seen them since 25 years before. We stayed in New Jersey a little over a week. Then we went to Washington to visit Linnea. We stayed a week with her. We also had a chance to visit the White House and the Capitol and many other places of interest.

From there, we again took the bus to the place where the children had stayed several summers before. We stayed with those people also a week. Pat had behaved very well. He told a lot of fantastic lies, which embarrassed me, but I thought perhaps the people didn't catch on as long as they didn't know him. So I didn't let it spoil my trip. I really had a good time – the first since I got married. And it was many years before I had a chance to get another vacation.

Then, almost before I knew it, we were home and things were back to normal. Harold was now in the C.C.C. camp.

Linnea knew how hard it was for Violet to get along with Pat, so she sent for her and got her into a dental nursing class in Philadelphia. After Violet finished the course, she worked in Washington for a while. The next year she got married. But they kept their marriage a secret. The boy was not 21. He was supporting his mother and two younger brothers. His mother always said that if he got married before he was 21, she would have the marriage annulled, so they didn't tell anybody. They had been married about a year and a half before she told us. Well, that was her business. It was all right with me.

Late one night, Linnea got very bad pains in her stomach. She got in touch with the doctor somehow and he said it was her appendix. He asked her what she had for supper and she said, "A very light one – spaghetti and meatballs." Well, they operated and had a hard time finding the appendix because it was not in the usual place. It was in the middle of the stomach. So there was another appendix out of the way. She was fine after that – no complications.

One day I heard Leonard screaming in the bathroom. He didn't seem to be able to tell me what was wrong. I took him to the doctor. The doctor said that he had to be circumcised. That was news to me. The other boys had never had any trouble.

Leonard had long curly hair and looked for all the world like a girl. The morning of the surgery, the nurse came into the room to pick him up; she looked at him and looked at the slip she had in her hand. She said, "This must be the wrong patient." I asked her what she meant. She said, "I'm looking for a boy." I said, "That's your boy. He looks like a girl, but he's all boy. Believe me."

This brings to my mind something that took place about 15 years before, when one of the other boys was about six months old. He had had a fever for several days. The doctor was asking for a urine specimen. How does one go about getting a specimen from a baby of that age? I had six little ones, all less than seven years of age. I couldn't spend all my time watching for one certain thing. The doctor was getting rather impatient.

Finally, I brought the bottle proudly into the doctor's office. The doctor's first question was, "Well, how did you get it?" My answer: "I tied a balloon where it did the most good." I thought the doctor would split. He called his two nurses in and repeated what I had just said. It sounded like the best joke that he'd ever heard.

Leonard had a lot of trouble in different ways the next few months. One evening, while I was visiting someone in the hospital, he fell off the couch and broke his collarbone. Mildred and Geraldine were frightened. They felt that it was their fault, as they were babysitting. They put him in the go-cart and took him outside. I couldn't find any of them when I returned. Finally, about 10:00 p.m., they came home. Leonard was still crying. I could see at once that his shoulder was out of order. It was too late to get him to the doctor that night, so I had to stay up with him all night just to keep him from crying out loud. It was a lot easier than to have Pat raising he--. I took him to the emergency room in the hospital the next morning to have it set.

He barely got over that when he came down with the mumps. After two weeks, he still had a large swelling below one ear. That didn't look right, so I checked again with the doctor. It turned out to be a large abscess. It took several weeks before that was cleared up, and then what should happen? He got whooping cough. He didn't have a severe case, though, not nearly as bad as some of the others had had it. But he had trouble with a sore throat after that. So it was tonsillectomy time again. He was the tenth one in the family. By that time, he was well acquainted with doctors, nurses and hospitals. There was no problem. He even played big brother to another little boy in the same room for the few hours that he was there.

Walter was driving the dump truck on a road construction job. One day it jackknifed on him, just as it had done for Pat and the other driver. Pat went out to the place of the accident, but his musician friend had gone with him, just for the ride I guess. Naturally, Pat was all for taking it out on Walter, but Pat's friend told him, "You should thank God with all your heart that your boy wasn't killed and don't you ever forget it."

Pat and Walter did have some words over it and Walter left town. Five of the children had left home by then. It was getting rather lonesome around the house.

I was reminiscing about the time when they were still very young, in grade school and under. There were several things that stood out very clearly, such as when they first started their music lessons. The first few weeks on the violin, saxophone and clarinet were the hardest on the ears. Cello, piano, guitar, accordion, etc., were not quite as bad, although there was still a lot of noise. Most of them played two or more instruments. At one time, we had 23 instruments in the house, including two pianos.

The six oldest belonged to a band at one time that was called, "The Teeny Weeny Band." It was for children between the ages of five and twelve. They played many different instruments, even ukuleles, fifes and mouth organs. There were about 30 children. They had many calls to perform, not only in our town but also in nearby towns. It was not that their music was anything special, but they had cute uniforms. I believe that was what made the hit. Anyway, practicing music gave them less time for mischief.

I also remember a couple of humorous incidents. One day when the house was exceptionally messy, the Fuller Brush man came and was trying hard to make a sale. He was giving me the applesauce about how nice the house looked and that I needed certain gadgets to make the work easier. Well, he asked for it, so I spoke my piece. I said, "Mister, I never clean house. When the house gets too dirty to live in, I move." He packed up and left. I haven't seen the same salesman since.

Another time, I had an abscessed tooth that was very painful. The only thing that would stop the pain for a minute or two was cold water. I had to get to the dentist somehow; it was a distance of about ten blocks. I filled a bottle with cold water and started out. I had to take a swig of cold water every quarter of a block or so. Everyone stared at me and wondered, "What gives?" One poor fellow driving a car was looking at me so intently that he almost had an accident. When I reached the dentist's office, he wasn't in.

There was an optometrist who used the same waiting room. He told me that the doctor wasn't in but would be there shortly. I went right into the doctor's office and sat down in the chair. I wasn't going to let someone else get there first.

The dentist was a very short fellow. It was a lower molar that had to be pulled. He didn't want to give me Novocain because of the abscess. I just told him to go ahead without it because the pain was getting worse by the minute and I wanted that tooth out. He tried to pull it, but being as short as he was and having to pull upward, the tooth broke. I grabbed the arms of the chair and said, "Now, pull." He finally got the root out. What a wonderful feeling to get rid of the pain.

Raymond was transferred to a submarine shortly after the Squalus went down, which had us all worried for a while until we got used to the idea. Nothing happened anyway. Walter returned to town after a couple of months and joined the C.C.C. camp where his brother was.

The next summer, Harold quit the C.C.C. and hitchhiked to California. He didn't have a cent when he left, but he took a chance anyway. He had tried to ride a freight train for a week before. He got into the next state where he tried to get off. He fell alongside of the wheels. His guardian angel was on the alert, because Harold wasn't injured. He could easily have been killed.

When he hitchhiked, he rode everything from a hearse to a truck. He reached the coast in less than four days. He got a sandwich here and a doughnut there to keep alive. Raymond had some friends who were connected with a nightclub in Los Angeles. Harold went to work there at once.

Walter cut his foot very badly with an axe. He was in the camp infirmary for a while. Before he returned to work, they let him come home for a week. His foot looked bad. I thought that he would have trouble permanently, but I was wrong. The next time he came home on a visit, his foot was fine except for the scar. He quit the camp the next spring when his term was up.

There was a lady and her invalid daughter who wanted to go to the west coast. They wanted someone to drive their car. Walter was only 16, but he had been driving for several years, not only cars, but trucks as well, so he got the job.

After his passengers were settled, he went to Los Angeles and worked in the nightclub with his brother during the summer. He hitchhiked home in the fall. Somewhere along the road, some fellow had held up a gas station. His description checked somehow with Walter's. The police picked him up and took him to the station 20 miles back. The man in the station took one look and said, "No, that's not the guy." Walter said that he didn't mind being picked up, but he did mind the 20 miles that he had to hitchhike all over again.

Not long after, Walter and a friend of his, only a year older, took a freight train clear to the east coast. I wasn't in favor of the freight trains, but the young punks didn't tell me until after they had reached their destination. Walter said that he didn't want me to worry. The mother of the other boy worried at all times, so it didn't matter which way they went. Walter told me in one letter; "There is such a contrast in the letters you write and in the letters Richie's mother writes. Her letters say, 'Darling son, won't you please come home?' Your's say, 'Stay where you are, you Mug, there's no work here,' " which was the truth. The depression was still on and there wasn't any work in Duluth. He was lucky enough to get a job with the Greyhound, driving the empty buses between the garage and the station in the town he was in.

There was an old fellow in his seventies who lived in our neighborhood. He played the violin and he used to come to the house and have Mildred accompany him on the piano. He always paid her a dollar.

One day this fellow had a friend of his along. The friend was also a violinist, visiting from another state. They were waiting when Mildred came home from school. She had been sick all day and was looking forward to going to bed, but she knew that it meant a dollar if she played.

So she played along with them for a couple of hours. After that, they sent Geraldine to the store for some ice cream and cake. The rest of us all had a little party, but poor Mildred excused herself and went to bed.

About an hour after the two fellows had gone, Mildred was so sick that I had to get a taxi and take her to the hospital. The doctor checked her and said that she had to go to surgery at once. There was a man who was supposed to be operated on in the operating room, but they wheeled him out and got her ready instead. Her appendix was ready to rupture. Surprisingly, she got along very well after the first three days.

Albert joined the navy. Every time one of the children left home, it brought back memories from their childhood. This time, I remembered when he was a little fellow of about five. He fell on a peashooter that he was playing with and cut a big gash in the roof of his mouth. When he was about eleven, he got the tip of his finger cut off in a car door. That time he ran right down to the hospital and the doctor sewed it back on. It healed fine. The scar still shows, but it has never given him any trouble.

I was getting ready for my tenth and last child. The depression was still on. I was sick for 23 hours. Pat was taking a short course in machine shop. It was a W.P.A. project and it was at night. I wasn't going to tell Pat that I was ready for confinement that night, because he was of no help anyway. But after suffering all day and the night before, I was afraid the time was getting too near.

I had to call the doctor just before Pat was ready to leave the house. He went to the class all right, but he wanted a good excuse to come home and sleep instead of being in class.

He told the foreman what was happening at home, so he let Pat go home. The doctor and the nurse were there when he got home, so he went right upstairs to bed.

He never bothered to find out how things were turning out. It didn't bother him any more than it did when "Depression," the cat, had kittens.

At the time, we were very short of everything. I had a mattress with a hole right in the center. I had stuffed some newspaper in there and covered it with a blanket and a sheet. Of course the doctor and the nurse couldn't see it. After the baby was born and everything was taken care of, the nurse put the baby in bed with me, and both she and the doctor left. After a while, I happened to sink into that hole in the mattress and my back was very sore so I couldn't roll out again. I was lying there about five hours and it was torture.

When the baby was born, she was blue. I thought that she had a heart condition, but the doctor said, "No, she is fine, but your organs are like an old girdle – no stretch. It just squeezed all the air out of her." Well, I thought, if that is the case, I hope that I never have another one.

I got my wish. She was the end of the line. I was just a couple months short of my 45th birthday.

The War Years

Walter came home on a visit. Pat was pouting about something and was itching for an argument.

Walter had an old car and Pat accused him of taking some of Pat's tools, Walter said, "Well, you can search the car. I'm not carrying them in my pocket." I saw Pat sneaking some tools from the garage and putting them in Walter's car. That man would stoop to anything just to win an argument. But I told Walter what I saw. They had a big row about it. Walter left again that afternoon, but he told me that he would have liked to "wipe up the alley with his father."

The war broke out. Albert was in Manila on a battleship. We didn't hear anything from him for over three months. One day I got a telegram. It just said: "Am all right; don't worry." That was a great relief.

Going back to Christmas two months before, Raymond was in town. He brought his fiancée home for Christmas dinner. Pat wouldn't have dinner with us. He went into the bedroom and shut the door. He stayed there until they had gone. They were getting married ten days later, but Raymond conveniently forgot to invite his father to the wedding, which was held in the parsonage of the church.

It was just a small wedding with closest relatives from both sides. The reception was held at the bride's aunt's house. Mildred and I went. Pat didn't know they were married until two months later.

Leonard got whooping cough for the second time, which is rare, but it happened that it was much more severe this time than the first. The doctor wanted to give Jean (the baby) a shot so she wouldn't get it.

The day for our appointment came and it was 13 degrees below zero. The doctor's office was 16 blocks away. As usual, no bus fare so I had to walk and carry her, She was then 10 months old. When I reached the doctor's office, I noticed that her face was a little frostbitten on one cheek. I went in the washroom, put my scarf in cold water and put it on her cheek until the white stuff disappeared. I didn't want the doctor to know that I had carried her all that way in that cold weather.

Since the start of the war, it was hard to get gas and tires for the trucks. It was also hard to get help as almost everyone was in defense work.

Pat finally decided to go to work after 17 years. I knew it wasn't going to help me much as far as money was concerned. He just wouldn't give me money for household expenses if he could possibly get out of it.

Linnea had bought clothes for all the children and me since she started to work. She also paid for graduation pictures and graduation clothes for the ones who graduated. When she graduated, I had to turn in my insurance policy to get a dress and coat for her. The insurance company had a crooked agent and I was cheated out of half of the money.

Anyway, it was less work for me when Pat no longer ran the trucks. I didn't have to keep the books and I didn't have to take those blasted telephone calls. Also, I no longer had to put up with people's bad natures every time Pat did something wrong on the job.

Every time I told him that we needed something for the house, I got the same answer, always in the form of a question. "Who's going to pay for that?"

It turned out to be an awfully cold spring. At the beginning of April, I ran out of coal. The house was cold and damp. Jean caught a very bad cold. I walked three blocks to carry two pails of coal that I borrowed from a friend of ours. Pat, however, hadn't thought of the colored lady that I mentioned before. When she got riled, her temper matched Pat's to perfection. Leonard and Jean were **her** children and if she thought they were neglected in any way, she was right there to explode. When Jean caught that cold and the lady knew it was because of Pat's neglecting to buy coal, she lit into him the very next morning. They had some very hot words, but Pat ordered coal that afternoon.

Pat worked in the steel mills for about three months. Then he changed to an ironworks company. He had only worked there a couple of months when he lost a finger. He had lost his thumb on the same hand when he was just a young boy in Europe. That also happened in an industrial accident. It was his right hand, so he was quite helpless for a while. It didn't heal right so he had to return to the hospital for a second operation.

We had now lived in our present home for 17 years. For the last ten years, Pat had never made one payment. The poor fellow with the one arm had even paid the taxes out of his own pocket. He was such a good Christian fellow, he hadn't wanted to foreclose because of all the children we had. He knew as well as we did that it would have been impossible to rent. But now both he and his wife were ill. He finally foreclosed. We would have had to move in the dead of winter if I had listened to Pat. He didn't want to pay anything. But Albert made out an allotment to me, so I paid rent from then on as long as we lived there, which was about 15 months.

Pat bought an old, beat-up house about a block up the hill. As I mentioned before, Pat was very handy and could do anything he wanted to do when he put his mind to it, which wasn't often.

He got another fellow to help him and they both worked in their spare time. But Pat always wanted everything his own way. I never had anything to say; it was always his way, and nobody else's. I heard him talking over his plans with a fellow next door one day. In passing, I heard Pat say, "Well, what my wife likes and what I do are two different things." I thought to myself, "Okay, big boy, you can do just as you want to, all by yourself; build it to suit yourself." I never went near the place until 15 months later when we moved in. And by that time, I didn't care if I moved or not. The place didn't even appeal to me any more.

Pat was working in the shipyard by then. He was making very good money. But those fellows were all taking Uncle Sam for a ride. They used to sneak in some corner every afternoon and go to sleep. Pat didn't tell me, but one of our neighbors did. We were talking one day and he came up with this: "Pat sleeps in the same place I do in the afternoons." I had heard some rumors to that effect before, but I didn't know that they were all that bad.

Pat was fixing a large fan one day and some fool turned on the current. He was strong enough to brace himself and he yelled for help. All he got was a broken ankle in the accident, but he could easily have gotten killed. Their safety methods were not very efficient.

Linnea was getting married. I wanted to go to the wedding but Pat couldn't see spending any money for such a silly thing as a wedding (when it wasn't his own), so there was nothing I could do about it. But I was thinking even at that time: "Someday, I won't have to depend on him for anything." Well, that day finally did come, some years later.

Walter joined the army/air force. He was sent to Texas. Harold was then in Oregon. A girl that he had dated in Duluth had moved out there with her parents. Harold and the girl got married. He was not of age, but he wasn't going to let a little thing like that stop him. We didn't even know until months later. Knowing Pat as Harold did, he did things his own way instead of asking for trouble.

They were hiring girls to work in a glass factory in New Jersey. Mildred signed up and went east. She was only 16. She worked there about six months. Then she went to Washington, D.C. There she worked as a cashier in the Statler Hotel. During the war, they didn't check on ages. If they looked old enough and could do the work, that was all that was required.

Leonard was nearly seven. He spent a lot of time at the YMCA. One evening, just before suppertime, he came home with a broken arm. He had fallen from an overhead horizontal ladder meant to strengthen arms and shoulder muscles. I couldn't take him to the doctor just then. If Pat had come home and no supper was ready, I would never have heard the last of that, accident or no accident.

Leonard started out for the doctor's office all by himself. We didn't even have a phone at that time so I couldn't call. When he got to the doctor's office, he discovered that our family doctor was out of town, but the nurses got in touch with another one who was still in the building. All the others had gone home for the day.

They had some trouble locating material for the cast, but they finally got it all together. When it was nine o'clock and Leonard hadn't returned, I was getting a little uneasy. I was just going out to get to a phone when the doctor drove up in front of the house. He was kind enough to bring the boy home.

Geraldine was working in the hospital collecting trays and such. She was not quite thirteen. If she had been at home, there would have been no problem. She could easily have gone with Leonard to the doctor, but as it turned out, he did all right by himself.

The next week, Leonard was supposed to go to camp for two weeks. I had already paid for him. Pat would never pay for anything like that, but the children all sent a little almost every payday.

I couldn't send Leonard by himself with the broken arm, so I arranged to have a boy twelve years old to go with him as a bodyguard. They went just for one week instead of two, so it didn't cost any more.

Pat had been acting very odd for some time. He didn't even want me to go out of the house to go to the store. Well, I wasn't going to take that from anybody. I just didn't pay any attention. I let him rave if he felt like it.

One evening, Geraldine got off early, so I decided to go a block down the hill to visit Pat's musician friend and his wife. As I will be talking about this fellow more in the future, I'll call him by his first name, which was Andrew.

We all went, the four of us, Geraldine, Leonard, Jean and I. We stayed until a quarter of ten. Ten minutes later, when we reached home, the door was locked. Not only that, but the windows were nailed down.

That simple-minded action was all I needed to set me off at the time and I'd had enough. We spent the night with some friends. Of course I knew that he was going to look for me, but I also knew that I could get in hiding some place before he could find me.

The first thing he did was go down to the hospital and raise Cain with the sisters. When Geraldine saw him coming, she scooted out the back door and came to the place where we had spent the night. I knew that he would be on our trail before long. We all hurried across the street to another family I knew. From there I called a taxi, which picked us up at the back door which was in the alley and hidden from view. The taxi took us out to a park. I had fifty cents in my pocket so I had the taxi stop at a store on the way. I picked up a loaf of bread and a small jar of peanut butter. My friend had given me money for the taxi.

We stayed in the park all day. I really didn't have any plans, but I knew I wasn't going back home. The man who was taking care of the park guessed that something was wrong. He could see that I hadn't planned for a picnic. The only way I could spread the peanut butter on the bread was with a small branch that I broke off a tree.

Finally, he came over and asked me if I was hiding from someone. I said, "Yes, but not from the police." He said, "I guessed as much."

It started to rain a little then. The fellow said that he had a little cabin about a half a mile from the park. He said that we could use that and he would stay in the tower, which was located in the park. He gave me the key and the directions, so we went to the cabin. Next morning, the man came with a big box of groceries and told me to help myself, adding, "Don't let the children starve."

Albert had some money in the bank, which he had sent home; it was in both his name and mine. But he said that I could use it if I needed it, so I drew $50.00 out. I took a test and got work in the steel mill. I knew I had to look for a place to stay because school would begin in two weeks.

Now, to get back to Pat. The first thing he did was to put an ad in the paper saying that he was not responsible for any of my bills, which was a big laugh since he had never paid my bills anyway. So, in turn, I put an ad in the paper and said that I was not responsible for his bills.

The first few days he was really the big shot. He was going to give a party the next Saturday night. There was a married woman, a little on the silly side, that he was hanging around with a little more than necessary. She promised to go there and make coffee and sandwiches, but everybody else said that they wouldn't go as long as I wasn't there. Then he began to think that it probably wasn't such a good idea after all.

When he first went down to Andrew's house and told him that I had left, Andrew told him that he didn't believe it and, knowing Pat as he did, he asked him point blank if he had locked me out, but Pat insisted that the door was open and he just couldn't understand what had happened.

Andrew came up to the house. The first thing he saw was the ration books lying on the table. Then Andrew blew up. He told him right then and there that he knew Pat lied. Pat went out and got drunk.

About eleven o'clock that night, the colored lady found him lying on the sidewalk in front of the house. He was a mess. He had even wet his pants. She thought that he had had a stroke or something, so she went down and got Andrew. Andrew came up and took one look at Pat. He said, "You're not sick. You're drunk. Now get up."

Between Andrew and the colored lady, they managed to get him in the house. The next day, he was crying all day. He asked Andrew if he couldn't do something to find me. He'd do anything, anything, if I would only come back.

I saw Andrew's wife a couple of days later downtown, and she told me everything that had happened. Well, I promised to have a talk with him, which I did. To make a long story short, I went back. He behaved a few months, but it didn't take long before he was back to his old tricks.

Harold joined the army/air corps; after some months' training, he was sent to Italy and then to somewhere in Africa.

Walter came home on furlough and wanted to get married. They had kept company since they were in junior high school. Walter was only 19 so he had to ask his father to sign the papers. It was really comical. I was in the kitchen; Pat was in the living room. Walter had been walking between the living room and the kitchen at least half a dozen times, trying to get up nerve to ask his father.

Finally, he came into the kitchen again and said, "I would rather face six generals than ask him that question." But finally, he told Pat what was on his mind. Pat must have been in a good mood because all he said was, "I'll sign it but I think you're making a mistake." Walter got married that weekend.

We celebrated our silver wedding anniversary a couple of years before this time. It was held in the same hall where we were married. There were about 150 people. We had a nice program, smorgasbord and a dance afterward. But it was during the war. Everyone was worried. Most of our children were too far away to come home. I really didn't enjoy it, but all of our friends celebrated their 25th wedding anniversary, so it was expected of us to do the same. Anyway, it was something to remember in the future.

Mildred was the type who always came to the point without always considering the whole "cause and effect" side of her decisions. One day we got a letter which said, in part, "You're not going to like what I'm going to tell you. I got married last night and I'm happy about the whole thing." She was three months shy of her eighteenth birthday.

It didn't bother me since I felt it was her own business, but Pat was "fit to be tied," as they say. That was the first time (that I knew of) that he was really angry with Mildred. He said that he was going to have the marriage annulled. I put him straight on that in a hurry. I asked him what he thought he would gain by that. In three months she would be 18 and all he would have for his trouble would be two enemies. They certainly would have married again.

The boy was from Duluth and if Pat had ever paid any attention to the young people that came to the house, he would have remembered him. It made it bad for Geraldine, though. I guess Pat just figured that he was going to keep all the boys away from her.

A couple of years later, she had a date with a boy one Sunday afternoon and Pat embarrassed her right in front of the boy and said that she couldn't go. She took it good-naturedly enough on the outside, but she must have been boiling within. She made the remark that Pat would never again have to be bothered with any of her boyfriends and that is just what happened. There never was another boy calling for Geraldine. It might have had something to do with the choosing of her work and her life later.

At the time, it was very hard on Geraldine. She was going to high school, playing in the school orchestra and also playing in the junior symphony orchestra and working four and five hours at the hospital six days a week. We had to live on what she made. Pat kept his money for himself, what little he made. He was not working steady then.

Leonard had a paper route from the time he was eight. I had to do all the collecting for him because some of the people just wouldn't pay. I had to cut out delivery of papers time and again. I also had to help him on Fridays and Sundays because the papers were too heavy for a little boy of eight. About a year and a half later, he had saved about $200.00.

There was a big warehouse to be torn down. A person could have the warehouse for nothing, but it had to be removed from the premises. Pat wanted to put it up in our backyard. It would cost $200.00 to move it. He wanted the bonds that Leonard had in the bank. Pat wouldn't have been fit to live with for either the children or me if I had refused, so I had to let him use them.

He was that way with everything. Anything he wanted, whether it belonged to the children or to me, he would just take it as if it was his without even asking. When Albert went in the service, he gave Leonard his toolbox. Pat took that and just dumped Leonard's tools on the floor. We didn't have a case for one of the guitars. Linnea sent some money for Mother's Day, so I bought a case for it. Pat sold the guitar and the case and kept all the money.

When we first moved into our new house, the people who were there before us had used rat poison in the basement. It was just a dirt basement so I didn't pay much attention to it. "Depression," our cat with her two kittens named "Kilo" and "Watt," were running in and out of the basement. They all got poisoned. Depression and Watt died.

I felt very badly about Depression. She was thirteen years old and she was such a smart cat. Since Watt died, I renamed the remaining one "Kilowatt." It had also been poisoned, but lived. It had fits, though, until it was about two years old. It was a beautiful cat and very large, as it was a male. Some years later, it got the mumps. There is nothing much funnier looking than a cat with mumps. It recovered from that just as the children did.

Leonard had a very good friend who lived right across the street from us. His name was Lawrence. He was ten. Leonard was eight. But they were both the same size and, most of the time, they wore similar clothing.

Lawrence's parents didn't want him to have a bike. I guess they were trying to protect him from accidents, which was only natural. They just had this one boy and an eighteen-year-old daughter.

Well, Lawrence didn't see eye-to-eye with his parents. He would borrow a bike whenever he could.

This particular evening, he had borrowed a bike from the boy next door. He came through the alley on the bike and a young boy with only one arm came driving a car down the hill. They crashed right in front of our house. I saw the boy fly over into the gutter under a parked car. My heart dropped down to the bottom of my shoes.

Wearing clothes somewhat similar to Leonard's, it appeared to be him. I ran across the street and, of course, I recognized him at once. I sat there until the ambulance came, which seemed an eternity. He never regained consciousness. He died five hours later. When Leonard found out that his friend was dead, he put his bike in the basement and he never touched it for a whole year.

Jean was having trouble with her tonsils. It affected her sinus. She coughed a great deal and it appeared as if she always had a cold. She was also running a temperature most of the time. The doctor wanted to take the tonsils out, but every time she was supposed to go to the hospital, she came down with a fever. Finally, the doctor decided to take her on short notice. I called him when her temperature was normal. I brought her into the hospital that evening and she had a tonsillectomy the next morning.

The trouble started after surgery. For some reason, they couldn't wake her up and it looked as if she was choking. The next half hour I was chewing my nails, so to speak. It seemed as if the whole world dropped off my shoulder when she finally woke up. Geraldine worked at the hospital, but the sister let her come and stay in the room until Jean woke up. Once she woke up, she was fine. The doctor returned after she had been awake for a couple of hours. He handed her a stick of gum and said, "Here. I've been chewing on this for the last two weeks; you can have it now." That made her laugh, and she still remembers that little speech.

Walter had a close call in the air force. He was coming in on a plane one day. They were supposed to refuel and take off again, but for some reason, they took him off and changed him to a later plane. When the plane took off again, it crashed and burned on takeoff. The whole crew perished. Walter wrote about it in a letter a couple of days later. He said, in part: "As I was watching, I could just see myself in there burning with my buddies."

A short time later, though, he was in a crash. He came out with broken ankles and an injury to his stomach.

The next spring, Violet came home for a vacation. She took ill while she was there. The old trouble again, which all stemmed from the beating she got when she was four years old. The doctor advised surgery. She went to the hospital.   When they got her ready for surgery, the doctor still hadn't learned to give the spinal anesthetic properly. He had already made an incision when Violet said, "Stop, doctor, the spinal didn't work."

The doctor said, "You're kidding; wiggle your big toe." Violet lifted up her whole leg. The doctor burst out, "Oh, gosh, give her the gas immediately!" She looked bad and I was really worried, but she came out fine after a few days. Although the operation didn't do her much good, it was necessary then. She had a more serious one later.

She was still in town when we received the most shocking letter one day. The whole bottom had just dropped out of Linnea's world. Her husband had been killed over in Germany. I sat down and bawled like a small child. He was such a wonderful boy. I just couldn't believe it. I was hoping against hope that it was all a mistake, but of course, there was no mistake.

Poor Linnea. My heart really went out to her. She had been going to college evenings, and the day she got the telegram, she had the final exam. She came out with a "C," the first "C" that she had ever gotten since she first started school. With the shock that she had just had, I was surprised that she got anything above a zero.

George, her husband, was a platoon sergeant in his army company and they had reached the Elbe River on Friday, April 13, 1945, just three weeks prior to V-E Day in Europe. Around midnight, he was making the rounds of his platoon which was dug in near the Elbe. They knew that forward of them the German army had been periodically seen from their position. Suddenly a burst of machine-gun fire exploded the stillness of the night and caught George in a partially standing position. He threw two grenades and collapsed as they found their mark. He stopped the machine gun, but it was already too late for George. He was awarded the Silver Star for his actions that night and given credit for saving the lives of his platoon members. It was also too late for Linnea.

Geraldine came down with a slight touch of pneumonia and had to go to the hospital for a few days. We had no hospitalization, so it was a strain on the budget to pay the bill, but I managed with Geraldine's check when she went back to work plus what the other children pitched in.

Pat was doing carpenter work, but by that time, he had Europe on his mind. He wanted to make a trip to his hometown, so it was almost impossible to get money out of him.

Geraldine graduated the next spring, at the age of 16. She immediately went into training to become a nurse. There was a course of three months at a college at first and then she went straight to the hospital. Linnea paid the initial payment for her, because I didn't have it.

The war was over. Harold came back with a bad case of malaria, which bothered him for several years after that. Violet's husband and Mildred's husband, as well as Walter and Albert, all returned from their wartime services. They all had their own families at that time, with the exception of Albert. He was still single. He came home to go to college. Junior college was just one block from our house, so it made it quite handy. Raymond also had his own family and property by that time.

Linnea returned from her government job in Washington, D.C. and entered the University of Chicago. In six weeks, she had passed all the tests for a B.A. degree, but she stayed right on to continue the courses necessary to get her Masters degree. But, she also had to work besides going to college, so it took a little time.

The Post-War Years

My income was getting mighty slim, so I decided to go to work. I knew there was plenty of risk involved. Jean was only six. But that was the chance that I had to take. We had to eat. Pat was no good as a baby sitter. He was out with his car, driving around at all hours of the night. Albert had his own interests besides his studying.

Leonard belonged to the Boy Scouts, the Optimist Club, the Duluth Ski Club and the Y.M.C.A. I couldn't curtail all his activities. So that left poor Jean alone some evenings until after ten o'clock.

One evening, she was just lonesome, I guess. She went half a block away to some colored children's house to play with them. That night, Pat came home at eight o'clock, which he usually never did. He looked for her and someone told him where she was.

Pat hated colored people, so he went right up there. When Jean heard him coming, she crawled under the bed. Pat went right in and dragged her out. When he got her home, he was beating her so hard that she couldn't breathe any more. I'm sure he would have killed her, but Geraldine just happened to drop in.

She grabbed Jean away from Pat and really told him off. Jean was black and blue the whole length of her body. Geraldine knew that if I saw her like that, I would have him arrested. She didn't want a scandal because she had just started in training at the hospital. I worked nights, so I didn't know anything about it until a couple of days later, when I noticed the marks on Jean's body. I went to the bottom of the whole thing. I told him then to keep his hands off, or else.

He tried something else some time later. The bathroom was at the end of the hall and every time Jean went to the bathroom during the night, he would get up and hit her. She didn't dare to go to the bathroom anymore, and naturally, she couldn't sleep.

I came home from work at two o'clock one morning and there she was, awake and crying because she didn't dare to go to the bathroom. I really lit into Pat the next morning. I told him that I had warned him once and he had better listen if he knew what was good for him. He didn't hit her after that, but he tried to make it as miserable as he could. As an example, when I bought her a bike for her eighth birthday, he told her, "I hope you run into a telephone pole and break your neck." Of course it hurt her feelings very much.

Pat got into trouble with Andrew's son about the cabin. The agreement was that Andrew's son and his family were to use the cabin when Pat and Andrew were not there fishing.

First, Pat sent some of his friends up there to fish and live in the cabin, which was not in the agreement at all. The next time he went there, he locked the cabin and took the key home. That made the fellow mad. He owned the land. He wrote Pat a letter and said that Pat would either have to sell the cabin to him or else tear it down. Pat tore it down, but he didn't clean up the mess; he just threw the stuff all over the place. Naturally, he wasn't on speaking terms with either Andrew or Andrew's son for about five years after that. I had nothing to do with it, so it didn't spoil my friendship.

Leonard and Jean got along fine, but sometimes Leonard wanted to show his authority. If Jean was in bed when he came in and he wanted something from the store, he would make her get up and dress and go to the store for him. But usually, he was very good about looking after her.

Once when Jean had a cold, Leonard was trying to use the remedy that he had seen me use for a chest cold. He was greasing her chest with Vaporub and he had the oven on. He was heating a flannel pad to put on her chest. Pat came in and roared, "What the hell are you kids doing?" Leonard spoke up, "Taking care of my little sister, that's what I'm doing; nobody else seems to."

I remember once when they were smaller, Leonard was eight-and-a-half and Jean was four. They were alone for a little while. When I came home, they were sitting by their little table with a deck of cards. She had on her panties and one anklet. He still had both of his anklets, t-shirt and shorts. Jean said, "Mom, Leonard taught me a new game, it's called strip poker." I could see by the way they were still dressed who was in the lead.

Only once I found Leonard to be a little careless of Jean. I found them both hitching a ride on the back of a bus. It was in the winter and she had lost one boot and was hanging onto the other one with one hand, also hanging onto the bus with the other hand. I had a talk with both of them and explained the danger. I also told them what happened a few years before just a block from our house. A ten-year-old boy took his six-year-old brother to hitch a ride on a semi-trailer truck going up the hill. The six-year-old fell under the wheels and was killed instantly.

I worked in a hotel. Sometimes I worked the whole night through, from seven in the evening until six in the morning, and sometimes only until 12 midnight. It all depended on when I finished my work. The worst part was to get some sleep at home. I could have slept a few hours after the children went to school. But the problem was Pat. He had always been a stinker for making things miserable and he was no exception then. He turned the radio on full blast, purposely to keep me from sleeping. I was so tired that sometimes I fell asleep standing up.

I had ulcers on my legs and arthritis in the balls of my feet. Any little pebble on the street would throw me off balance. Pat had a car, but he would never pick me up, although he was always out with his car at night. Most of the time, I had to walk because the buses had stopped running by the time I got out. It was 16 blocks from home.

One night, I was crossing the street. There was a dip in the street where I couldn't see the cars coming down the hill. I struck a slippery spot on the street and couldn't move. The car was bearing down on me. The driver couldn't stop. He had to go in the ditch, but there happened to be a big snow bank there. He hit that, so his car wasn't damaged.

Another night, I took the bus to within a block of my home. It had thawed during the day and then frozen up at night, which made the sidewalk very rough, but also very slippery. It was two o'clock in the morning and there wasn't a soul in sight. I couldn't walk, my feet hurt too much. I crawled the whole length of the block. My mittens were in tatters and my knees were bleeding. I was the biggest mess imaginable.

Pat had all of his papers ready to leave for Europe. I was glad to see him go. He wasn't working, he didn't give me any money, and he certainly wasn't worried about how I was going to get along while he was gone. I was making an average of $15.00 a week after taxes. This was 1948 and things were not cheap any more, although it didn't cost as much as it does today. But $15.00 for the three of us was a chore to keep everything within the budget.

Ten days before Pat left, one of Leonard's newspaper customers gave him a puppy. Pat hated dogs, cats, kids, and anything that wasn't of any use to him. I would never have been able to let Leonard keep the dog if it hadn't been so close to Pat's trip, but I thought that I would try my darned best to keep the puppy out of Pat's way until he left.

It was in the middle of March and still quite cold. After school, the children took turns sitting outside with the dog until they both came down with bad colds. At night, we put the dog in the ash barrel in the backyard. We wrapped it in old blankets. If it was warm enough in the barrel, "Susie" was reasonably quiet. Finally, Pat left, which was a relief to all of us. I had only one letter from him in the four months he was gone.

One night, a friend of Leonard's spent the night at our house, which happened often when Pat wasn't there. They couldn't have company when Pat was at home. Well, this time the children heard some strange noise on the rear porch. They thought that someone was trying to break in.

I came home from work about one a.m. Instead of walking right in, I always put my hand in to snap on the light. It was a lucky thing that I did. If I had stuck my head in, I'm afraid this story wouldn't have been written. All three of them were standing on the stairway, three feet from the door, each holding a baseball bat ready to swing.

One weekend, Leonard had gone to Chicago on an excursion with some boys from the Y.M.C.A. Jean was alone. She didn't mind being alone so much after we got "Susie" because Susie gave the alarm if someone stepped on the porch. That evening, it was brewing up to a big storm. I got through about 11 p.m. I was lucky enough to get a bus, but that time of the night I had to walk two blocks to get home. I hurried and thought that I could make it before it really started. I was about a half a block from the house when everything broke loose. There was a 60-mile-an-hour wind and I have never seen such rain. I was going uphill, so I couldn't run.

When I finally got inside, I ran upstairs to check on the windows. The hall window was very high and that happened to be on the windy side. There was poor Jean standing in her pajamas, soaked to the skin, trying to close the window, but she couldn't reach it. The water was all over the floor clear to the other end of the hallway. Jean kept repeating, "I tried, Mom, but I just couldn't reach it."

Kilowatt got pneumonia. An odd ailment it was for a cat to get. I had an idea that he was going to die. One day, he wanted to go out. He was so weak that he staggered, but he walked away someplace. I never saw him again.

Pat returned with the same disposition that he had when he left. Still, he hated Susie. But it was summer and the dog stayed outside, so he only got a kick at her once in a while.

A mouse had strayed into the house somehow. I set a trap for it in Jean's room. One night, the mouse got caught, but only the leg was trapped. The mouse was jumping all over the place, making a terrific racket dragging the trap around. Pat yelled to Jean to cut out the noise. Of course the mouse just kept on going. Pat came charging into Jean's room ready to swing. She didn't dare to say anything, but she pointed to the mouse in the corner. He picked up the trap with the mouse in it and threw the whole mess out in the yard. I found it there the next morning, but by then, the mouse was dead. The foot was still caught in the trap.

Pat wouldn't go to work. He didn't even look for any. I had to feed him too, on my small wages, which was really a headache. Then, two months later, he decided to go back to Europe.

He had the warehouse in the backyard that he had moved up there the year before. He had it full of tools and machinery. It was worth about $3,000.00. He got a buyer for it. He included the truck, the car and a lean-to off the garage, and was ready to sell the whole thing for $1,500.00. He wasn't going to give me any of it. That time, I objected. I asked for $500.00. He refused.

I got my lawyer on the trail. I knew when the man was supposed to come up with the money and I had the lawyer right there. The lawyer told him that he was getting off easy. According to state law, I could hold out for $750.00, and there wouldn't be any argument about it. I got the check for $500.00 and I handed it right to the lawyer and said, "Take care of this until I have a chance to put it where I want it." The lawyer left with the check. Pat was mad enough to chew nails. He left for Europe a few days later.

I was very happy because I thought that he would stay over the winter and be out of my hair. But I guessed wrong. He had taken the boat over, but he flew back three weeks later. He never explained to anybody why he did it. That was an easy way to get rid of $1,000.00 in a hurry. Naturally, he was broke when he returned, but he did go to work for a couple of months. Then it turned cold and, of course, he couldn't do carpenter work outside in the winter.

Albert was in Minneapolis going to the University of Minnesota. Linnea was still going to the University of Chicago. Her scholarship had been renewed every year. Meanwhile, the U.S. Army had brought George back from Belgium for re-burial in Arlington National Cemetery.

Violet had surgery for the third time. She was very low for a while and the doctors didn't think she was going to make it, but she did. There are times when she still has to be careful about what she eats but, considering the rough time she has had health wise, she is fine.

The hotel I worked in was supposed to be an up-to-date hotel, but it was filthy. I could never understand how they got by with the inspections. They charged me for the meals, but I refused to eat them. I brought my own sandwiches. There were roaches and water bugs all over the place. They had rats and mice too. When they put poison out for the rodents, they went behind the cabinets and died. The smell was enough to kill, if one's stomach wasn't insulated.

The mice gave us a performance one night in a big lard bucket. They were sitting on their hind legs, washing behind their ears, just like cats.

The manager was a wonderful person and the chef was a jewel, but the assistant manager was something else, but I could never figure out just what. In my opinion, "A dog like that shouldn't happen to anybody." The poor fellow died two years later from throat cancer. Ssh – don't speak ill of the dead.

Christmas came, and Linnea came with it for the holidays. There had been some hard feelings for some time between the assistant manager and me. On New Year's Eve, there was a show that I wanted to see. Linnea came to the hotel to help me with the work. Ray (the assistant manager) came in and gave us a hard time. I blew up for the first time and let him know just how I felt, and I didn't mince any words. I just about told him to drop dead. Then we walked out and went to the show.

I went back at two o'clock to finish my work. When I thought of all the things we had to put up with, such as the pot washer going in our dressing room and sleeping off his drunk and us having to change clothes with him lying there, and the mice running over the dishes, it made me madder by the minute. I didn't care if I had a job or not.

The next day, Ray told the chef that he was going to fire me. The chef knew how I felt about the place and he was on my side. He sent someone to my house in the afternoon to tell me what was going on, and in that way,

I had a chance to beat Ray to the draw. That is exactly what I did.

I went out and called the office and asked them to please send the check and that I wasn't coming back. I saw Ray once about a month later. Neither one of us spoke, but if looks could kill, we'd both be dead. Two days later, I went to work in a restaurant right across the street from the hotel. I was there for five months. Then the place closed.

A few days later, I found the nicest place to work. It was a seafood restaurant. They were the nicest people I've ever worked for. They did more favors for me than anyone has ever done, outside of my own family. Since it is now closed and I don't expect it to reopen, I'll name it: **The Jolly Fisher**, the most wonderful owners and the best place I've ever worked in. The world needs more places like that one.

For Easter, I bought a rabbit. It was a female. We called it Lily. Susie was very fond of Lily. It was fun to see them play. Lily had one trick that Susie didn't like. She used to get hold of the tip of Susie's tail and hang on. Susie never bit her, though. Both of them were neighborhood favorites. During the summer, Lily was outside in a cage, and all the children brought her lettuce, carrots, clover and what have you. She was the fattest rabbit in town.

I was having a lot of trouble with ulcers on my legs, but I never stayed home from work, no matter how painful it was, and I also had arthritis, which made it worse. If I sat down, it took at least a half an hour to get walking again. I never dared to sit down at work because of that. I always had to stand up in the bus, even if I was the only passenger. If I sat down, I couldn't get up in time to get off.

One day Jean accidentally touched my ulcer with the heel of her shoe. A piece came right out of the leg. I

163

saw stars for the next half hour. The next day, I went to the doctor. He told me that if I hadn't come, I might have been spending three months in the hospital in the near future. I had hospitalization by then through the union, so I knew that I could afford an operation for the first time.

After the ulcers were healed, the doctor made arrangements with the surgery in the clinic to have the veins cut and tied. I was to have surgery one morning at 10:00 a.m. Just when the nurse had gotten me all ready for surgery, the doctor was called out on an emergency case. They put me to bed until one o'clock.

So I had surgery at one that afternoon. I had planned to be home at lunchtime, but as surgery was delayed, I couldn't make it. Jean came home for lunch. She could easily have made herself a sandwich, but Pat decided to make pancakes. Well, he didn't know any more about making pancakes than a hog knows about the Jewish Sabbath.

He mixed up some flour and water and tried to fry it. It just made a mess. Jean couldn't eat it. She gave some to Susie and Susie turned up her nose and walked away. Jean just said that she wasn't hungry, and she didn't dare to eat anything else, so she went back to school without lunch.

When I returned about 3:30, all he— broke loose. We had no phone, so I hadn't been able to call. Pat was in a worse mood than a Spanish bull just before the kill, simply because he didn't get his lunch. When he didn't quit raving, I told him that he could go without supper, too. I gave Leonard and Jean money to get some hamburgers for themselves and then I went out.

I hadn't planned on going to work that night, but I just knew I couldn't stand Pat's raving all night, so I went to work. It wasn't too bad in the beginning, but about ten o'clock, my legs were pretty sore. I never used to sit down, but I finally sat down for a while. The boss came in and asked if I didn't feel good. I told him that I had had surgery that afternoon about one o'clock. He asked, "Then what are you doing here?" I could have gone home then, but I knew that I would have to listen to that raving at home, so I stayed until one o'clock in the morning. The other girls did the work for me the rest of the evening. They were a wonderful bunch. They always did what they could in a pinch.

Pat was mad for several weeks. Once, when I came home from work, he had emptied all the dresser drawers on my bed. There were some common pins in a box that had come open and they had spilled on the bed. So I was picking common pins for an hour before I could go to bed.

He would do all the crazy things that he could think of. Sometimes when I came home, I would find that he had taken all the clean dishes and put them in the sink. They were all messed up and had to be washed over again. He also took the dirty clothes out of the clothes hamper and put them on the dining room table. He might have been sane, but he certainly didn't act like it. If any of the children over three years of age had pulled off a stunt like that, I certainly would have paddled their seats, but what could I do with a grown man that acted like a spoiled brat?

The children all lived so far away and were scattered in different directions. We had never had the family all together at one time. Christmas 1949 was approaching. Linnea had been trying for weeks to round them up. Finally, they all promised to be there on Christmas Eve and, more than that, each one kept that promise. The last ones came at eight p.m. and ten p.m. Raymond had to leave, so that gave us just two hours. But we managed to get a family picture taken during that time. I was always happy that we did, because we would never again be able to get together all at the same time. Two hours for a family reunion in a lifetime is very short, but it was something for the family to keep in its collective memory.

In the next few months, small, annoying things kept cropping up; Geraldine had an appendectomy. Leonard tipped over on his motor scooter and came out with a hernia, for which he later had to have surgery. Jean broke her big toe by playing "kick the can." She kicked a brick in the gutter instead. She also broke one of her fingers by loading a B.B. gun. All those little things kept life interesting for a while.

The next summer, Albert graduated from one college, Linnea from another one, and Geraldine from nurses' college. Linnea sent for me to come to Chicago for her graduation. I had not had a vacation since our trip east in 1938. I had a week's vacation with pay coming where I worked, so I decided to go. I left Leonard to take care of the dog and the rabbit and also to make the meals for Pat. He was only 14, but he was very dependable. I took Jean with me.

Linnea graduated with honors. She was also awarded the Phi Beta Kappa pin. Her former boss from Washington sent her a dozen gladiolas with stems five feet long. We all got the biggest bang out of that. I had the most fun all that week and hated to go back home when my time was up.

I had had an icebox for many years, but I never had money to buy the ice. I guess it didn't matter much; there was never any food in it anyway until I went to work. I tried to keep both food and ice in it after that. In the winter, I tried to cut down on the expenses by freezing the ice I used for the icebox. I froze it in a small pail and then put the whole thing in the ice compartment. It lasted 24 hours.

I had to cut corners every way I could. The fuel bill came very high in the winter. We heated with a coal stove. Six rooms took a lot of coal when the temperature dropped to 35 below and, once in a while, even 40 below.

The next Christmas, the children all got together and bought me a refrigerator. Geraldine got me out of the house for several hours while the others had the refrigerator brought in. I came in the back way and when I saw the refrigerator, I was so happy I could have screamed, but I didn't dare stop, or say anything because I didn't want to show an emotional outburst.

I walked into the other room. Walter was sitting there with the camera. I believe they were all disappointed; they probably thought that I didn't appreciate it, which was the farthest thing from the truth. I just didn't want to break down. Walter spoke first. He put it like this: "You are the most unemotional woman I have ever seen." I agree; if I can possibly help it, I try to hide what's on the inside. I had the same trouble several years before when Linnea bought me a beautiful set of dishes for my birthday. I couldn't even thank her until half an hour later.

Leonard was playing the clarinet in the school band, but he also wanted to play the accordion. He went to work in a bowling alley, evenings from eight to twelve midnight. There was an eighteen-lesson course at a music studio. He was the first boy to finish the course in the shortest time. A girl had finished in the same length of time shortly before.

As Jean was now entirely alone every night, I kept her busy. She had no time to play out after dark. She took swimming, figure skating, dancing, singing, violin, piano and she also got in on the accordion lessons. Three months later, she won an accordion competing with several adults. She still had a straight "A" in school. I know that it was a little hard on her, but I couldn't take a chance of letting her play out on the street corners. The next year, both she and Leonard played in the junior symphony. I still believe it helped, keeping them out of mischief. There was always something to practice and get ready for a program of some sort.

Violet and Mildred lived in Philadelphia at that time. I had a two-week vacation coming. They invited us to come east for the vacation. Pat didn't work steady so he could go any time he wanted to, so the four of us went.

I knew that Pat was jealous of Mildred's husband, but I had no idea how jealous until two days after we reached Philadelphia.

We had been sightseeing all day. In the evening, we went to a show. We came home about eleven p.m. Pat went right to bed, but the rest of us decided to have some coffee. It was Saturday night and nobody had to work the next day. Jean had gone to bed, but there were Violet and her husband, Mildred and her husband and Leonard and I. We were talking very quietly so as not to disturb Pat because we all knew his temper.

About a quarter of twelve, he came into the kitchen raving mad, yelling and swearing at the top of his voice. "Didn't we have sense enough to go to bed and why all that racket and blah, blah, blah." Then he announced that he was going home. I was taking care of the bus tickets and he said, "Give me my ticket." I threw the bus ticket on the table and said, "Enjoy yourself." He picked up the ticket and his suitcase and walked out. Violet's husband wasn't sure that Pat would be able to find the depot, so he took the car and scouted around until he found Pat and took him to the depot. As soon as Pat got to Duluth, he went on a vacation with someone else and only got home the day before we did.

Leonard, Jean and I went to New Jersey and also to New York. Violet went with us as far as Washington. We met her in Washington on our way back. We also stayed in Washington a few days. On the way out, we had breakfast at the bus station. I didn't have any money left. Violet had a dollar and some cents. There were four of us. We were in line. Violet and Leonard were about ten people apart. Leonard called, "Vi, what's the limit?" She called back, "25 cents." It just about brought down the house.

We came to a rest stop in a small town in Maryland. There were three busloads of people. We had all just gotten seated in the bus when the sheriff came in and announced that we were all under arrest. It seemed that someone had lifted a wallet with $300.00 in it.

They herded us all back into the restaurant and it was a tight squeeze. Leonard was on the other side of the room. I called, "What did you do with that wallet?" Everybody stopped talking for a minute, but then they realized that it was all a joke. The poor sucker that stole the wallet didn't have time to hide it very well. He hid it in the seat where he was sitting. They searched all seats. They found the wallet and then checked to see who sat there. Evidently he wasn't an experienced crook. So we were all on our way again, minus the fellow who thought he had struck it rich.

When we reached Duluth, Leonard and Jean had a big disappointment. "Lily" had gotten out of the cage that morning. The children who were taking care of her had been chasing her rather fast to catch her. She was too fat and she died from a heart attack. She had just died when we got there. Poor Susie missed her as much as the children did.

I noticed that Pat was still mad at his son-in-law. He had taken their wedding picture off the wall and hidden it in a drawer. Mildred wrote her father a rather stiff letter, telling him that it was all right to throw a fit in his own home if he felt like it, but it wasn't exactly the thing to do when he was visiting in someone else's house.

Pat was getting more violent and did more crazy things. Every day was getting worse. If I set the table and told him that lunch was ready, he would walk around the table and look it over. Then he would say in a nasty tone, "You can eat that yourself." Then he would go out and buy his lunch in the restaurant.

Sometimes he would eat, but then he would leave something on his plate and dump that back on the meat platter or in a casserole or something, just so that I would have to throw the whole thing out.

Some mornings, he would get up at five o'clock, go down to the basement then start pounding on something just to wake everybody up. I didn't get to bed until 1:30 or 2:00 o'clock in the morning. It was hard on the nerves.

Other mornings, he would walk nude through the house, go to the kitchen window, turn on the lights and then pull the shade up. We had neighbors only about ten yards away who could see right into the kitchen. I reported that to the police. The police said, "He might be a case for the psychiatrist, but then again, he might not. A lot of fellows in their sixties do crazy things just to get attention."

Then he started to turn off the lights on me. Every time I got home at night, he would come downstairs and turn off the light. I liked to read the newspaper. I paid for it, but I could never read it in the house. There was a church across the street with a bright streetlight in front of it. I began to go over there just to read the paper. That didn't suit him either, as I'll explain a little later.

He was fixing an old porch for someone a couple of blocks from our house. He had all the time in the world. Those people didn't care when he got it ready. One morning, there was a big parade in town. The high school band was to play in the parade. Leonard had to be at school at 7:00 a.m. for band practice. If he didn't get there on time, he would get a low mark in conduct and he would also have to be in school at 7:30 a.m. for a whole week as a punishment.

That morning at six o'clock, Pat came storming through the house yelling and swearing for Leonard to get up and carry over some lumber for him. There was no excuse in the world why he couldn't have asked Leonard the night before to carry that lumber. What chance did the boy have? He carried the lumber of course, but he was a half-hour late for school.

I sent a note to the bandmaster, but I wasn't so sure how much good it would do. I went down to the hospital to talk to Geraldine. The attendant principal thought that Geraldine was the school's number one student while she was going to school. In fact, she had skipped school one day but he didn't know it and he never found out. But what made it so funny is this: some girls skipped school the next day and were caught and he said to them, "Why don't you girls be like Geraldine? She never skips school." Well, anyway, she talked to him about Leonard's problem and Leonard got off without trouble. But the whole mess made me so nervous that I just couldn't take any more. I left a note for Pat when I went to work that night and told him that I was suing for separate maintenance.

That night when I came home, he attacked me. Leonard was sleeping at someone else's house, but Jean was in bed upstairs. I ran down to the hospital to get Geraldine (she was on night duty most of the time). When I went, Pat naturally thought that I went to get the police, so he disappeared. But Geraldine went to the house and took Jean out.

The next day, someone talked me into suing for a divorce. I signed all the papers the next day, but we were having an awfully big snowstorm. It was hard to drive anywhere. The sheriff asked if it was absolutely necessary to get Pat out that day. I said, "No, I wouldn't even put the dog out today. Let him stay until it stops."

The day after he was put out, two policemen and a police matron came down to the restaurant where I worked. They came walking through about 10:00 p.m. They didn't say anything to me, but they talked to the boss. He said, "She'll be through at twelve." They went out. I didn't know what it was all about.

At twelve o'clock, they came back. They handed me a paper. I looked at it and it was an order, signed by Pat, for me to be taken to the state hospital. According to him, I was insane because I was reading the newspapers on the church steps by the streetlight. I knew that there wasn't any use putting up an argument, so I smiled sweetly at the police and said, "Okay, let's go."

The police didn't mention the case in question, but we talked about several other subjects on the way to jail. I found out later that one of the officers had remarked to someone, "I don't understand this. She's just as sane as I am." When we got to the jail, I asked to use the telephone. I called Geraldine. I said, "Hold on to something now. I'm in jail. I'm supposed to be crazy. Imagine me, who was pointed out as the smartest kid in the village and I end up in the crazy house." When I put the receiver down, the fellow by the desk was laughing out loud. He asked me who put that charge against me. I said, "My husband did, so you'd better lock me up."

Geraldine called my lawyer in the middle of the night. He said, "They can't do that." She said, "I don't know if they can or can't, but they did."

The next morning, they brought me my breakfast. A greasy doughnut and some black coffee. I had no appetite for the doughnut. I left that, but I tried to drink the coffee. It tasted of tin or iron or something, so I wasn't very successful in getting that down either. I hadn't been able to sleep, so they gave me some old, torn magazines to read. I was tired, so I laid down on the cot fully dressed.

About eight o'clock, the lawyer came. He asked, "What are you doing here? Put your shoes on." He had a doctor with him. The doctor asked me a couple of questions and then said, "All right." The lawyer said that I could go.

I went to the restaurant where I worked to get a good breakfast. When the girls saw me coming, they all lined up and started singing the "Prisoner's Song." It was all in good fun and I took a ribbing for the next two weeks.

There was to be a trial three days later to clear up the mess. Geraldine called Linnea. She came on the next train. Raymond and his wife drove in the morning of the trial. Leonard was there, too. I wasn't in the room during the first part, but my boss was there and also a couple of other people from the restaurant. They said that the judge asked Pat what made him think that I was insane, and Pat answered, "Her feet hurt."

They called me in later. The judge asked me when we first started to disagree and I said, "On our wedding night he pulled a gun on me because the best man kissed the bride." The judge smiled and said, "That's all." Two days later, Linnea and Geraldine took Pat to a psychiatrist. He was supposed to go back again, but when he found out that it cost him $15.00, he wouldn't go.

Well, he cried in his beer and cried on everybody's shoulder until I dropped the charges. He promised to behave. Of course I knew he wouldn't, but it was hard to get away from him because he tried to make all kinds of trouble for both the children and me. He told so many lies to everyone, and he had even called the welfare and said that the children stayed out all night, which certainly was one of the biggest lies he ever told.

Another big whopper was this: He had told his lawyer that the boys had sent money home during the war and I had spent it all. He must also have told the lawyer that the children's marks were poor in school, because the judge asked me what Jean's marks were. I said, "Straight 'A'" He smiled and looked at Pat. Then he said, "Takes after her mother."

I found myself between the devil and the deep blue sea. When I thought of all the nights that Geraldine had to go to the house and take Jean out when I wasn't there, and also the nights that I had to get out myself and go to stay somewhere else because we didn't know what he was going to do next, I hesitated about taking him back. Then again, I thought perhaps he had learned something from all the mess that he had just created.

He behaved for exactly nine months. Then he got mixed up again with the same woman that I mentioned before. At first, I didn't pay very much attention, although things looked rather silly to me. I had bursitis in my shoulder and couldn't work for a couple of nights. I asked her to work for me because she needed the money.

Pat had never picked me up at work, but he went to pick her up. She was through at twelve. It was a distance of eleven blocks. Pat brought her home at 2:15 a.m. He came home at 2:30. He never explained why all the delay. She was more talkative. She had mentioned to a friend that they had gone out to a park and "watched the moon." Imagine, two goons in their sixties, both married to somebody else, watching the moon at two o'clock in the morning. Well, I let it go. I never mentioned it. I just didn't ask her to work again.

Then we were going to drive to California. That woman had a son, daughter and brother in California. She wanted to go along, but she didn't want her husband to go. He was a good-natured soul, so he stayed at home.

A short while before, she had played a rather bad trick on her husband. She always managed to go along whenever we went someplace. One Sunday afternoon, we went to a National Picnic in the Park, where Jean was dancing in the program. After the program, this woman said that she wanted to go to a city 160 miles away. Pat wouldn't have cared to drive me six miles if I asked him, but when she asked him to make that drive after the picnic was over, he couldn't have been more ready.

I thought she should at least have called her husband before she went. He was in his late seventies and he was all alone. But, she didn't call him and that poor soul was waiting up half the night for her to return. Worse yet, we were all captive participants on the drive since we had to go where the car went, so we also didn't get back until one o'clock in the morning. He thought there had been an accident or something. He didn't even scold her. If I had done anything like that, Pat would have killed me for sure.

We were all ready to go to California. She was supposed to pay $50.00 to help with the gas, but I'm sure that she never paid anything.

Things were going from bad to worse. We were not supposed to leave until midnight, but Pat went to pick up his "passenger" in the afternoon. Albert was in town for the weekend and he was supposed to ride with us back to Minneapolis so he could be ready for work on Monday. We told him we were leaving at midnight, so he depended on that and then went out for the evening.

Well, Pat was getting jittery. He wanted to leave at ten o'clock. So we left, but that made it bad for Albert. All the buses were gone by then and he had to be in the office at eight the next morning. He had to hitchhike through the night. I didn't blame him for being disgusted.

Pat was getting very cranky with the children and me. We couldn't say anything. He would snap at us like a rattrap. But he talked very nicely to his "lady love." The next day out, we stopped for lunch someplace on a picnic ground. Leonard and Jean went swimming in the pool. The other two disappeared.

After I cleaned up the mess, I went to look for them. I found them on the playground. She was on the swing and Pat was pushing her. It looked so silly that I almost ruptured something just to keep from laughing.

Pat was continually picking on Leonard's driving. Leonard wasn't even supposed to be driving because Pat refused to sign for his driver' license. He wanted Leonard to drive alone without Pat in the front, but I put my foot down to that. As long as he wouldn't sign for his license, I thought he could sit there as the law required. When we got into the mountains, Pat was driving 25 miles an hour. A truck driver reported him, so he had a little trouble when we got to the border.

We stayed a week with this woman's daughter. There were nine in the family and there were five of us visiting. They didn't have very much to eat so I bought groceries for all fourteen of us. That took all the money I had. The woman we took with us to California went everywhere with us. There wasn't one place we could go without her. We went to Knott's Berry Farm one day. She and Pat had chicken dinners. Pat paid for it. I couldn't afford it so Leonard, Jean and I had hamburgers. I never said anything. I always figured that someday "my time" would come.

There were six rooms in the house where we stayed. But the son-in-law of our passenger was a semi-alcoholic. He wouldn't fix anything. He had all the material for completion of the bathroom. The pipes were lying in the bathtub awaiting his installation but he wouldn't do it. They had an outdoor toilet with a very stiff spring on the door. It was an odd thing – it would snap backward. One day I was slapped right into the hole. The only time I swore on the trip.

They carried water for the house from a hose in the next-door neighbor's yard. One day, I went there to get some water. There was Pat holding the hose and his "girlfriend" was standing in her slip washing herself. That's when Leonard really got riled up. He said, "If I see any more of this, I'll hitchhike home." I believe he would have, but we left the next day. A couple of nights before, the whole family had gone out to visit some other relatives and the lady in question had gone with them for once. They returned about midnight. That time Pat wasn't anxious to sleep like he did in Philadelphia. He got up and stayed up talking until three o'clock. One just can't win.

Since I had this woman under foot for the next four years, I'll call her by her first name, which was Alma.

On the way home, we drove through the desert. It was very hot. Alma complained of the heat and Pat obligingly reached over and unzipped her dress the whole length and helped her pull it off her shoulders. He didn't give a darn about the rest of us or how hot we were. I could see by the expression on Leonard's face that he would have liked to slug him.

I ran out of money on the third day, so the three of us didn't have anything to eat that day. Only Pat and Alma went in when we stopped by some restaurant. The next noon we reached Walter's place in Iowa. Our daughter-in-law made dinner for us and she packed a lunch to take along, so we were fine until we got home.

I quit going to Alma's place after that. We had been friends for many years, but I just couldn't "swallow" it any more. Her husband came to our house sometimes. He was a nice old fellow and I always liked to talk to him.

I just told Pat that I didn't want to go in the car if she was going everyplace with us. She had a nephew in town that had a brand new car. He and his wife were willing to take her anywhere that she wanted to go, but after Pat started taking her around, she wouldn't go with them any more.

They went to the same church and they would have been glad to pick her up on the way going there, but Pat was there every Sunday morning and drove her to church. He didn't go to church, but he went to pick her up again after the sermon was over. Alma's husband went to a different worship and he had to walk. Pat never once took him.

Sunday afternoons, Pat went back to their house again and they went somewhere in the car. If Alma's husband was there, they had to take him along to make it look good, but if he wasn't there, they went and they were usually gone until eleven p.m.

Jean and I had to entertain ourselves. Lots of people asked us to go along on picnics in the summer, but I wouldn't have dared to go because of Pat's unreasonable disposition. As jealous as he was, I was never sure of anything. I tried to stick it out until Jean was through school.

One Sunday, Jean and I wanted to go to another town about 60 miles away. We started out in the car and we got about five miles out of town. Pat said there was something wrong with the car and we had to go back home. Jean and I both laughed because we knew that he was stalling. We went back home. He dropped us off in front of the house. Harold was still living in Duluth then and Pat said that he was going over to his house. I knew better, but I let it go at that. I called Harold later and asked if he had been there. Harold said that he hadn't seen him for three weeks.

Jean and I went to visit Walter's in-laws. They lived in the same house as Alma and her husband. About 10:30 p.m., Pat and Alma came driving up. I let them go into the house. Then Jean and I went home, but I stuck a note on the front seat which said "The car seems to work fine when you're with somebody else."

When Pat came out and found the note, he came rushing home, charging into the house like a bull. I wouldn't talk to him. Jean had already gone to bed, Pat started to make all kinds of excuses so I put my coat on and walked out of the house. I walked downtown and he was right behind me. I walked back home again and there he was, right behind me like a shadow. I pretended that I didn't even see him.

Another time, I wanted Pat to drive us to Raymond's house, which was about 50 miles away in Wisconsin. He wanted to pick up Alma to go along. I said, "Count me out." Then he wouldn't go. He certainly couldn't go to Raymond's house with Alma, but without me. There would have been trouble if he did. I never asked him again to go anyplace while Alma was in town.

Just before Christmas, Pat took off for California again. Geraldine asked someone if Alma had gone with him. Pat ran into a big snowstorm so he had to return home. Someone told him that Geraldine had asked about Alma going with him. She hadn't gone of course. He was alone. But it wouldn't have been a surprise to anybody if she did, because she had been talking about going back again. But Pat tried to act the innocent lamb that had been injured. The scandal was all over town anyway.

The first thing Pat did when he returned was go to the hospital and start a scene with Geraldine in front of several doctors and a couple of nurses. She was very disgusted with him by then. She had promised to buy him new seat covers for the car, but when he pulled that stunt, she wouldn't buy him anything.

That was the only Christmas throughout our whole married life that I didn't make him a Christmas dinner. Some friends invited Leonard, Jean, Geraldine and me for dinner, so we accepted. They had no use for Pat. By that time, I felt just about as they did.

The next summer, Pat took off for California again without even telling me that he was going. It was almost my vacation time anyway. So Jean and I went to Florida. Leonard was then working as an orderly in the hospital. He took care of "Susie" and the house. He even painted the kitchen for me while I was gone. I thought that was very good for a sixteen-year-old. Pat was gone for two months; then he returned to where he left off. Alma had been in the hospital before that with a nervous breakdown.

Something rather spooky happened while Leonard worked in the hospital. He worked nights. If someone died during the night, he had to bring the corpse down to the morgue, which was in the basement.

One morning about three o'clock, a man died. Leonard was getting ready to take him to the morgue. As it was during the night and no people were around, he wasn't very careful about how he wrapped the corpse. He just tucked the sheet in on the side and started off. He was on the basement floor going at a merry clip when, suddenly, the stretcher gave a jerk and the man sat up.

Leonard said later that if that had been the first one that he had taken down, he would have gone right through the wall and never even bothered to look for the door. But he said he knew there must be a reason. He checked the stretcher and found that the sheet was loose on one side and got caught in the wheel. The other side was tucked tightly around the man's arm and it jerked him into a sitting position. It was still a little hard for a sixteen-year-old to cope with. He was very pale when he came home that morning and he didn't want any breakfast.

Something similar happened the same week in the same hospital. One of Raymond's classmates in college was also working there as an orderly a couple of days a week. He was 22 years old so it shouldn't have been as bad for him, but he fared worse. He lifted the corpse onto the stretcher and somehow it pressed the wind out of the lungs and the corpse said, "Ahhh." He took off right then and there and never went back to the hospital.

The next night after Leonard had told me his experience, I had a scare almost as bad. About one o'clock that night, I was walking home from work. It was very dark. I was thinking about what Leonard had related that morning when suddenly a man came flying through the air and hit the sidewalk two feet in front of me. If I had been one step farther, I would have been a dead duck.

It was almost in front of a lodge hall where they also served liquor. The first thing that came to my mind was, "Well that's a funny way to throw a man out." I looked at the man a little closer and I noticed that he was bleeding from the nose and ears. I ran into the hall and told the man at the bar that a man had been hurt and to call the ambulance and the police, which he did. Then he came running out.

The man had just left the bar, so he knew him. The bartender asked, "For gosh sakes, Bob, what did you do?" The man was out cold but I answered. I said, "I don't think he did anything, but I believe I know what happened." There was a stone wall about five feet high. When the man came out, he mistook the wall for the sidewalk. He made a misstep and was thrown over. It was dark and there was a large bush in front. That way I didn't see him until he almost knocked me down. I stayed until the police came and explained to them. The poor fellow lived after all, but he lost one of his eyes. It was a miracle that he wasn't instantly killed.

Albert had served in the navy for six years but, after he was discharged, he had signed up for the naval reserve. His time was almost up and he was almost sure that he wouldn't be called back in. So what happened? The last day, he got a notice. It was a windy day and when Jean took the mail out of the box, it blew out of her hand. She had to chase it for a long distance before she finally caught it. I still wonder what would have happened if he didn't get the notice. He had served in the Pacific during the war. This time they sent him to Europe, so he wasn't too disappointed. He served for one year. Then he returned home, got married in a very big church wedding and then took off for their new home in Minneapolis. The company held his job for him, so he started right in where he left off.

Pat was getting worse again. I believe he was worrying about losing his ability to boss everybody. One day, Leonard playfully picked up a cork from the vacuum bottle and bent it. That evening, Jean noticed that Pat was sitting in the corner with the same cork, trying to bend it, but he couldn't make a dent. After he lost his fingers, the hand wasn't as strong as it had been before. But it bothered him that Leonard could do something that he couldn't do. It was foolish, of course, but that is the way he was.

One Saturday evening, while I was at work, Leonard brought home another orderly and two nurses.

182

They were singing and playing the piano when Pat came home. He felt that this was a good chance to embarrass Leonard. He started right in about kids not being any good nowadays. They were all going to the dogs, etc., etc.

So, naturally, Leonard talked back. Then they all went, including Leonard. He stayed with someone else. On the fourth day, he came with some papers to sign. He had joined the paratroops. I thought that Pat would put up a fuss about signing, but he didn't. He probably thought that Leonard was getting too big for him to handle, which was the truth.

Leonard liked the paratroops, although they had their rough moments. He said there was usually someone hurt during their jumps. One day we got a letter, which he had written just before a jump. It said, in part: "We're getting ready for a jump, but I'm not going to mail this until after the jump is over. If you get the letter, I'm all right.

He drove the ambulance for a while. Then he got into the band. He loved that. He was in Germany for a year before he was discharged.

Geraldine had gone to Washington, D.C. to work in a hospital. Jean was the only one left in town. She missed Geraldine and Leonard. When school was out, Geraldine said that she could come to Washington to spend the summer, which she did.

Linnea wanted Pat and me to come to Chicago and spend the 4th of July with her. It was a little hard on my pocketbook, because I bought the bus tickets for both of us. I also bought a new jacket and hat for Pat. For all the credit I got, I could just as well have saved it. One of the neighbors commented how nice he looked in his new jacket and hat. He said, "Oh, the kids buy me everything." It was always "The Kids." He would never admit that his wife gave him anything. Although I spent a fortune on the guy, he would never say anything.

Well, we went to Chicago. I always had a wonderful time there. I enjoyed my vacations in Chicago more than any other place. Violet was in Florida, Mildred and Walter were in California, so I didn't lack places to go for a vacation and, usually, I changed off from year to year. But Chicago was my favorite spot, although I wouldn't have liked to live there.

At the end of August, Geraldine and Jean returned from Washington. Jean was such a little thing when she went. That summer, she had grown about three inches in height. I didn't recognize her at a quick glance. She is now the tallest of the girls.

Geraldine had converted to Catholicism just before she was eighteen. We are Protestants. I could tell from the time she changed that someday she would enter the convent, although no one would have thought that when she was about ten. I remember once when a bigger girl was picking on her. She came home and got a golf ball, put it in her mitten, went out and finished the fight and won. Anyway, before she returned from Washington, she had a choice to make. She could marry a lawyer in Washington or come home and join the convent. The convent won. But this is a few months ahead of my story again.

Geraldine went back to work in the hospital where she graduated. I still had trouble with my legs. My veins had been cut and tied six times, but the ulcers always returned. A few months later, Geraldine insisted that I have vein stripping done.

I asked for a week off from work. I thought it would be something like the cutting and tying had been. But I had a surprise in store. It was nothing like that. I entered the hospital one afternoon, had surgery the next day, but they only operated on one leg. Then I had to wait a whole week before they fixed the other one. Then I still had to wait another week before they let me go home. Then it took another week before I was able to walk.

Pat came to see me twice in those two weeks that I was in the hospital. He tried to start a fight both times. I was too sick to argue, so he went home. After I came home, he didn't stay home even one evening, so I knew then that when I retired I couldn't look for any company from him.

After I had been home about three weeks, I asked the doctor if I could go to Florida. He said it would be good for me. I would just as soon have gone alone, but Pat was all ready to go as soon as I was.

He was all right on the trip, but when we got there, he had another one of his nutty spells. We got in about eleven p.m. At five a.m., he was mad about something; I didn't know what about, and I still don't know. But he wanted his bus ticket and said that he was going home. I gave him the ticket and told him to get the he— out of there and not to tag along the next time.

Then he changed his mind and didn't go. About nine o'clock, he wanted me to show him the way to the beach – I had been there before; he hadn't. He behaved very nicely the rest of our stay.

I went back to work nine weeks after the operation. The boss laughed because I had asked for one week off. He had the same trouble with his legs, but after he saw how long it took me to get back to normal, he decided against an operation.

One night, Pat didn't come home at all. So the next night I decided to stay out a little later than usual. When I didn't get home at the usual time, Geraldine got worried and called the boss. They had just moved into their new home. The floors were waxed and they had not as yet put the rugs down. The boss had only the top of his pajamas on when he ran for the phone and he slipped and fell on his bare end right on the floor.

He told Geraldine that I had left work about three hours before. He was so worried that he couldn't go back to sleep. I got home about an hour later. And, of course, there was the usual brawl. In Pat's opinion, it was all right for him to stay out all night without any explanation, but it was all wrong for me to stay out a couple of extra hours. But, I stood my ground. I don't need anybody that bad that I have to take anything. The boss came to the house about eight a.m. to see if I was all right. That's a pal for you. How many bosses would bother enough to see what happened in a case like that? But he was always there to ask if he could help if something was wrong.

Pat disliked Catholics and, speaking of priests and nuns, well, he simply hated them. A friend of Geraldine's was a Catholic, but I don't believe he took it seriously. He told me one day that he had seen Geraldine go into a Catholic church. I didn't answer because I was not in the mood for a scene. About a week before Geraldine was to enter the convent, she told him. He didn't say anything right then, but he was stewing over it all week.

When Geraldine was about fourteen, I could see that she was leaning towards the Catholic religion. It hurt a little at first, which was natural for any mother of a different religious persuasion. But after all that time, it didn't bother me anymore. She was then 24 and certainly old enough to know what she wanted in life.

The night before she was to enter the convent, Pat suddenly developed a "brainstorm." He tried to hit her with his fist. She ducked and it only grazed her shoulder. He ordered her to take her trunk out at one a.m. Of course, she couldn't get a deliveryman in the middle of the night, so she had to leave the trunk there until morning. But both Geraldine and Jean left the house. Geraldine didn't go back there for over two years.

Anyway, the girls were both on the street corner when I came from work. Jean was hysterical. A nurse from the hospital picked Geraldine up and I finally got Jean in the house and got her to bed.

Pat was just like a maniac all week. He disowned Geraldine and said all the nasty things that he could think of. If anybody had believed him, which they didn't, her reputation wouldn't have been worth a nickel.

Pat was a case from then on. He had made up with Andrew and they were playing their instruments together again. Alma's husband played with them, too. But when they played over at Alma's house, Pat spent all the time in the kitchen with her, when he was supposed to be in the living room playing with the other two. Finally, Alma's long-suffering husband had had enough. He told Andrew not to bring Pat over again. He didn't want him in the house and he didn't even want to see him.

Some times Pat would see her if she went over to Andrew's house, but I don't know if he went to her house anymore, at least not when her husband was there. It was really a mess before Alma's husband clamped down on them. He wouldn't even shovel the snow at home. We had six feet of snow one morning on our front steps. Pat got up at seven o'clock and went over to Alma's to shovel snow. Jean had to crawl through that drift to go to school.

Finally, Alma and her husband moved to California. I guess Pat still has a soft spot for her. Every time he goes to California, he makes an extra trip of 150 miles to go see her. Her husband died and the last I heard of her, she was living in a home for the aged.

After Alma left, he spent a lot of time at Andrew's, always trying to make me look bad, but they never took him seriously. Sometimes Andrew would give him a good talking to.

One time, he planned to take Andrew and his wife to a fancy restaurant some 35 miles out of town. It was my day off and Pat had not mentioned a thing to me about it. I made supper as usual, but Pat disappeared just before supper. He went down to pick up Andrew and his wife. They asked him where I was. They knew it was my day off. Pat said, "She's working." Andrew lit into him right there. He said, "We're not going any place unless you bring your wife." Pat got furious. He went out and slammed the door. Then he jumped in the car and drove around the block at least fifteen times. It didn't make sense, but that was his way of doing things. I couldn't understand why he didn't want me to go along. Shortly before, on Father's Day, I had taken Pat, Andrew and his wife to the same restaurant and I paid the bill.

Jean was spending the summer in California. When it was time for my vacation, I got ready to go to California, too. Pat said that he was going to stay home. I stocked up the refrigerator with food, such as he could use without cooking. He was supposed to go out for his meals. I also got a case of dog food for Susie. About three hours before I was ready to go, Pat said, "I guess I'll go along." So I had to rush getting his clothes packed and taking Susie to the kennel.

Jean went to Texas shortly after we got there. There was a convention from her church that she wanted to attend. She got to our hometown a week before us and she stayed alone. She was only fourteen, but she was very dependable, so I didn't worry. Pat went to visit Alma, of course, but he behaved very well on the trip. I can't say as much for his behavior after we returned home.

I had a severe hemorrhage and the doctor ordered me to the hospital, pronto. He thought it might be cancer. My first worry was for Jean. She was only fourteen and Pat was not a good father. If something happened to me, it would be hard on her. The others were all grown and on their own, but they had their own problems. Linnea was going to law school and working besides. The others had families of their own.

Leonard was in Germany. And of course, I was sure that this was the end of the line for me. I was in the hospital for three days. The tests came back negative. What a relief. Pat never came to the hospital even once.

He was very jealous of a Greek cook that we had in the restaurant. The poor fellow was older than I was. I used to go to the bakery every Saturday to pick up some goods for Sunday. The old fellow asked me to bring him two dozen cookies because he would have had to get off the bus and walk three blocks, and since I had to go there anyway, it was no problem. He gave me the money.

Pat was with me when I picked up the stuff. I bought two dozen cookies for us as well. Pat wanted to know why the two boxes of cookies. I told him that Charlie had asked me to bring him a box and I explained why. Pat almost had a fit. He was griping all the way home. I just let it ride. After I had made supper, I left for work. I took Charlie's cookies and put the others in the usual place where I kept the cookies.

I had been at work about a half and hour when Pat came stamping into the kitchen at the restaurant. He looked like a wild man. He had taken the cookies out of the jar, put them in a bag and brought them to the restaurant. He slapped them on the table in front of the head cook and said, "Give these to Charlie. They are from my wife." Talk about embarrassing. There were about eight people in the kitchen at the time. Pat stomped out. How was I to explain such behavior?

That wasn't the only trick that he had up his sleeve. Shortly after, he pretended to have a stroke one evening. He couldn't make up his mind whether it was supposed to be a stroke or a heart attack. I asked the doctor and he said that it was neither. Walter's in-law called the ambulance and Pat was griping later about having to pay for that (which he knew beforehand).

He was very much awake when he got to the hospital. He told Walter's mother-in-law that he wanted to see someone from the family, but he didn't want me. Jean was the only one there so she went. Geraldine was in the hospital as a patient at the time. She was then "Sister Emily." She went down to see him when someone told her that he was there.

He said to her, "I guess I'm on the way out." She said, "Don't worry about that, they'll have to shoot you on doomsday." He didn't want to see me (or so he said), so I didn't go near the hospital. When Walter's father-in-law came to tell me that Pat had had a light stroke, I was still so burned up with all the things he had pulled off in the past, I said, "I hope the S.O.B. dies." Not another word.

Pat was there three days. On the third day, he sent me a note. "Come and see me. Forget the past." So I went. He seemed all right. The doctor let him go that afternoon. Two days later, he drove 200 miles. He wasn't sick then. Well, that little trick didn't get him anywhere. It just cost him a little money.

A few days later, when I went to a union meeting, he locked the door on me. I made so much noise that he had to let me in. But he was storming all day.

One afternoon, I had gone to the hospital to see a lady friend. When I came home, he had all the furniture piled on the middle of the floor. He was going to sell everything. Andrew happened to come to the house and saw all the disturbance. He asked Pat what was going on. Pat said, "Might as well sell everything, nobody is ever home." Andrew said, "What's wrong with you? Now put the furniture back where it belongs."

Near the restaurant where I worked, there was a grocery store that used to sell chances on football games. Well, all the girls from the restaurant took chances and sometimes we won. Once I won $25.00. Pat needed a new jacket. So I bought him a new winter jacket and spent the whole thing. I had told him about the $25.00. Did he appreciate the jacket? He did not. I hadn't told him who sold the chance on the football game. He thought that I had bought it at the restaurant. He went to the police station and said that they were running a "gambling joint" at the restaurant. Well, the police knew better, but they told the boss what Pat was trying to stir up.

The boss knew several members of the family. Leonard and Jean had worked there a few hours every week since they were eleven years old. Jean was still working there in her spare time. It was just helping out with little things, but that's how they got their pin money. Linnea always came in to say, "Hello," when she was in town. So did Albert. After Pat had pulled that boner, the boss said to me one day, "You have a wonderful family, except for your husband. I believe he has a screw loose somewhere."

I had worked a double shift one day because one of the other employees had been called out of town in an emergency and they were stuck. We all pitched in, in a case like that. The boss forgot to put the extra pay on my check, so he put the cash in an envelope with my name on it, and the amount inside and gave it to me. I took the money out and stuck the envelope in my pocket and forget about it.

Pat always went through all my pockets. He found the envelope, took it to the union office and said that I was accepting cash, so I wouldn't have to pay tax. I was called into the union office. When the business manager told me what it was all about, I said, "That sounds very much like one of my husband's fantastic stories. There is nobody else in this whole town with a gift of gab like him." The manager admitted that it was Pat who had brought in the envelope and told him the story.

Pat also objected to my wearing white blouses to work. He wanted me to wear some old faded housedress. Sometimes when I had washed the blouses and hung them up to dry, he would put his dirty hands on them so I would have to wash them all over again.

There was a plain dirt basement under the restaurant where they stored things that were not used at the moment. But Pat didn't know that. He thought that it was a full basement with cement blocks. He started a story that they had gambling devices down there – and a red light district. And I was also supposed to be involved. Of course I was used to his accusations. There isn't a crime in the book that he hadn't accused me of, but it was a little hard to listen to because of the other people involved. Those stories came back to me time and again.

Pat bought a TV set **for himself**, not for the family. He had been a pain in the neck with the radio while the children were still in their early teens and some in the preteens. They didn't have an awful lot of time to listen to the radio because of their homework and their music, but they loved to listen to Amos and Andy. Once there was a program that was continued and it was time for the climax of the story that evening. The children all hurried with their lessons. They all came trooping into the living room, all excited. I turned on the radio. Pat came hurrying in – and took out the tubes. The children were near tears, but of course they didn't dare cry. That could have meant a beating for the first one who tried it.

But, to get back to the TV, he bought it just before Christmas. It was all right when Pat sat there himself watching it, but if Jean turned it on, he would turn it off pronto and say, "Don't you have any school work to do?"

In the first place, it was Christmas vacation. In the second place, nobody **ever** had to tell Jean to do her homework from the time she started school. Pat did that a couple of times. Jean never bothered again. She was satisfied with her radio in her own room.

I worked nights, of course. I had no time to watch TV. I tried it a few times on Sunday nights, but Pat would always switch channels in the middle of the program, so I didn't bother with it at all. Some years later, one Sunday evening, Pat had watched the programs for three hours straight. There was one program that I was interested in at that time. He turned off the TV when that program was ready to come on. I said, "Leave it on. I want to listen to the next one." Pat said, "No you don't!" in a very nasty tone. I didn't say anything, but I thought to myself, "O.K., big boy, that's the last time I'll ever bother your TV and if I told you where to put it, it wouldn't look very nice in print." I never watched it again.

I loved symphony concerts. Linnea bought me a season ticket. The concerts were held once a month. The boss let me off three hours to attend the concerts. Of course, I always went alone, but Pat wouldn't believe that. He was always somewhere in the neighborhood of the restaurant watching when I came out. When I took the bus, he would follow the bus to the concert hall just to see if I met someone there.

I loved to ice skate, so I used to go to the skating club on Sunday afternoons where they had indoor skating. It was about 16 blocks away, so I usually walked. When I got to the club, there was Pat's car outside. He was checking to see if I had met someone else. I was in my middle sixties and I can just see myself chasing men.

Sometimes on cold nights, the boss and his wife used to give me a ride home. One night, it was 22 below. They drove me home. Pat was always hiding in some corner to see what I was doing when I got out. He followed right behind us. When I got out on one side of the car, he went up to the boss on the other side and yelled right into the boss's face, "You don't have to drive her home. She can **walk** home." The boss just shook his head as if to say, "What a nut."

Pat was always outside of the restaurant when it was time for me to go home, but he would never offer me a ride. He was always hiding, and the minute he saw me start walking, he would beat it home and jump into bed. As soon as I got inside the door, he would come downstairs swearing that I woke him up. And he would keep up the racket sometimes for three hours. I began to hate to go home. But I had Jean to think of. She was getting to be a nervous wreck. She was skinny as a rail and she couldn't eat.

One weekend, Jean went out in the country with some friends. It had thawed and then it had been snowing again. It was slippery. The trip out was fine, but after she got out there, she slipped and fell. She broke her arm. That happened on Saturday afternoon. She didn't complain, so they didn't bring her in until Sunday night, when they were supposed to return anyway. I had an idea that it was broken as soon as I looked at it. Monday morning, when she went to the doctor, he said that just one bone was broken. He thought that he wouldn't have to put a cast on it. He put her arm in a sling. Then she went to school.

194

It's no secret that teenage boys seem to have an inbred streak of meanness, especially in exhibiting their powers of superiority to similarly aged females. Most people have run into it at one time or another, although the teenagers wouldn't necessarily want to exhibit that behavior to their own parents.

While Jean was walking down the hall toward her locker when she returned to school, one of the aforementioned teenagers mentioned above came from behind her, ramming her injured arm with the full force of his motion while continuing on without stopping. The pain was enough to almost make her pass out. She finally managed to come home. I called the doctor and told him what had happened. He said that he would put a cast on it.

So she went back to the doctor and he put a cast on it. She had that cast on for six weeks. That little incident caused Jean to lose out on being valedictorian three-and-a-half years later. She got one "B" on her report card for the six week period she was in that cast. It was the only "B" she received in her four years of high school. But she did come out a salutatorian.

Pat had been working for a few months, but was idle at the moment; however, his group insurance was still good for another two months. I sent in the doctor bill for Jean, which was $85.00. I waited over two months and I didn't hear anything from the company. I asked Pat several times and he said that he hadn't heard anything. I sent a letter to the company office and asked about it. They said that the check had been sent to Pat six weeks before. When I confronted Pat with the evidence, he said, "Well, it was my check. It was made out to me, so I kept it." Of course, I had to pay the doctor. Pat had spent the insurance check for his own use. If he was able to cheat me in any way, he would do it.

He would also cheat anybody else if he had a chance. Once the colored lady bought a bed from him that he had taken in on a moving job. The bed looked very nice and she was glad to get it for the price he asked, but when she came to get it, he didn't give her the one she bought. He gave her an old beat-up one that she couldn't use. She had the man take it right to the dump when he picked it up. What could the poor woman do? It wasn't worth starting a lawsuit over. Pat knew that and that was all the reason he needed to pull those crooked deals.

Once, I borrowed $20.00 from him. I paid it back at $5.00 a week. I marked it on the calendar every time just for my own convenience so I wouldn't forget. A day after I had paid the last $5.00, I noticed that it was erased off the calendar. I knew at once that Pat was trying to get an extra $5.00 out of me. But of course, that didn't work. I just told him that he could erase the whole thing. He just wasn't getting any more money from me. Several times he had borrowed from me, but he never paid it back, so I quit loaning it to him. Now I wouldn't trust him with the time of day.

Jean spent the next summer in Florida. She got a little vacation from Pat's ravings. At least she could sleep nights.

Pat found a new "girlfriend," a widow with a retarded daughter. She bought the house right behind ours, but across the alley. He made himself at home in her house from the very beginning of her occupancy. This widow also had a married daughter living in Duluth. She didn't approve of her mother's new "boyfriend." One day when she came there, Pat was lying on the living room couch with his shoes off. She told her mother off, so to speak, and she didn't come back for several months.

The woman's name was Selma. She was smart in a way, in that she got most of her work done free of charge, and that kept on for four years. Pat was at her house much more than he was at home. He would walk around the whole block so I wouldn't catch on that he was there. What a joke. I knew where he was the minute that he was missing.

She was also a little odd in the way that she played him. She tried to be friends with me. She would sometimes come to our house when I was alone. She would bring ice cream and cake, rolls, cookies and what have you. Of course, I would make coffee for her although I would just as soon have ignored her, but after all, she was a neighbor, so I tried to be nice. She would repeat all the lies Pat was feeding her. I recognized the line the minute she opened her mouth.

It was the Centennial Celebration of Duluth that summer. I belonged to a club and we were going to be in the parade. Everybody was to wear centennial dresses and bonnets. I picked up a cotton dress and bonnet for $9.00. Pat went to Selma and said that I had paid $60.00 for the dress I was going to wear in the parade. She came to my house and wanted to see the $60.00 dress. I just couldn't stop laughing. When I showed her the dress, she laughed right along with me. The men were wearing vests, the kind that they wore in the eighteen hundreds. I bought Pat a very nice one for $8.00 but, of course, he wouldn't tell anybody about that.

Jean returned home in time for school. It was time for my vacation, so I was getting ready to go to California. Pat was still jealous of my son-in-law, so he didn't trust me to go alone. The winter before, Mildred and her whole family came home for a visit. Sometimes they would have liked to use Pat's car to go around and visit their friends, but Pat stayed out in the car all day so they wouldn't have a chance to ask him.

Pat told Selma that I had given our son-in-law $1,000.00. I still wonder where I got that kind of money. At the time, I couldn't have given anybody 1,000 pennies because I didn't have that much to spare.

When they were ready to leave, Pat drove them to the depot because I insisted, but he wouldn't talk to them and he went on the other side of the waiting room and sat down. He wouldn't even say. "Good bye." Mildred was so disgusted, she said, "The next time he comes to visit, I'm going to the mountains." But, of course, she didn't. She still treated him nicely although he didn't deserve it.

We were gone three weeks. Jean stayed alone. One morning, she had a scare. A neighbor girl called for her every morning on the way to school. Her name was Lynn. This particular morning, Jean had unlocked the door so that she wouldn't have to go downstairs again. She was in her slip, at the head of the stairs when someone rapped. Jean asked, "Lynn?" It was a deliveryman and he thought that Jean said, "Come in," so he opened the door. Of course he saw Jean in her slip. She dashed in her room and grabbed her bathrobe, then came out again and asked what he wanted. He was all right, though. He was looking for another family, but had the wrong address. Jean never again unlocked the door until Lynn got there.

Pat behaved fairly well on the trip. Of course I had to be careful never to be alone with my son-in-law in the kitchen, living room, or even out in the yard for even a minute, because it would have caused an explosion.

We returned through the state of Washington. When we reached Seattle, Pat had the "Asiatic flu," which was raging at that time. I wanted to stop at a fairly good hotel, but Pat wanted the cheapest one he could find. He finally found one for $3.00 a night. It was terrible. The bathroom was in another part of the hotel half a block away. There was an "L" shaped hall to go through and men that looked like bums sitting all over the place. I was just plain scared.

Pat got an awfully high fever during the night. The first time that I ever knew him to run a temperature was then. I doped him up with aspirin and I had to keep cold towels on his head all night. Luckily, there was a washbasin in the room where I could get the cold water, but the basin was leaking so I put the wastebasket underneath. It happened to be a metal basket.

I got Pat out of there early in the morning on the first bus out. I didn't want to be stuck with a hospital bill in a strange town. I rented a pillow and propped him up against the window. His temperature went down but he developed a very loud cough. It was embarrassing and I thought surely that they would make him get off the bus. I was keeping my fingers crossed, so to speak. We got a through bus and it was a few hours faster than the other one. I was relieved when we reached Duluth.

When we got home, we discovered that Jean also had the Asiatic flu. Sister Emily had taken her to the infirmary at the convent. I thought that it was very nice of them to do that. It would have been very hard for Jean to keep the place warm, sick as she was. At that time, we still had the old coal stove and she would have had to carry the coal up from the basement.

After a while, things were back to normal again. Pat was back to watching me as to what time I came out from the restaurant at night. One night, I rode home with a waitress and her husband. Pat was right behind. On one corner, they didn't come to a full stop – they just slacked off for a minute, then continued on. There wasn't any traffic to interfere with anyway. Pat did that all the time, but it was different when someone else did it.

When they stopped in front of our house, Pat rushed up to the driver. "It's going to cost you ten dollars for bringing **her** home. You went through the stop sign," he blurted out. They just laughed at him and drove away.

The only thing he could do to me was to slam the door in my face. I guess that gave him a little satisfaction.

Raymond had gone back to school some years before. He finished three-and-a-half years of high school in two years. He worked nights and went to school in the daytime. He still managed to come out with a "B" average. By that time, he had a daughter and son in high school and funds were running low, so he decided to wait until they got through high school in order to finish the rest of his college courses. He had a lovely property out in the country and he built a nice house where he raised his family.

When I think back on our very poor years, it's surprising that the children didn't miss school because of illness. The house was like a refrigerator during the winter. Clothes were not always plentiful. I know that they were cold most of the time during the cold weather. But I guess they just got tough after a while. Linnea never missed a day during her four years of high school.

As the years went by, the children drifted back to school. Several are still going to college (night school) at this writing.

When Linnea graduated from law school, she asked Pat, Jean and me to come to her graduation. We went and spent a week there. Pat was on his good behavior that week so I enjoyed it very much.

Jean stayed in town that summer. She was going to a business university, taking a special course in shorthand. Unfortunately, she was working for a scholarship in high school and had to take more academic courses, which left no time for shorthand.

I had my most embarrassing moment about that time. I've made many boners in my lifetime, but I never felt like I did about this one. I had worked with two different girls at different times. They looked enough alike to be identical twins, but were not at all related.

About a year after I had worked with them, I saw in the paper that one had gotten a divorce. I knew that she had trouble with her husband the year before. In the same paper there was also a death notice. The other girl's husband had died. Some time later, I met one of them downtown. Of course, I **knew** which was which. I bounced up to her very cheerfully and called out, "I see that you finally got rid of your old man." She looked stunned for a moment. Then she replied very sadly, "Yes, the poor fellow passed away a month ago."

The next fall, I had not as yet asked for my vacation. Pat had given me a hard time for some weeks, which the boss knew. One Saturday night, he handed me the vacation check and said, "Get out of town for a couple of weeks and see that you aren't followed. You need peace and quiet for a few days." I took his advice.

I left for Florida on Monday without telling Pat. I knew it was going to be hard on Jean to take care of the house and make the meals for Pat. She had plenty of homework. She also had Junior Symphony practice, shopping for groceries, etc.

Pat was no help at all. He was worse than a small child. He pulled off the same stunts on her that he had practiced on me all through our married life. He would go to Selma's and eat supper. Then he would come home and not say anything. He would sit there and watch Jean setting the table and put the food on. Then he would say, "I don't want anything just now. You can put it away again." Jean told me afterward, "I was so disgusted I would have liked to throw the whole thing in his face."

Of course Pat exploded when I got home, but I didn't care in the least. I had had my vacation and it was a pleasant one. I was ready to return to work the next day.

Leonard returned from Germany a few months later. The second day after his return, he had a run-in with Pat. Leonard almost slugged him, but he had self control enough not to. That had happened twice before, once with Raymond and once with Albert. Pat almost brought them to the point of "no return." If they had ever hit Pat, I'm afraid it would have been serious for him. They were all husky fellows and I can't say that any of them had much love for him at that time. Of course, Leonard moved out of the house. He got an apartment of his own.

Leonard also told me some of things that had happened to him while he was in Europe, but that he wouldn't write about them because he didn't want me to worry about him.

One was a parachute jump that he made near the small village of Gabligan, not far from Augsburg.

He said that he was number four in the "stick" position (the order in which they exited the airplane), and he asked a friend of his from Florida if he would change places with him so he could stand in the aircraft's open door during the flight to the jump area.

His friend agreed, and Leonard became number one and his friend became number four in the "stick." That was also the new position for drawing their equipment, so Leonard drew his friend's parachute, and his friend drew Leonard's parachute.

When they finally got the green "go" light to jump, Leonard was the first one out of the airplane. His parachute opened just fine and he had no problems. But his friend's parachute failed to open and Leonard watched him zip passed him on the way down.

Fortunately, another friend of theirs from Canada whose parachute had already opened saw the risers and shroud lines of the failed parachute going passed him, so he reached out and grabbed a handful of the lines.

He was a big guy and was able to hold onto those lines and stop Leonard's friend from Florida from falling all the way to the ground with the failed parachute. He held them to a safe landing for both of them and all was well. Leonard never told me while he was there because he knew that I would worry about all of his future jumps after that.

All the girls in high school used lipstick, so Jean did too. One morning at breakfast, Pat snapped at Jean, "Take that lipstick off." Jean said, "And if I don't?" Pat said, "Take it off. I don't like it." Jean said, " I don't give a damn what you like and don't like any more." Pat said, "So, you swear, too." Jean said, "You're enough to make an angel swear." Pat stomped out and slammed the door.

Jean told Leonard that afternoon what had transpired at breakfast that morning. Leonard was looking for Pat but couldn't find him, so Leonard left him a note saying," Stop picking on Jean, or I'll have to take some drastic action." I honestly believe Pat was afraid of Leonard, because that evening when Jean came walking through the hall, Pat called from the bedroom, "You look so nice without lipstick." He wanted the last word and he never referred to her lipstick again.

About two weeks later, Leonard was planning to get married. The invitations were all ready to go in the mail. He was six months short of 21. Pat refused to sign for him. Leonard went to a lawyer who, after looking through the books for several hours, found a clause which stated that if a young person had not been supported by his parent within the last two years, he did

not need his parent's signature. The lawyer charged him $25.00.

During the time Leonard was overseas, the parking rules in Duluth had been changed, so when he came out from the lawyer's office, he found to his consternation that his car has been towed away, for which he had to pay $7.00. Needless to say, he was getting more furious with his father by the minute. To top it all off, after all the expense, Pat came up with this one: I'll sign for Leonard because his future mother-in-law asked me to." She said that she had not seen Pat for six months. Pat came to the wedding, but he went alone. He wouldn't go with Jean and me. He bought his wedding gift separately from ours, as if anybody cared. They had a large church wedding. Jean was one of the bridesmaids.

A few months later, Leonard was contacted by an old friend that he had served with in Germany who told him about a pioneer military program in the missile field that he would be eligible for, if he wanted to be based in California.

Leonard caught a plane to California the next day, after making interim living arrangements for his family, so he could process and go through the multiple briefings necessary for the work. He shipped out to Fort Bliss, Texas in April, 1958 for what would eventually turn into a military career of 30 years and multiple educational tiers in the missile field. He eventually retired from the U.S. Army with the rank of Major.

The next year, Jean was chosen as a foreign exchange student. I was wondering where to get the money. It cost about $800.00.

I talked it over with our family doctor. He was such an understanding person, just like one of the family, and he had always liked Jean very much from the time she was born. He haunted all the doctors in town and collected about $400.00. My boss contributed $50.00. My union gave $25.00. I belonged to several clubs. They, as well as Pat's union, each gave a few dollars. Even Pat gave $135.00 for which I was thankful and very much surprised. I borrowed from the credit union to make up the rest.

The only one who didn't contribute anything was Jean's church where she was baptized and confirmed and had played the piano for them every Saturday morning for two years straight. It was because the minister's son was one of the three first chosen and Jean won out over the other two. They had a bake sale in the basement of the church about two weeks before the final results, of which the proceeds were supposed to go to the exchange student's account. I gave five cakes to the sale. But of course, when Jean was chosen and not the minister's son, they gave the money to the church. It amused me no end. I believe the reason Pat gave the $135.00 was this: He thought that Jean could go to his hometown and stay with his sister. Of course the students had no say in the matter. They had to go to the country where they were sent. Pat was a little disappointed when she was sent to Finland.

She lived with an obviously loving family and she had a wonderful time. The first day that she was there, they drove 200 miles southeast to visit her aunt, whom she had never seen. They also spent two weeks in Lapland, camping out, climbing mountains, etc. Jean had always been very thin, but she gained 20 pounds during those three months. It was one of the great experiences of her life.

The next winter, Jean applied for a scholarship in Michigan. She had to go there to take the exam. I didn't say anything to Pat because he acted strangely at all times and he didn't want to pay for any of our expenses. He was already on pension but he worked in addition to that. He was collecting $45.00 a month for Jean from Social Security and I had to put up a big fight to get some of that. I even had to report him once to the Social Security office.

When he noticed that Jean was gone, he put up a big scrap. He wanted to know why I didn't **ask** him, because he was still the master of the house. I told him in plain language that he didn't pay for the trip and he certainly wouldn't pay for her college education, and I wasn't going to let him spoil her chance of getting a scholarship. I said that he could be the master of the universe just as long as he stayed out of my hair. Jean passed the exams and got a four-year scholarship. She was also granted a government loan.

In the spring, three weeks before graduation, the day Jean was eighteen, Pat threw a ten-dollar bill on the table in front of Jean. He said, "You're eighteen now. That's all the support you'll get from me from now on – you're on your own." Jean smiled and said, "Thanks." She had three weeks left in school and she was going to work in a hospital some 130 miles away from Duluth, which meant bus fare. She also had to live for two weeks in the new place and pay room and board before she would get her first paycheck. All that had to come out of my wages. I have often wondered if Pat ever stopped to think that those things would count against him later.

Jean was concertmistress of the high school orchestra and also of the Junior Symphony Orchestra. Pat wouldn't go to either one of the concerts. Jean had never missed a practice in the symphony orchestra and she had been there for seven years. Even when she had the broken arm and couldn't play, she was there in her seat, turning music pages.

When it was time for graduation, Pat wouldn't go, and he wouldn't give his ticket to anybody else. Harold's wife was in Duluth that night, and she would have liked to go, but Pat wouldn't give her the ticket. I almost didn't get there myself. I just couldn't find anyone to work in my place. It seemed that everybody had someone who graduated. I went to work as usual. The boss's wife came in and saw me there. She said, "Your place is with your daughter tonight. I'll take over and don't you come back until tomorrow night." Jean was so happy to see me and said that she felt like an orphan until I showed up.

Pat hadn't paid anything towards the support of the house for three months, so I quit cooking. I ate in the restaurant where I worked. He acted like a maniac every night when I came home. He had kept that up for some time before Jean's graduation. The night before her final exams, he got her into hysterics. She kept on screaming, "I can't take any more. I can't take any more." Imagine a teenager having to take a final exam in that frame of mind.

Linnea had moved to California a year after she graduated from law school. She came home for a visit in July because Geraldine took her final vows in the convent. Linnea was planning to take me to Europe in the fall. I was keeping it a secret because if Pat had found out about it, he would have made trouble in some way, so that I wouldn't be able to go. He was quite handy at such things.

Geraldine was sent to another town to work in a hospital. Pat was getting more violent by the day. One night he attacked me when I got home from work. He was standing there with his eyes looking like boiled onions and with his fist raised. He told me that he was going to knock me through the dining room window. He never took the storm windows off in the summer, so that meant that I would have **sailed** through a double window.

207

I used to snap the lock on the door when I came in, but for some reason, I didn't that time. I don't think that he expected me to run out, but as scared as I was, I was outside before he had time to lower his fist. It was about 1:30 in the morning and our town wasn't very safe after dark for anybody to be walking around.

I had no money and there were no buses running anyway. It was fifteen blocks to the police station. I ran all the way. All I was thinking about was to get away from Pat. If there were any thugs and hoodlums around, they just had to look out for themselves. I didn't give them another thought. I told my story and the police asked if I had some place to go for the night. I said that I had some friends living about 18 blocks away. The police took me there.

The next day, I had Pat picked up at work and taken to the hospital. They put him in the psychopathic ward. I called Geraldine and Jean long distance and also Albert. Geraldine went to the hospital to see Pat. He was very much worried.

Three days later, they had some form of a trial right there in the hospital. They asked me a few questions and then they called Sister Emily (Geraldine). They didn't ask the others any questions. Pat's friend, Andrew, was there too. Sister Emily asked him why he was there. He said that he was going to tell them that Pat was a good driver and that he had never seen him drunk. Sister Emily told him that her father was not in the hospital on a drunk-driving charge. He was there because of his strange behavior.

The judge asked if we wanted Pat committed to the State Hospital, but we were all against that. We really didn't think that he was bad enough for that. I offered to move out of the house and let Pat live there, but his lawyer (not mine) said, "Let him get out." So they released Pat from the hospital and gave him two hours to get his things out of the house. The lawyer asked me to stay out of the house for those two hours. It was my birthday, so Albert took me out for dinner. We stayed out about four hours.

Pat took his TV, his mandolin and a few things to wear. Then he went to stay with Walter's in-laws. They had a large apartment and there were just the two of them. Pat was not supposed to go near the house after that.

I didn't bother to have the lock changed, so he went there when I was at work. I didn't say anything until he started on his old tricks. One night, he had taken the fuse plugs out – no light. I tried to get the fuse box open but it was too tight, with my fingers half crippled with arthritis. I couldn't do much. I just used the flashlight that night.

The next morning, I called one of my friends. She sent her husband over. He brought some fuse plugs along and fixed it up. Pat, of course, was watching the house night and day. I don't know when he had time to sleep. When the fellow went outside to get in his car, Pat was right there, ready for an argument. He went up to the guy and yelled, "What were you doing in the house with my wife?" The fellow said, "When you get so rotten mean that you come and take the fuse plugs out, somebody needs to take a hand." I called my lawyer and he sent Pat a very snappy letter telling him to stay away from the house,"or else."

Pat told someone that he didn't even know there was such a law that they could put him out of his own home and he didn't see how it could be done. Well, he found out. He didn't do any damage after that, but of course he still went to the house when I wasn't there and he watched every move I made. I was a little uneasy coming home at night as I knew that he was insanely jealous and I was thinking back about 30 some years.

Pat's youngest brother did a foolish and fatal stunt because of jealousy, and just when he had everything to live for.

As for Pat, I didn't put anything past him, or about how he felt at the time. I had a phone put in as soon as Pat was out. Of course, he saw the phone when he went there in the evenings. He took the number and then he began to call at all hours. He wouldn't say anything, but I could hear him breathing on the other end of the line. I always hung up, but it was annoying. I probably had just fallen asleep and the phone would ring. Finally, I put a pillow over the phone and let it ring.

Once when Jean was in town, Pat called and she answered. Of course he didn't say anything as usual. She hung up and she called the house where he lived. She told the lady, "Tell my father to stop calling at all hours of the night if he wants to stay out of trouble." He didn't call during the night after that, but he didn't lose any time in the morning.

I was planning for my trip to Europe, but I had to keep everything a secret. I asked my boss for three months' leave of absence and I asked him to keep it quiet. He didn't tell anybody but, about ten days before I was to leave, he had to hire someone to take my place for three months. That caused some talk. Everybody knew then that it wasn't an ordinary vacation. They didn't know what was up, but they knew it was something. One girl knew, but of course she wouldn't tell anybody. But all the others were guessing and talking. Finally, something leaked out to Pat. Of course he didn't know what was up, but he began to watch closer than ever. About three days before my departure, I took Susie to the kennel where she was to stay in my absence. I didn't see Pat around, but he was somewhere, because he knew that I had taken her there.

I was to leave on Monday. Saturday night, he was parked half a block away, sitting there for hours, waiting for me to come home. One of Jean's friends could tell he was waiting for me. She called the place where I worked. She told me what was up and asked if I wanted her sister to pick me up. I told her that would be fine. They were there about a half hour later and the boss said that I could go. I went to their house to spend the night. When I hadn't reached home by three o'clock in the morning, I guess Pat saw red. He didn't know where to find me, but he had to take it out on someone. So he drove 130 miles to the town where Sister Emily was. He got in there at six a.m. He went right to the hospital and raised the devil with her. Of course she didn't have anything to do with it and she told him that very plainly.

Jean had left for college the week before. The day before I left, I got a telephone call from California. Walter was in the hospital with bleeding ulcers and they didn't know just what to expect. He had already lost fifty percent of his blood. That was his third brush with death. They were not supposed to move him, but he was an employee of the railroad and the railroad hospital was 300 miles away. They gave him a private coach, a doctor and a nurse, but moving him from one place to another didn't do him any good. I was worried sick, but we had the reservations on the plane and I had to get away from Pat while it was at all possible, so I had to take the chance. The only thing I could do was pray. Walter came out all right, but he had to be on a very careful diet for several years after that. He still has to be careful of some things.

Now my biggest problem was getting away without running into trouble with Pat. I was to meet Linnea Monday night at Albert's house in Minneapolis. We were going to take the plane from that airport on Tuesday morning. On Monday morning, about 9:00 a.m.,

Pat came to the house in Duluth. I didn't let him in the house, but I did talk to him on the porch. I had called the plumber to come and shut off the water and gas, and I was afraid he would show up momentarily.

Pat wanted to know all about my vacation plans. He definitely knew that I was going someplace because I had taken Susie to the kennel. I told him that I was going to Florida, but I wasn't leaving until Wednesday. Then I asked if he would please excuse me, that I had to go downtown right then, but I would talk to him at three o'clock that afternoon. So he left. Ordinarily, I hadn't planned on leaving until three o'clock, but I knew then that I would have to leave on the twelve o'clock bus, if the plumber came in time. Luckily, he came a few minutes after Pat had left.

I had everything packed and ready to go. I took a chance on taking the local bus in front of the house at 11:30 a.m. I was hoping Pat wouldn't be watching the house, since he thought that I had gone downtown. I don't know whether he did or not but, at any rate, I didn't see him and by 12:15 p.m., I was on the Greyhound a mile out of town.

About eleven o'clock that evening, we were just about ready to retire when the telephone rang. My daughter-in-law answered the phone. I could see that something was up because she had such a queer look on her face. She said to Albert, "It's your father. He's at a gas station two miles away. He doesn't know the way and he wants you to come and get him." There was nothing for us to do but go to a hotel. Albert took us into the center of town to a hotel and then he went to pick up Pat.

I was afraid that Albert's children would "spill the beans." There were then three of them and all great talkers, but I guess they slept through the whole thing. Pat had discovered that the water and gas were shut off and he knew I had left for someplace, so he decided to go to California. But he had had a minor accident on the road, so Albert talked him into leaving his car there and taking the bus. Albert took him to the depot for the six o'clock bus. Then he came to pick us up and took us to the airport.

When we first came into the hotel, I met a friend of ours in the lobby. He was from Duluth. It gave me a scare for a moment, but then I realized that there was no chance of him meeting Pat before we would be on the plane and on our way.

Tuesday night we spent in New York. We left there on Wednesday afternoon. On Thursday afternoon, we landed in Helsinki. Then I could give a sigh of relief. Our vacation had begun and it was wonderful.

My nephew and niece met us at the airport. We spent the night at my nephew's place. The next morning, my nephew produced a Volkswagen. Four of us got in with all of our baggage. We drove 56 miles out in the country. We felt a little bit squeezed, but it was fun. I had never been in a Volkswagen before. There were no paved roads, only gravel. The pebbles were flying every which way. Every time one hit the window, I ducked.

I had gone that same road 46 years before. I had walked, skied and ridden with a horse and buggy, but never in a car. Forty-six years before, it was an overnight affair. Now it took less than an hour.

But, please allow me to take a moment to backtrack a bit to our flight across the Atlantic.

It was a beautiful night. We were watching the northern lights most of the night. There were only fourteen passengers on the plane and it seemed as if we had the whole plane to ourselves (which was, I suppose, pretty much true).

There was a young Norwegian steward tending to our section of the airplane. He took a fancy to Linnea and he was treating us like royalty during the entire trip. Every half hour or so, he would come around and ask if there was anything we wanted. We were the best-fed passengers on the whole trip.

We had a little trouble with the language now and then in most of the cities in Finland. I had lived in Finland for nearly fourteen years as a child, but I didn't learn to speak Finnish because, at that time, the whole southern part of Finland was Swedish. I also went to Swedish school. But now, in most of the cities, the general language is Finnish. Of course, in the most southern part and on the outlying islands, Swedish is still spoken.

Fanny, my sister, lived on the mainland, but on a point way out in the gulf. There was no indoor plumbing and, at that time, she didn't even have a telephone. We were doing our personal washing and bathing every morning in the gulf. They had a steam bath, but that was heated only on Saturday. There was also an outdoor toilet, but it was quite some distance from the house.

We stayed at Fanny's sister-in-law's place. She had a little two-room cottage about a block from Fanny's house, so we had our meals at Fanny's place, but we slept in the other cottage.

In the summer, there were poisonous snakes around, but this was in the fall. We didn't think that they would be around that late, but my cousin had seen some the week before. We didn't want to take any chances on going to the outdoor toilet during those dark nights, so we used the "golden pot" in the house.

One night, Linnea accidentally tipped the pot a small degree. We were washing the rug at two o'clock in the morning. It was so funny that we had a hard time keeping quiet so we wouldn't wake the landlady, who slept in the next room.

We carried water from the well every morning and we had to skim the insects from the top of the bucket before we brought it in the house. I was very thankful that the government had insisted on typhoid shots before we left the United States. And although the shots made me very sick at the time, I can only imagine what it would have been like if I had gained a first-hand relationship with the germ itself.

The whole neighborhood was just like one big happy family. Every afternoon, we were invited out someplace for coffee and everything that goes with it. They were great for baking cakes and coffeecakes and all kinds of pastries. They all insisted that we have three cups of coffee and something to go with it. We had a hard time keeping our weight somewhere within limits. It's no use kidding anybody – we gained, whether we wanted to or not.

We spent a week at my cousin's place. She lived on an island about four miles long and about two miles wide. She was in her late sixties and was the only person on the whole island. Since her husband's death about six years earlier, she had not used the motorboat because that was large and hard to handle. She used a small rowboat and she could handle that thing in and out between the rocks, in small straits and even in the dock. She had a built-in stove which used wood. Every morning, she was out there chopping wood like a lumberjack.

One evening, she and Linnea went to the mainland. It would have been a little risky to overload the small boat in the dock, so I stayed home alone. I bolted the door when they left, but there were no window blinds and I felt a little uneasy. Then I began to think about being the only living soul on the island. The nearest neighbor was on the next island two miles away and I didn't have a boat. Then I began to imagine that I heard steps outside of the house. There was no place to hide and I didn't want to be in the dark. I was sitting there sweating it out when they finally returned. I unbolted the door and put on my biggest smile as if it was the most natural thing in the world for me to spend a dark fall night all by myself on an island out in the gulf. Naturally, I wouldn't tell anybody that I was scared – of course not.

It seems strange now, how forty-six years on another continent had made a coward out of me. As a child, I had spent many evenings alone under the same circumstances.

We also spent a few days on another island with a childhood friend of mine. They had a half-grown cat that always went to sleep every afternoon on the stove in a kettle that they used to cook potatoes for the pigs. I knew that the kettle was used for the pigs only, but Linnea didn't. When we came to the table in the evening, they had boiled potatoes. Linnea looked at the potatoes, then she turned to me and remarked, "I wonder about that cat." Of course they didn't understand English, but I wanted to explode. I didn't even dare smile for fear that they would think that we were making fun of their dinner or something. We excused ourselves after dinner and lost no time getting outside. When we got away from the house, we just sat down and howled.

Shortly afterward, we took a trip to Lapland, which was about 400 miles north of us. We rode on the train for the first 200 miles. It was an all-night trip. The seats were something for the birds, with just plain boards up and down. I felt like I was broken in two. For the next 200 miles, we traveled by bus. The seats were a little better, but the roads were terrible. A rock flew up and cracked the windshield right in front of the driver.

The comfort stations were little shacks along the road – no soap, no water. But someone had been very thoughtful. The tissue had been used, but they had put it back for someone else to use. Now wasn't that nice of them? Once, the bus stopped along the road and some of the men got off to answer the call of nature. They didn't care if we saw them or not, and that was that.

When we came to the hotel, we got along fine as far as the rooms were concerned. Everything was nice and clean. But in the dining room – that's where we had a little trouble. We couldn't read the menu. The only thing I understood was vegetable soup, and that was only because it was printed in Swedish. The rest was in Finnish. So I had vegetable soup four times in a row. One morning, I tried to get something different, so I ended up having pickled herring for breakfast. But it was fun. I wouldn't have missed that trip for anything.

I went there for the purpose of seeing reindeer, but it was late in the season and the only thing I saw that even reminded me of a deer was a couple of hides tacked up on a barn wall to dry. What a disappointment. There was snow on the ground but it wasn't cold. It was foggy and dark the whole time we were there, so our pictures didn't come out very clear.

On the return train trip, we took a sleeper. Somewhere along the road, they unhitched the sleeper without telling us and we almost missed the connection. Somebody told us just at the last minute.

A man committed suicide that night by jumping off the train. The train was delayed one hour because of that.

The Lapps were the friendliest of people. We couldn't have a conversation with them, but they certainly had the biggest smiles. At one station, we saw two female gypsies. They were dressed differently from any gypsy I had ever seen before. When I first noticed them, they were picking up cigarette butts from the floor and smoking them.

The pheasants were tame where Fanny lived. They would come right up next to us. They would even take bread out of the hand of Fanny's little

217

granddaughter. But it was against the law to shoot them. It was also interesting to stand out in the yard and watch the ships and the boats go by within a few yards of the shore.

The sunrises and sunsets were beautiful. It looked like a big red volleyball in the sky, with all the brilliant colors around it. Linnea was out there bright and early in the morning to take pictures; the same in the evening when the sun went down. Sometimes when a steamer came by, she would run for the shore to get a close-up.

Fanny had a son who was Linnea's age. He was still a bachelor and stuck around to take care of his mother. He and Linnea got along famously, although neither one spoke the other's language. Each had a small pocket dictionary. I believe they talked in sign language, because they seemed to understand each other perfectly. We would get the biggest charge seeing them take off arm in arm along the shore.

It was very interesting out on the island, but we couldn't stay there very long. The snow came early that year, and was accompanied by big storms. We didn't want to get stuck out there so we flew to Sweden to visit Pat's sister and a few other relatives. The roads were better in Sweden and the food was excellent.

Linnea had never been able to eat onions, even when she was a child. One day, at Pat's nephew's house, they had a dish of onions fixed in a certain way, and peculiar to Sweden in particular, that didn't resemble onions in any way, nor taste like them either. Linnea asked for a second helping. It seemed like a very big joke when we discovered later what she had been eating.

On our return trip, we stayed one day in Stockholm. I was glad to finally get back to the city where I was born. I went through there as a small child with my parents, but I didn't remember seeing anything in particular from my past; only the things that I'd been told about it. The castle grounds and castle itself were most impressive.

We spent one day in Hamburg. That city had the most beautiful harbor of any city I've ever seen anywhere. It was very chilly, but the harbor fascinated me (all harbors do). We were sitting there for several hours. It must be in my blood. There were sailors among my relatives for many generations.

It was Thanksgiving Day, by the way, that day we spent in Hamburg. We only had a few pennies in German money and we didn't want to change any more dollars into marks because we were leaving that evening. There was a small coffee shop at the airport where they sold hotdogs, and I mean just hotdogs. No buns, just the wiener. So we had a wiener and a cup of coffee. That was our whole Thanksgiving dinner. Of course, we got our dinner aboard the airplane that evening, although it wasn't turkey.

We also spent one day in New York City. The Christmas decorations were already up in the stores, so there was a lot to see.

We still had our plane tickets to take us back to our respective residence cities of Duluth and Los Angeles, but wanted to see Violet and her family, so we took the bus that evening for West Palm Beach, Florida.

They had a cold spell when we got there, the first one of the season. They had not as yet turned on the heaters. All the others went to bed and covered up with blankets, but I sat in a rocker the rest of the night, reading, with my coat on. I wasn't in the mood to get ready for bed in a cold room. They turned the heat on the following morning.

After six days in Florida, we took off for home after an absence of almost three months. I went right to work the very first evening I was home. It felt good to look forward to a paycheck again.

Pat was back in town again. As soon as he noticed we were back, the telephone calls started again. Linnea decided to stay over the holidays, and Jean came home from college to spend Christmas and New Year's with us. Harold and his family came on Christmas Eve and stayed overnight. I invited Pat for Christmas dinner. He came, but somehow he felt out of place. I felt sorry for him in a way. He looked rather tacky. His clothes were not pressed, and his jacket looked sorely in need of dry cleaning. Every time I saw him, he would say, "How about it, Ma? It isn't right to break up a marriage after so many years. Should we try it again?"

Both Linnea and I told him that he would have to see a psychiatrist. He was always afraid that we were going to play some kind of a trick on him. Finally, he consented to go. We made the appointment with the doctor. We were there waiting, but he didn't show up. Finally, he called and said that his car was stalled way across town. I told him to take the bus, but he never showed up.

He didn't come to the house any more while Linnea was there. Jean had already left to go back to college. After Linnea left, he began to come to the door and ask for certain things that he still had there, which was just an excuse to talk to me, because he could go there and get anything he wanted at night while I was working.

He had been out almost six months. He was begging to come back every time he came to the house. He promised that he wouldn't cause any trouble. I felt sorry for him, but I hesitated because of the many odd things that he did that didn't make any sense to anybody. Here are a couple of examples: While Jean was in her senior year in high school, he told her one night that she couldn't take a bath. She said, "Sorry, you're too late. I had a bath an hour ago." I could never understand his point of view. He didn't pay for the water or the gas.

Another time, a club that I had belonged to some years before had a banquet. I was invited to the banquet. Naturally, I intended to take Pat. But the morning of the banquet, he told me, "They don't want you there." So what did he do? He went and picked up Alma and took her there. She wasn't even invited.

Andrew came and told me that he had picked up Alma. I knew then where they went, so I didn't go. I certainly didn't want any man so badly that I had to chase him, husband or no husband, and I knew that I couldn't stand to put up with that again.

In the meanwhile, Selma thought that I had sued Pat for a divorce. I don't know what Pat had promised her, but she was just as friendly as she could be until the day I finally told Pat I was giving him another chance and he moved back home.

She wouldn't talk to either of us. I didn't care. I just simply ignored her. She wrote me a couple of nasty letters and I mailed them back to her. One day she called me and pretended to be someone else. I recognized her voice and told her to see a psychiatrist and then I hung up. She didn't bother me after that.

She began to talk to Pat again. I knew that she had plans of some sort. Then she told him that she wanted some work done on her porch. I knew that she was up to "no good" and I told Pat not to touch it, but he wouldn't listen. The job was worth $40.00. When he was through, she didn't pay him. He waited three months before he tried to put a lien on her property. But it was 90 days and too late to do anything about it. She sold the house and moved to Florida. That was the last I heard of her.

Pat behaved wonderfully for four years. He didn't start an argument. He picked me up at work every night. Of course I paid him for that. He got about $140.00 a year out of the deal, but I didn't begrudge him that as long as he behaved like a human being. He also painted the whole inside of the house the first two months after he returned. It had not been painted for seven years before that. It was really a mess. I had tried to wash the walls at least once a year but, with soft paint, it wasn't very successful.

During those four years, Pat also drove me to various stores to pick up groceries, which he had never done before – nor since. Those were the only happy years of my whole married life. There was never a cross word said on either side. It was wonderful just to be living.

I know now that Pat can behave if he wants to, so I don't feel sorry for him any more. What happened later he owned in its entirety.

In the spring after he returned, we went to Michigan where Jean was going to college. We went to pick her up for our summer vacation. It was a nice trip, the weather was beautiful and Pat was in a good mood all the way. It kind of brought me back to the days when we went on the long-distance trips with the trucks.

Jean went back to work in the hospital where she had worked the summer before, about 130 miles from home.

There was some kind of mix-up with the government loan in the fall. It was not granted until a month after the school started. Jean didn't wait for them to make up their minds. She took off for California and got work in an office. She worked there until Christmas. Her scholarship was still good and the loan had been granted, so she returned to college in January.

She also worked 40 hours a week, but I realized in the spring that that was entirely too many hours. She was very nervous and had lost weight, which she couldn't afford to do. She was too much underweight as it was. She cut down her working hours and stayed in college during the summer to make up the semester she had missed in the fall.

Pat was helping Harold on his new house. One day, he fell off a ladder and came home with a compound fracture of his arm. He stayed in the hospital overnight. He was almost helpless for four months. The arm was crooked and it wouldn't heal. I had to give him baths, dress him and cut his meat, etc. The arm never did get back to normal.

Susie was almost fourteen years old, which is an old age for a dog. She had dropsy; her legs were getting stiff. Finally, she refused to eat. The vet was out of town and his assistant didn't seem to know much. She was lying there for several days and was getting too weak to move. Finally, the vet came back. I had to wrap her in a blanket to get her in the car because Pat could only use his good arm. We took her to the hospital but she died that afternoon. It felt just like losing a member of the family. I couldn't eat and I couldn't sleep for a whole week. All I could see was the dog.

I expected Jean to come home for a couple of weeks as soon as she was through with her final exams. I called her and asked if she was through with the exams. She said that she had two more to go. I said, "Call me when you're all through." She got suspicious and asked, "Is Susie all right?" I said, "No." She just said one word: "Dead?" I said, "Yes."

I knew it was a very bad time to tell her because she felt the same as I did about Susie. The dog had been Jean's companion from the time we got her until Jean left for college. I didn't want Jean to come home and discover that Susie had died and I hadn't told her, and I couldn't lie to her after I had called her and she suspected it anyway. Even Pat also felt bad when Susie died. He couldn't stand her when we first got her, but he got used to seeing her around.

Linnea came home a couple of weeks later. Pat bought a new car. We took Jean back to college and the rest of us went on to Florida. I got a kick out of Linnea and Pat. They were criticizing each other's driving. Once, down in Georgia, Pat passed a truck on a double line. The highway police were right behind. They picked Pat up and he was fined $20.00. He was lucky to get off that easy. Sometimes they put them in jail.

We had a very nice vacation in Florida. On our way home, we stopped at Raymond's place. He was playing a small part in a movie as an extra at the time. It was a story about Ernest Hemmingway as a young man. Raymond played a policeman at the homecoming of Hemmingway at the end of World War I. The movie was made just a few miles from Raymond's home.

The next summer, Jean got married. They had a big church wedding, with a big reception afterward. Raymond's daughter and Harold's daughter were two of the bridesmaids and Leonard's small daughter was the flower girl. Linnea brought her along with her when she came to the wedding from California. The wedding was held in the town where Jean went to college.

Pat gave Jean away at the wedding. He is so emotional at times, when he really doesn't have to be. At other times, he is a brute. He broke down at the rehearsal and again at the wedding. They gave him tranquilizers, but it didn't help. He still came down the aisle with tears streaming down his face. At times like that, I could put my arms around him and sympathize with him. But there are other times when I could cheerfully wring his cussed neck.

Jean and her husband both still had four months left of college, but they both graduated in December of that year.

About a month after Jean's wedding, I broke three toes. I worked every night, but it was very painful even though I wore bedroom slippers.

Then Harold's daughter was getting married, in a church wedding also. I had to wear shoes, of course. I managed to squeeze the shoes on after much struggle. I didn't really walk, in that sense of the word, but I managed under my own power until after the reception. We stayed at Harold's place that night. It was dark and I stumbled over something and got a three-inch rip on my leg. And I didn't even have one little drink to blame it on.

In those four years, Pat didn't show any signs of jealousy. We took a trip to California, but he didn't watch me when our son-in-law was around, the way he used to.

That son-in-law, Mildred's husband, had had several heart attacks, and he had one while we were there. Pat seemed to feel bad about those attacks.

His first attack had come years before when he was still a very young man. It happened when they were driving over the mountains enroute to California on their first trip there. A big boulder had fallen down and blocked the road. Mildred's husband tried to get it out of the way. He was able to move it enough for the car to pass, but he had a mild heart attack right then and there. Mildred knew how to drive, but she hadn't been driving very much and she didn't even have a license. But it was an emergency, and she had to drive. She said it was a nightmare, with a sick husband and two small children in the back of the car. And the mountain road frightened her to no end.

For several years before Pat got so bad that I had to put him out, I didn't dare to accept a ride home from work. If I couldn't afford a taxi, I had to walk, even in a snowstorm. When I consented to let him come back home, I told him strictly that I didn't want any more of his silly outbursts, and I wasn't going to walk home. If he didn't pick me up, I would ride home with the others from the restaurant if they were driving my way.

After he broke his arm, he didn't pick me up any more and I didn't make an issue of it. He was able to drive by then, but as long as he didn't throw a fit when I rode home with the others, I let it go at that.

The boss's wife was out of town. She was supposed to come home the next day. We were closing up for the night. The boss was the only one left going my way. When we were ready to go, I said, "Are you driving my way?" (Sometimes he didn't go right home.) He said, "Yes. Do you mean to tell me that you dare take a ride home?" I told him that Pat hadn't bothered me since he came back. The boss went to get his jacket. When he came back, he said," Well, what are we waiting for? Let's go."

He was very cheerful and seemed happy about his wife returning home the next day. He talked all the way home. He let me out in front of my house and said, "See you tomorrow." When I stepped out of the car, a huge black cat walked right in front of me. I laughed, as I'm not superstitious. When I came in the house, I told Pat about the black cat. He's a little on the superstitious side. He asked why I didn't walk around the block. I said that the poor cat couldn't help it that he was black, and it didn't bother me.

The next noon, a girl from the restaurant asked if I had heard anything from there. I said that I hadn't. She asked, "You don't know what happened last night?" Somehow, I knew before she told me. Call it a premonition, or anything you like, but I knew. The boss had died from a brain hemorrhage early that morning.

Someone had talked to him about 9:30. He was still alive at that time. It was a business call and the same person called him back at 10:00 but there was no answer. I was the last person to see him alive.

I felt guilty in a way because I always said that he would die suddenly when he did. His brother had died from a heart attack two years before, and I had the feeling that the boss would go the same way. I don't know why I felt that way, but I made that statement to a couple of the girls in the restaurant the day before.

The people that were to start work at ten o'clock that morning couldn't get in, of course, since the boss wasn't there to unlock the door. They waited until eleven o'clock; then they called one of his nephews who had his place of business just a couple of blocks away. He drove out to his uncle's house to check on him, but he had to break the glass in the door so he could unlock it. He found his uncle on the floor, dead.

It was an awful shock to the boss's wife when she returned that afternoon. Several of the relatives went to the airport to pick her up. They hadn't been able to notify her and she didn't know a thing about it. When she got off the plane and saw several of the relatives there, she looked bewildered. She asked, "Where's Paul?" His nephew told her what had happened. She kept on saying, "He can't be dead. I talked to him last night. Let me get to a phone. I have to call him."

She felt lost for months afterwards. She ran the restaurant for awhile, but finally she turned it over to one of the boss's nephews, whom they had brought from Greece several years before.

He was seventeen when he came there, but he was no larger than a fourteen-year-old and he couldn't speak a word of English. He started by coming to the kitchen to help out. He began by asking questions immediately. He would ask, "How do you say this? What do you call that?" We always said that we brought him up. To me, he was just like one of my own boys. He was a very smart boy. He started in junior high school; seven years later, he graduated from college. We knew that he would make a wonderful boss.

I enjoyed those few summers. We used to go someplace on Sunday in the car and we always took Andrew, our neighbor who played the guitar, and his wife along. They were getting old. He was nearly ninety and she was in her early eighties, but they were still very alert and kept up with all the latest news and happenings around town. But they were lonely. Their children lived far away and all their friends had passed away. I used to have them to our house for dinner several times a month.

Finally, Andrew got cancer. He hung on for a year and a half. He never knew that he had it though. The last four months, he was in and out of the hospital. I couldn't understand Pat's attitude after that. He talked as if Andrew was his best friend and how bad he felt about Andrew being ill, but he wouldn't do a thing for him. Although he knew that Andrew liked company, he only went there a couple of times a week and then only for a very few minutes at a time.

One day, when Andrew was coming home from the hospital, Pat made it a point to go to a Golden Age meeting, which he had not attended alone before or since. He just made the excuse so he wouldn't have to drive Andrew home. They had to take a taxi, which they could ill afford. I was very much disgusted with Pat, because I remembered the many times Andrew had gone out of his way to do favors for Pat. I didn't want an argument, though, so I didn't say anything. I did what I could to make their life more pleasant. If Andrew wasn't able to go out, I would bring something to their house.

Sometimes a roast, a steak, ice cream, coffeecake, etc. The things that I knew they liked.

I didn't go to Andrew's funeral, because I can't attend anybody's funeral. But the people who were there said that Pat made a big show of crying. Those kinds of tears I could do without.

Mildred's husband had been ailing for a long time. He couldn't work anymore. He suffered a lot, but he was such a patient soul and we knew he suffered a lot, but he was always cheerful and always joking.

Mildred had a couple of weeks' vacation. They hired a trailer and their whole family was going camping. They had the trailer all packed and they were talking over their plans for the next morning, when they were supposed to leave. They were still talking at one o'clock in the morning when he finally said, "We had better go to sleep so we can get an early start." Mildred walked out into the kitchen and when she came back into the bedroom, he was dead.

Linnea called me at three o'clock that morning. I knew it was to be expected sometime, but it was still a great shock.

Then about two months later, I had a very disturbing dream, the same type that I had just before my mother's death. I also had it when my brother Frank died. My brother Andrew died from a heart attack a few years before this. I also had an odd dream then, but a different type; however, this dream disturbed me very much. This was on a Friday night. On Sunday, we went to visit Harold and his family. I told my daughter-in-law about my dream and I remarked, "I don't like it. I'm afraid that something is going to happen." She told me not to worry; perhaps I was just nervous about something.

On Monday night, just before quitting time, the boss came and told me that they wanted me in the emergency room at one of the hospitals in Duluth. He said that my son was there. I said, "None of my sons are here." He said it was Raymond, I remarked that he was the healthiest one in the family and the only thing I could think of was that he had been in the area and had been in some type of an accident.

One of the boys from the restaurant drove me to the hospital. My daughter-in-law and my granddaughter were there. I asked if it was an accident. They said, "No, a heart attack." I just couldn't believe it. Sister Emily was an anesthetist in that hospital. She came in then and said, "It doesn't look good." I knew then there wasn't much hope. She would never have told me that unless she was trying to prepare me for the worst. A half-hour later, she came back and told us that the doctor said that he couldn't do anything more. Raymond was dead. And although I was as prepared as Sister Emily could make me, it was still something my mind was not prepared to handle. It was a terrible ordeal.

I stumbled out of there rather blindly. I knew that the dark streets were not safe at night for anybody, but that was far from my mind. I stumbled home somehow and then I had the very hard task of telling Pat. I woke him up and told him. Well, neither one of us slept that night. Pat went to lie down after a while, but I didn't even sit down. I walked the floor most of the night. I still couldn't believe it.

Raymond had seemed in the best of health. About six weeks before that, Jean and her husband were there with their three-month-old baby. Raymond was a great one with children. They took a dozen different poses of him holding the baby. After that, he took us all for a long drive all through the country around there. Jean's husband had never been there before.

One Sunday, about two weeks before Raymond's death, Pat wanted to go to Harold's house. But this time, I objected. I had no particular reason. I just wanted to go to Raymond's instead. There wasn't much difference in the distance. Pat said, "All right." So we went to Raymond's. He was so very cheerful. After dinner, he took us for a fifty-mile drive. He even took us to the cemetery where his father-in-law was buried. He had died a few months before. (That's where Raymond is now, right next to him.) I still have no idea why he took us there. Cemeteries have always given me an uneasy feeling, and I steer clear of them whenever I can.

We were talking about going on a vacation in the next few weeks. There is a place about 75 miles from Raymond's place that I had never seen, but I had always wanted to go there. The last thing Raymond said that Sunday evening, just before we left, was this: "When you return from your vacation, come early some Sunday morning and I'll drive you there." I'm so glad that we went to Raymond's that day instead of Harold's. I will always remember Raymond as I saw him then. I didn't see him after that. To me, it seems that he is still alive.

He was always a great one for coffee. At our house, the coffee pot was always on the pilot light because Pat drank at least 15 cups a day. Every time Raymond came to visit, his first question was, "Any coffee in the pot?" He would drink coffee as long as there was anything left. As long as I lived in our home, I was always looking for him to walk in any day and ask for coffee. Then suddenly I would remember. It was a pain that never went away.

Sometimes, when I'm alone, I remember certain periods from Raymond's childhood. Once, the doctor prescribed some ointment for Violet for a skin rash. Raymond ate half of it and smeared the rest on his shoes. When he was four, I asked him one day to keep an eye on the twins while I was hanging the wash out in the yard. He either forgot, or disobeyed on purpose. At any rate, he went out. The twins had gotten up on a high shelf that I thought was out of their reach. They had disposed of half a bottle of castoria, internally, of course. That was another call for the doctor, naturally.

About the age of six or seven, Violet and Raymond had a race on their scooters. I don't know who won, but Violet came home with a large gash on her forehead. She had run into a cement wall which had a protruding spike. The doctor took several stitches and she carries the scar to this day.

Linnea also has a small scar on her forehead. She was knocked down by a boy on a bike at the age of two. Raymond was a very good-natured child. I never heard him complain about anything. Sometimes one of the other children would remark that someone else in the family was treated better or he didn't get as many things, but Raymond never said anything. Although he got the brunt of his father's bad nature at all times, whatever he felt, he kept it to himself.

He was rather rough in his play. If he had a fight with the neighborhood boys, he usually came out the winner, and he never said what happened to his opponent.

When Raymond was ten, one day Linnea picked up his saxophone and put it to her mouth and pretended to play. Raymond threw a pillow at her, which knocked a tooth loose and split it in half. It took a lot of money to fix it, which we could hardly afford. He was sorry afterward, but the damage was done. He tried hard to earn a few cents whenever he could. He got up at five o'clock every Saturday morning and walked 13 blocks to turn on the gas for a Jewish rabbi and he only got five cents. He did that for a whole year.

One of his teachers didn't like him and, I must say, the feeling was mutual. One period, she gave him all failing marks, even the subjects that he had gotten an "A" in the year before. I took him out of that school and put him in another one. His first report card in the new school was very good. He took his report card and went back to the old teacher and said something that wasn't very nice. He called her a "Snake in the grass." Of course, he got a lecture from his old principal, but it didn't bother him at all. He was happy to get it out of his system. He had no trouble in the new school.

When he was in the sixth grade, the band leader from the junior high school heard him play the clarinet one day. The band leader was very interested and got Raymond excused once a week to get him some special instruction.

After Raymond's death, I wanted to get away for awhile. Linnea stayed on after the funeral, so we three went on a long vacation. – Linnea, Pat and I. First we visited Jean and her family. Then we went to Niagara Falls, followed in leisurely sequence by the New England states, New York, New Jersey, Washington, D.C., Florida and New Orleans. It would have been a wonderful vacation, but I couldn't forget what had just happened. That **pain** was always there.

From New Orleans, I had to return home since it was time for me to get back to work. Linnea was returning to California so Pat went with her.

Raymond's widow came to work in Duluth after his death and she was alone then. Her daughter was in college and her son was in the Marines. I told her that she could live at our house and help herself to anything in the house. I didn't charge her anything. I wanted to help her all I could. I knew that she felt lost. She worked days and I worked nights. She went to her home on weekends, so I hardly ever saw her.

233

The Last Straw

Pat began to change for the worse more and more from then on. He didn't help getting the groceries with the car. I had to carry everything most of the time. I had to make two trips to the grocery store every time I went shopping. He began to hang around a couple on the other side of town, several miles from where we lived. They were once friends of Andrew's but, when he died, Pat stepped in to take over.

The woman's name was Lil. Pat wasn't interested in the man. He never went there when she wasn't at home. I can't say that she encouraged him. She was different from Alma and Selma. But, on the other hand, she didn't discourage him either. I leaned over backwards to keep the atmosphere pleasant.

The next spring, I paid for a trip to Jean's house for Pat and Harold and his wife. I really couldn't afford it because I had paid for the vacation (the bus fare that is) for Pat and me. Linnea paid for the rest. I didn't want Pat to drive because his arm wasn't very strong, so I asked Harold to use his car. But I paid all the expenses. I thought Pat might get his mind back on doing something around the house. But it was useless effort.

He began to spend most of his time at Lil's house. He got up at six o'clock nearly every morning and was out at Lil's house at 6:30 because he never took time to wash. He acted as if he was hypnotized. He expected me to be in the house at meal times every day and have his meals ready on a moment's notice, but he never bothered to call and tell me that he wasn't going to be home.

It cost a fortune to keep that up, because most of the food had to be thrown away. I had to leave it on the pilot light to keep it warm in case he came home after I had gone to work. He didn't know how to heat anything and he never put anything in the refrigerator. After it had been left on the pilot light a few hours, I had to dispose of it all. And that went on day after day. If he came home at all before I went to work, he would flop down on the sofa and go to sleep in the living room without saying a word.

He painted Lil's house on the inside – every room. But he wouldn't even wash the kitchen walls for me. I worked out six nights a week. It was a little hard for me to get everything done at home. The stand for the clothesline broke. I asked him to fix that - no result. The light in the living room went out of order. He didn't fix that. I waited a year, then Albert came to town one day and I asked him to fix it. As soon as he started, Pat was right there trying to help. He was just underfoot. Albert had built several houses and was perfectly capable of fixing it.

I had a second vein stripping on my legs. Pat came to the hospital a couple of times, but he went right to sleep in the rocking chair in my room and sat there without saying a word. As soon as he woke up, he went home. The day that I was ready to go home, he spent the whole day at Lil's house. A girl from the hospital finally brought me home.

I was home three weeks before I returned to work. I thought that Pat would at least stay home in the evenings after spending all day at Lil's. Where was he? You guessed it. He was out at Lil's house playing cards until 11 o'clock at night. In the whole three weeks, he was at home exactly two evenings. And those two nights he was dead to anything but his TV. If he ever stayed home during the day, he would go to sleep with the radio on full blast and always playing rock and roll, which almost drove me insane.

I had given some thought to retiring, but I realized that I would have no company from Pat and he didn't want me to have anybody else for company, even for a little while.

There was a fellow Pat's age that we had known for nearly 50 years. He came in to see us if he was in the neighborhood, which usually happened about once every six months. I always asked him to stay for coffee when he came. He read a lot and was an interesting talker. I enjoyed discussing things with him. One day, Pat saw him downtown and told him point blank: "I don't want you to come to our house any more." I saw the fellow some time later and he told me about it. He just couldn't understand it.

During Easter, I asked a friend of Sister Emily's to spend a few days with us. She was from another town. She was good company and I liked to have her, but Pat had different ideas. The second day after she came, he began to ask in a stage whisper, "How long is she going to stay? When is she getting out of here?" She was supposed to stay eight days, but she left on the fifth. She had had enough of Pat's insults.

Lil went to the hospital for an operation. Pat visited her twice a day for the whole time of ten days that she was there, even the day of the surgery. The next day, she was not supposed to have visitors, but Pat went just the same. The nurse told him that he couldn't go in. He came home very unhappy and cussed down the whole hospital and their system.

Pat began to make snide remarks to me that I was spending hours alone in the kitchen with the boss, which was a laugh in itself. Nobody had time to spend alone with anyone; besides, the boss was just one of my own boys, even if he was married and had two small children. He treated me like one of his aunts.

Pat also began to watch me coming home at night. He was usually standing on the porch when we drove up. Then he would go in and lock the door, even though he knew that I would come in within a minute or two. Of course I had my own key, but it was just the idea that I didn't care for.

Sometime before, Pat had gone to the town where Jean lived, some 800 miles away. He offered his services to help them build a house. He was supposed to be gone three months, but he got into some small disagreement with Jean's husband. He returned home in three weeks. After that, he was very cool to both Jean and her husband. They visited us once, but Pat didn't want to talk to them.

Linnea came home for a visit. She hadn't spent any significant length of time with us since she left home when she was just a very young girl. So she decided to stay a few months. I was very happy, because I knew that I would have company at least part of the time. But I'm not so sure that Pat relished the idea. He had never wanted me to take an interest in anyone. I never dared to show any of the children that I even liked them, let alone loved them. He always said that I paid too much attention to them and that I spoiled them. I don't think any of them are spoiled. They all have good jobs. They are well educated, well read, wonderful people and I'm proud, and I mean proud, of every blessed one of them.

About this time, the restaurant where I worked moved into larger quarters. We got a lot more trade than we had before which, of course, resulted in having to work longer hours. Every time I came home an hour later than usual, Pat would sit there watching the clock, just itching to start an argument. Linnea told him several times to behave himself. She also told him that there were a lot of things that he could do around the house. His only answer was, "Like hell I will."

One Friday night, he threw a fit when I came home. He got up and sat in the living room all night. The following week, he told me several times that I wasn't going to live very long. That bothered me a little, as I didn't know what he really had in mind.

He had been going to the doctor for a carbuncle on his neck. The next time he went to the doctor, I called the doctor's office and told them to check Pat a little closer, as he looked to me like he was coming down with a nervous breakdown. I don't know what happened during the doctor's visit, but the next morning, Pat was black in the face with rage. He told me that the doctor found his head just perfect and now I could stop making fun of him in front of my friends. Whoever made fun of him, I have no idea, but I'm sure I'm not the one. I still think there is a mental problem someplace, but it isn't anything to make fun of.

A week or so later, Albert and his family came for a visit. They stayed over the weekend. Friday night, I came home late, as usual, because we had been swamped with orders all night. Pat had already gone to bed, but the rest of us sat around and talked. It was very late when we got through, so I didn't go upstairs as I knew Pat would cause trouble. I threw a couple of old coats on the dining room floor and slept there a couple of hours.

Pat didn't talk all day Saturday. He was just building up for an explosion. Saturday night, I was very tired and I went right to bed. I thought that I might get a good night's rest. But how foolish can one be? The minute I got inside of the bedroom door, the explosion came. Pat jumped out of bed. He was swearing and ranting. Then, finally, he yelled, "Why don't you get out?"

That was music to my ears! I had wanted to do just that for years. Pat went down to the kitchen and sat there until seven o'clock the next morning, turning the pages of a magazine; not reading, just turning the pages all night in the same magazine. He also had a very dangerous look on his face, enough to scare anybody.

That afternoon, after Albert and his family had left, Pat really let loose to Linnea and me that he hadn't received anything for Father's Day. Linnea told him that Father's Day was still a week away. He said, "Bull - - - -!" He also said that I made him miserable and that I woke him up every time I came home late. I told him that I would sleep in another room which I did from then on. I knew he didn't like it and I never slept soundly. There was always that fear of him doing something crazy. I wish that I had a dollar for every time he woke me up. I could take a trip around the whole United States. But, really, I didn't wake him up at all. He was awake all the time, just looking for trouble.

I had made up my mind by then to leave at the first opportunity. I told him when I took him back six years before that I wasn't going to put up with any more of his foolishness. I had no desire to spend any more money on him. It cost me a small fortune every time I put him out and as long as I was in town, he would never leave me alone. I knew that I would have to leave the bulk of my things. Also, the house was worth about $8,000.00, but it was worth the price to get rid of someone that cannot be reasoned with.

He'll never change, and I have no intention of spending the rest of my life with a dictator. I'm not a child, and there is no reason why I should run to Papa and ask him how late I can stay out. If I have brains enough to work, I have brains enough to go home when I'm through. I've never chased after **any** man. The one I have is already one too many for me, at the rate he's behaving. So Pat need not have worried that I'd be sitting out in the park **watching the moon** with some fellow after work.

Jean was expecting another baby. Linnea had promised to go there and help out while Jean was in the hospital. I could see by Pat's actions that he was just lying low until Linnea had left. I knew, instinctively, that he was back to his old miserable self, where he had been six years before. I also knew that as soon as I was alone with him, he would be dangerous.

Our daughter-in-law had left to go to California just a couple of weeks before. I had just about had all I could take.

I wanted to be with Jean anyway, when the time came, because she had had a very, very rough time with her first baby and I was worried. I told Linnea that I was ready to "get out," as Pat had suggested that night in a fit of temper.

Linnea began to take some of my things out of the house, which wasn't hard because Pat spent most of his time out at Lil's house. One day, however, Pat was in the back yard talking to a neighbor when Linnea walked out the front door with two suit cases. But he was so busy talking that he never saw her.

I hated to leave my place of work with just a few hours' notice after I had been there for 16 years. But there was no other way. If I had told anyone at all, it would have gotten back to Pat within hours. There was a certain person in the place that was better at spreading the news than the front page of the daily paper.

Pat and Lil had been making plans for a whole week to visit Andrew's son and his family in a city about a hundred miles away. Pat never told me until Saturday evening, five minutes before I was ready to go to work, and then he just said, "We're going to Stan's tomorrow. Do you want to go?" I replied, "No, thank you." He said, "That's what I thought" Then he turned around to Linnea and said, "How about you?" She gave him the same answer.

That was the last I saw of him. He left for the trip the next morning about five o'clock, but I didn't see him as my door was closed. I heard him moving around though. Linnea and I knew that this was a good time to leave without a big argument.

Some good people loaned us $200.00 so I could finish up all my debts in town. I had made arrangements with the gas and light companies to transfer the services to Pat's account. The telephone service was to be discontinued ten days later.

That afternoon, we picked up our things. A friend of Sister Emily's drove us to another town to buy our bus tickets. We didn't want to leave any trace as to our whereabouts. On the way going there, we had to drive a stretch on the road by which Pat would return. I didn't take any chances. It was a hot day, but I sat in the back of the car wrapped up in a big shawl; but, of course, we didn't meet him. I felt a lot better after we were on the Greyhound bus and 50 miles away.

Pat knew that Linnea had gone to Jean's, but he had no idea where I was. But he thought that I was hiding somewhere in town. I'm sure that he was moving heaven and earth to find me. The day after we got to Jean's, he called and talked to Linnea. He told her that I left a light bill of $15.00 which, of course, was a big lie. I had paid everything in full. The money that he had given me towards his board for the month I left with Sister Emily and she gave it to him as soon as she saw him. I never answered the phone at Jean's house for fear it would be Pat. If I was the only one at home, I would take the receiver down and say nothing. If it was someone from Jean's family calling, they understood and would start talking. I went out every day for a walk, but I kept to the back roads. I was still very nervous though. Every time a car was approaching, if the color resembled Pat's car in any form, I went for the bushes.

We had been at Jean's house about two weeks. She had been having pains all week, but did not pay much attention as she had had them off and on for several weeks. It was her day for the weekly checkup with the doctor. Jean drove 20 miles to the doctor's office. After he examined her, he told her that she was in labor and had to go right to the hospital, which she did. The baby was born that night. It wasn't easy, but it was nothing like the first one, so we all felt very much relieved when it was over. Linnea and I stayed two more weeks. Then we went to the west coast.

Linnea told Sister Emily before we left that she could have Linnea's piano. When Sister Emily came to get it, Pat was in a rage. Sister Emily said that she was sure that he would have struck her but for the other sister that was with her. Pat disowned Sister Emily all over again, just as he had done at the time that she entered the convent. But, whenever he was ill, she was the one he sent for. Also, at Raymond's funeral, who was the one he asked for? Why, Sister Emily of course. But because he knows that Sister Emily knows where I am but won't tell him, he will have nothing to do with her. That's a gross mistake on his part, because she is the only one there to look after him if he should take sick, or if anything else should go wrong.

Sister Emily was teaching a class in anesthesia at the hospital every afternoon. Pat knew just where to find her and he didn't hesitate to barge in there at any time and embarrass her with his problems.

First, he hired a lawyer. Then he told Sister Emily to tell me to turn over the house to him or else there would be a court trial. As if I cared. I knew that he couldn't do a thing inside of a year. Furthermore, I wasn't interested. If he wanted to spend money on a lawyer, that's his affair.

He didn't only hire a lawyer; he also hired a detective. He got so bad that the detective told Sister Emily to stay off the street, that her father was a dangerous man, and her safety was in doubt if he found her alone. She had to leave the hospital and go to the convent. She is still there.

Linnea and I had been on the west coast a couple of months when we got a telephone call one night from Sister Emily. She said, "I believe the detective has picked up some kind of a trail. You'd better get out of town." She told us a place that she had in mind, in another state. I left the next day. Linnea was supposed to stay two more days to check on a position. That same evening, she got another call from Sister Emily, urging her to leave town also. Linnea was on the bus inside of two hours after the call.

We've been in this town now about eight months. Nobody has every found us and no one outside of Sister Emily knows where we are. I don't know what happened to Pat's detective, but I presume Pat ran out of money. The year is almost up since I left, so there should be some action soon. Well, it really doesn't worry me. I'll never go back.

Raymond told me a couple of times that he believed Pat would go back to his old mean nature sooner or later. I didn't believe it at the time. I thought that Pat had learned his lesson, but I know now that he will never learn. I'm through trying.

I hope Pat settles everything to his own satisfaction and gets off my back. I want to be free and travel. I want to go to Florida first of all. I haven't seen Violet for almost three years. About a year and a half ago, she spent six months in a T.B. hospital. She is well now, but I'd like to visit her because I had promised to go down there when she was released from the hospital; but then my troubles began and I couldn't go. I can't go anyplace now, as I don't know where Pat will show up. I don't want to run into him.

Pat always talked about a golden wedding. It would not be a golden wedding for me. It would be a memoir of a fifty-year war. I have enough miserable things to remember without having a celebration about it.

Of course, there are nice memories too, some humorous, some sad. It was fun watching the children grow. The first six came within six years. If we hadn't been so terribly poor, and Pat hadn't been such a brute, it would have been wonderful. Then there was the time there were eight in school at the same time. It was always a scramble.

When Linnea was about six, a nun came to our house one day. Linnea took one look at her and said, "You have teeth as big as a horse." I felt about two inches high. I didn't need to correct Linnea verbally, I just gave her that famous look of mine which put them all in their places, and that was about all I needed until they grew up. Another time, Linnea brought a classmate home from school. She introduced me as follows: "This is my mother. She has been downtown today; otherwise she doesn't look so good."

One Christmas vacation, when Violet was about six, she volunteered to wash and iron all the curtains from her classroom. She brought them home, so what could I do. I had to wash them and iron them. With all the work I had and Christmastime besides. For a fleeting moment, I could have sold Violet cheerfully to a carnival or something, to put on exhibition as something out of this world. But nobody could stay mad at her for very long – she was such a lovable soul.

Another time is still very fresh in my memory, although it was over twenty years ago that it happened. We had been to Raymond's and, on the way home, there had been an accident where one man was killed and several others critically injured. All traffic was stopped on the highway. There were 14 cars lined up ahead of us; we were the last in line.

I had Jean on my lap and Leonard was standing right in back of me looking ahead towards the accident. Suddenly, there was a big crash. Leonard flew up to the top of the car like a rubber ball. I was thrown against the door handle. Two drunks had rammed us from the rear. Our rear seat was crushed. If Leonard had been sitting down, he would have been dead. Jean was screaming. I was so concerned about the children that I didn't know that I was hurt until I realized that I couldn't see out of my right eye. It was swollen shut. I was the only one hurt. The others were all right.

To add insult to injury, the drunk driver stepped out of his car, came up to Pat and asked, "How are you going to pay for this?" I thought for a moment that Pat was going to slug him but, for once, he controlled his temper. The man was asking for it of course, but it would have been bad for Pat.

I have a lot of time to reminisce about days gone by. Incidents crop up from time to time. Sometimes I read about an occurrence in the newspaper which brings back a similar incident in my life.

I just read about an explosion in New York harbor. The one I remember happened when I was about eleven. One evening, right outside of our harbor, a large motorboat carried a cargo of benzene and blew up. No one knows what caused the explosion. The skipper, his wife and the engineer were all thrown clear of the boat, but it didn't help them because the water all around them was just a sea of fire. We watched, horrified, as they burned to death and sank. There was no coast Guard at that time. The rowboat didn't get there in time, although it tried mightily to make it.

Then there is the war in Viet Nam, which brings back memories of the Russian-Japanese war. We had nothing to do with the war itself, but I remember when it started. To put it in perspective, "It scared the heck out of me." I was about nine years old at the time and there were no radios to broadcast the news.

My cousin was eleven. One evening, we walked to the village about three miles away to get the mail and the newspapers. We opened the newspaper and there it was in bold, black type with letters 3 inches high: "THE WAR IS IN FRONT OF YOUR DOOR." It didn't make any difference to us that it was thousands of miles away. All we could see was that the war was right in front of us.

We had read in the history book about all the cruel things that happened in the war of 1808-1809 between Russia and Sweden, where they didn't bother to shoot the children. They impaled them on the pickets of the fence. We were sure that was just what was going to happen to us. My cousin spent the night at my house, but we didn't sleep a wink. We were trying to find a way to hide, but how, and where? That was the question.

My cousin did witness some of the horrors of war nine years later, but by that time, I had already left for the Unites States.

War and hatred seem to be the natural state of humankind. There were people who called themselves the "Red Guards" when I was growing up. They were something like the Communists. They were very cruel and hated people with money. It was a reign of terror while it lasted. On one occasion, they captured three bankers. They skinned them alive and left them to die on an island about three miles from my cousin's house. Another man tried to hide in a tree. The Red Guards tracked him down and shot him like a buzzard. I knew that man when he was a child because we had had many fights together while we were going to school.

Many people committed suicide rather than being tortured.

During World War II, Fanny was strafed by a plane one day while she was in a boat on the gulf. She was not hurt, but a boy in another boat a few yards away was killed.

One day, a dead Negro floated up on the shore just a little way from Fanny's house. They didn't know where he came from, but evidently, some American boat had been torpedoed because there were no Negros that we knew of, within hundreds of miles from where she lived. The people in the neighborhood rowed 15 miles to get a minister to give the poor guy a Christian burial. He is buried right there on the small island where they found him. Linnea and I could see the little white cross when we rowed by the island, but we didn't go ashore.

One evening not long ago, I watched a television program about spiritualism. I don't believe in it myself, but it did bring back to me the memory of an incident from my childhood.

There was an old fellow in the neighborhood. He was in his late seventies. He had been very mean all of his life. His frail wife had ulcerated legs. One day, in a fit of temper, he kicked his wife's leg. Now, anyone who has ever had an ulcer on the leg can almost feel the pain just by thinking about it.

The man had three husky daughters who worshiped their mother. They had also felt the brunt of their father's whip while they were growing up. That was the last straw when they saw the old man kick his invalid wife.

They gathered a bunch of nettles and made a bouquet. They grabbed the old man, took his pants off and spanked him properly with the nettles. I've been accidentally blistered with nettles, which is painful enough, and I can imagine what it would be like to have one's whole back lambasted with a whole bouquet of nettles. He couldn't sit and he couldn't lie on his back for several days. He went to stay with an old-maid sister until his blisters healed. But it worked. He never touched his wife again. Unfortunately, she died shortly after the incident.

In that part of the country, everybody had a banquet in the evening after a funeral, for which they were baking and preparing several days in advance. The old man made a nasty remark about his deceased wife. He asked the girls, "Why all the fuss about an old carcass?" He was very fortunate that he didn't get another blistering. Some people just won't learn, no matter how hard the lesson.

Well, about two years later, the old man died. They found him dead in the morning in his bed. In the funeral sermon, the minister said that the old man died as he had lived, apart from family and friends.

Another man lived right across the road from the old fellow's house. That man was not the type that would make up stories and he was not the nervous type that would imagine things. But he insisted that he saw the old man go into the house the night after the funeral. It was midnight, but it is light during the summer and, of course, it is light all night for three whole months. It stirred up the neighborhood for while. It took months before anybody ventured near the place in the evening.

But now, let me return to Pat and the present, or at least the present for me as I know it.

I went to work because I was tired of bill collectors always bothering us. I was the only one at home most of the time. I had to take the brunt of their insults. But, of course, Pat could never see it my way. He would much rather have lived as people in shantytown.

Until I went to work, we could never use anything but newspapers in the bathroom instead of tissue.

Curtains and windows blinds had rips in them. I could never afford to send clothes to the cleaners. I always had to wash everything. Many things were ruined after the first washing.

Pat had tried to have me fired at every place that I worked. Of course he didn't succeed, and then he told everyone that I worked because I didn't like housework. Well, who was doing the housework when I worked? Yours truly, naturally.

Pat didn't lift a finger to help and never had, whether I worked in or out of the house, or was sick or anything else. I had been half-starved for many years. I had to eat what the children didn't finish. Pat, of course, got his first and then the children. I did for them what I could. It hurt to see them go to school in nothing but hand-me-downs. It wasn't so bad in grade school, but in high school, the others looked down on them and made cutting remarks.

After I went to work and got the bills out of the way, I tried to have good food and decent clothes for Leonard and Jean. I remember what a big rumpus Pat made because I didn't let Jean go to the prom in a black dress. I bought her a light green one. It took months for him to get over that.

Pat never took any interest in the boys. He has never played ball with them or taken them fishing. The four older ones were all born within three years and they stuck pretty much together. Nobody cared too much to tangle with them, and Raymond was the big brother that they always looked to for support.

Leonard, of course, came along after the others were grown. I was glad when his band leader in high school took a fatherly interest in him. When Leonard went into the service, they exchanged letters regularly. When Leonard returned from Germany, he went to see Tommy (the band director) the same day. They were having a band concert within the next couple of days. Tommy asked Leonard to conduct a couple of numbers, which he did.

While Leonard was still on stage, Tommy wanted to inject a little humor. He asked Leonard why the paratroopers always called out "Geronimo" before they jump. Leonard said, "We don't say 'Geronimo' ". We shout "I don't wanna go! And if we hesitate, there's a jumpmaster there to kick us out!" That little "bit" made a hit with the audience.

I have never been able to have any kind of social life in all the years I've been married. I didn't have a life. Period. I just existed.

Pat had the bedroom manners of a bull moose; or the manners of a moose – period. He has always been careless about his person. He never washes his hands before he goes to the table, no matter what kind of work he has done. He must surely be immune to any kind of germ. Anybody else would have died long ago. The cleanest he has ever been was during the four months that I took care of him when he had the broken arm the last time.

Pat's mother died when he was eight years old. He had three stepmothers before he was nineteen, at which time he left Europe. I honestly believe that, for some psychological reason, he has been striking back at me all these years because he hated his stepmothers. There could be no other reason. I never nagged at him. I never made trouble. I stood up for myself, of course, when he tried to treat me like a doormat. I do not believe in the "master and slave" proposition. My idea is a fifty-fifty deal. Pat knew that from the time I met him. I left Europe because I rebelled against the kind of laws they had there at the time. It was nothing more or less than a mild form of the caste system. I was not about to start that all over again in America.

251

It appears to me that Pat has wanted to be a bachelor for a long time. For the last fifteen years, he has been trying to shove some woman or another down my throat. I finally began to choke. He was sitting on top of the world, but he couldn't stay there. After I put him out once, he knew exactly what was going to happen if he went back to this old tricks. I know that the minister said for better or for worse, and that I was willing to go along with it, but he didn't say anything about "impossible" and that's just what Pat is – **impossible.** Anyway, Pat did me a favor. I'm the one that's sitting on top of the world now!

All things considered, it's probably time for me to wrap up this narration. To do so properly, I should go back about nineteen months and explain what has transpired during that time.

Pat tried to locate me all that time. He had no more money to hire a detective but he went to every one of my friends several times each month and asked if they had heard from me and if they knew where I was. They knew better than to tell him anything; however, they didn't know where I was anyway. I wrote to them, but my letters were never sent direct and I never gave them my address.

Pat made up such fantastic stories. At first, he said that I was in the convent to become a nun. Then he said I was in the hospital and was supposed to come home after eight months when I got out of the hospital, but he could never explain to anybody why I was supposed to be in the hospital. The last story I heard was that I was supposed to be in an old peoples' home.

About a year ago, I asked Harold to go there and get my trunk. I had a lot of important papers and also a lot of things that I treasured. Pat wouldn't give it to him. He said that the trunk belonged to him. Some more of his pipe dreams. He had broken into my trunk though. I had told Harold's wife that she could have all my clothes, as she is my size. There were several hundred dollars worth of dresses, coats, jackets, skirts, slips, blouses, sweaters, shoes, etc., etc., some brand new and never used. Pat threw an old coat at her but wouldn't give her anything else. She didn't take the old coat. She said, "I don't want any of it now." Pat and Harold had a big row. Harold and his wife left and they have never gone back since.

Pat went to visit Mildred in California about eight months ago. He didn't like her friends, made some unfavorable remark, and stayed only one day. So Mildred is fed up with him too. A couple of months later, he went to California again, this time to visit Walter. He stayed one week and then returned again to Duluth. Walter is the only one Pat hears from at all, since Walter does call him at rare intervals.

Linnea and I lived in Logan, Utah for nineteen months while Linnea made some contacts in California. Over that period of time, she made some eight trips there for interviews and personal contacts, until she finally achieved what she was looking for with respect to a professional position. At one time, she had to make the same trip three times because of someone else's mistake, but she finally got settled where she wanted to be.

About a week ago, I decided to follow her, that is, go live with her. She had already rented a lovely apartment and had everything ready. I took the bus and was on my way. Everything went fine until we reached Reno, Nevada. Then we ran into a snowstorm. The roads were closed and we were delayed for seven and a half hours. I didn't mind the delay, but I did mind an incident that occurred.

We had just boarded the bus before we knew that we would be delayed for some time. I had a seat next to the window. There was only one empty seat in the whole bus, the one next to me. A big burly fellow about six feet two and 200 pounds, who had had a few drinks, got on the bus and "flopped" himself down next to me. Within minutes, he was asleep on my shoulder. I was "fenced in" from five a.m. to ten a.m. The smell of whiskey made my stomach go like a roller coaster. The bus driver seemed to have trouble of his own because of the snowstorm. There was no other place to put the fellow anyway. After five hours, they split the load. My sleepy friend was transferred to another bus. Glory be. I finally reached my destination. We're now living in our new apartment and I love every minute of it.

Some weeks ago, I heard, indirectly, that Pat had been granted a divorce last December on the grounds of desertion. I was never served with any papers, but it suits me fine. I'm glad to be free without going to court and listening to a lot of mud slinging. Fifteen years ago, I served papers on Pat for a divorce, but I dropped the charges after he promised to behave. Of course I should have known that his promises didn't mean a thing. But what makes the whole thing seem like a joke is this: For the whole fifteen years, Pat was griping that I put a "black mark" against the children because of the divorce papers. He didn't believe in divorce. Oh, no, not Pat. I wonder which color the children have against them now?

As I was not served with any papers, I made no claims to any of the property. He got it all. That's all right with me. It was worth every cent of it, just getting rid of Pat. He can take it all with him when he leaves this good old world, if St. Peter will let him.

It would have been our golden wedding anniversary on Good Friday, which was March 24, 1967. I couldn't have a golden wedding, but I wasn't going to be cheated out of a little celebration. Linnea and I had dinner in one of the good restaurants in town. The dinner was delicious and I enjoyed it. I will always remember my 50th anniversary dinner.

On Easter Sunday, Linnea and I took a walk down by the river which runs through town. We were walking at a merry clip when, suddenly, I saw Linnea freeze like a pointer. I looked down and there, in front of us, was a snake about three or four feet long. We didn't stop to investigate what kind it was. I took off in the opposite direction like a cross-country sprinter. We took the highway on the return trip. There was a lot of traffic. But I feel much safer dodging an automobile than dodging a snake. No more walks on the river for me.

Life goes on. I'm very happy now. Compared to the things I've had to contend with in the last fifty years, this is heaven. I have everything now that I've always been wishing for, but never could afford. There is so much of interest in this world to do that nobody needs to be lonesome (if they're in good health).

In the first place, I have many interesting books. I read a lot. I study a foreign language. I listen to symphony concerts. I have a small organ on which I practice an average of two hours a day. In the near future, I plan to get two more instruments just to break the monotony. I walk from six to ten miles every day. I take trips, go on excursions, see shows and stage plays. There are picnics and dinners. Not a dull moment.

Yes, life is wonderful.

Of course, there is always a little sadness mixed with the happy times. After almost four years, I still miss Raymond. I wish that he could have been with us a little longer. But God had other plans. I think of him often, and I feel that he is with me in spirit.

This just about covers the story of my life. What will happen in the future will be another book and a new chapter, one I hope to fill with travel, adventure and happiness!

Acknowledgements

As a general rule, I only rarely read acknowledgements, mostly because they are written on a page not visible at the end of the book; however, the acknowledgements section is still an appropriate place to say "Thank You," something I think we too often forget. I also believe most of us have friends we can call upon when an extra hand is needed and we, in turn, are happy to reciprocate in kind when we're called upon to do the same. Here are a couple of my extra hands:

I wish to thank friends, family and colleagues of some sixty years for their efforts on my behalf: Colonel Carlos Ramirez and my sister-in-law, Helen Hermanson who certainly made the book more readable with their expert editing suggestions, and Lt. Colonel Jack Howell, who still shows concern for my spiritual development after all these years. We have worked through multiple assignments together in the same military organizations since the late Fifties.

Ron Barnes and his daughter Paula taught me compassion, coffee and conversation while introducing me to the works of various local writers and artists while living at our 8,000 foot elevation during my Colorado years.

My neighbors, Dave Kriska and Roxanne Rodgers, taught me how to properly live through a forty-below-zero Minnesota winter without ending up talking to myself, something I had forgotten over the years.

Finally, my only surviving sister, Dr. Gloria Heinemann, and I grew up together. We were the last to leave the nest and, as events proved out, Pat never changed his stripes right through his last breath. We never believed he would. If I hadn't taken on this project, I'm sure my sister Gloria would have. I also believe that Mom and our brothers and sisters would approve, given the means to do so.

Bud Hermanson

9 780999 231609